The Italian Revolution

The Italian Revolution

The End of Politics, Italian Style?

Mark Gilbert

Westview Press

BOULDER • SAN FRANCISCO • OXFORD

Copyright © 1995 by Westview Press, Inc.

Published in 1995 in the United States of America by Westview Press, Inc., 5500 Central Avenue, Boulder, Colorado, 80301-2877, and in the United Kingdom by Westview Press, 12 Hid's Copse Road, Cumnor Hill, Oxford OX2 9JJ

Library of Congress Cataloging-in-Publication Data
Gilbert, Mark.
  The Italian revolution : the end of politics, Italian
style? / Mark Gilbert.
    p. cm.
  Includes bibliographical references and index.
  ISBN 0-8133-8788-4—ISBN 0-8133-2685-0 (pbk.)
    1. Italy—Politics and government—1976. 2.
Political corruption—Italy. 3. Political
parties—Italy. I. Title.
JN5451.G48 1995
320.945'09'049—dc20   94-35984
                                                                 CIP

Printed and bound in the United States of America

The paper used in this publication meets the requirements
of the American National Standard for Permanence of Paper
for Printed Library Materials Z39.48-1984.

10   9   8   7   6   5   4   3

Contents

Tables and Figures

Acknowledgments

A large number of people gave me invaluable help and advice while I was researching and writing this book. Most of the research was undertaken in the libraries of the University of Trento and the *Museo del Risorgimento* in Trento: I would like to extend my heartfelt thanks for the kindness and flexibility shown by the staffs of both institutions. I would also like to thank Martin Bull, Stephen Hellman, Bob Nilsson, Gianfranco Pasquino and Douglas Stuart for having read and commented upon draft versions of several of the chapters included in this book. They made a large number of worthwhile suggestions and detected a number of minor errors: If any are left, it is my fault, not theirs. Bob Nilsson also most generously put his meticulously compiled card index of Italian governments and ministers 1946-1994 at my disposal.

I did my graduate work at University College, Swansea, under the guidance of George Boyce and Richard Taylor of the department of Political Theory and Government. My thesis work was on a topic very different from this, but I would like to take this opportunity to say how much I learned from them.

I need hardly add that I would like to thank my editor at Westview, Susan McEachern. She made many useful suggestions for the improvement of the book and put up with my constitutional vagueness with remarkable grace. Anne Rodman, my Charles A. Dana intern at Dickinson College, Kristofor Sargent and Dan Buchan, the College's resident computer wizards, assisted me in getting the manuscript into publishable shape.

My family, especially my mother and father, have been a constant source of support and encouragement. I know this book will mean a lot to them: Their having been such marvelous parents means more to me. I must also thank my wife's family, who have greeted the *straniero* in their midst with typical Italian warmth and affection. My love and admiration for Italy and the Italians will, I hope, be obvious from this book: It derives, in no small measure, from having been accepted into an Italian home.

The person to whom I owe the greatest debt, however, is my wife, Luciana. This book is dedicated to her.

Mark Gilbert

1

Introduction

This book grew in the telling. Its original title was the very scholarly sounding *Powers that Were? The Decline of the Party System in Italy 1976-93*. The pace of events soon rendered this title impossibly conservative. I toyed for a while with the idea of simply removing the question mark, but eventually came to the conclusion that Italy's political convulsions were too dramatic for such small changes; the book became the *Italian Revolution: The End of Politics, Italian Style?* and retained the title even after the victory of Silvio Berlusconi's *Forza Italia* movement in the national elections of March 1994.

I have tried to blend comparative politics and chronology in my narrative. The first five, essentially thematic, chapters deal with major events that occured within the Italian party political system between (approximately) 1976 and 1991. The last three chapters are an account of the tumult of the last three years.

There is no chapter that attempts to explain why the Italian party system collapsed so comprehensively. In part this is because I have not fully digested the voluminous literature on the subject; in part because I think my provisional answer to this question is clear from the narrative itself. Italy's seemingly perennial political system fell apart largely because of the hubris, excess and venality of its leaders. This is not to say that outside events played no part. Hundreds of thousands of northern Italians, in particular, felt sufficiently liberated by the fall of Eastern European communism to switch their allegiance away from the Christian Democrats (the bastion of Italian anti-communism), notably in the local elections held in May 1990. The requirements of the Maastricht process and the world's financial markets prevented Italy's politicians from buying as many votes as they would have liked with public spending and inflation, though by the standards of most countries they still spent freely.

Yet neither of these events (and the first, especially, has been loaded with significance by a number of writers), in my view, was decisive. More important, I think, was an enormous miscalculation made after the end of the Cold War by the parties of government. The Christian Democrats and the Socialists, in particular, appear to have assumed that the domestic effects of the 1989 revolution in Europe would be beneficial for them. The Italian Communist Party, the chief party of opposition, was immediately plunged into a profound and potentially terminal identity crisis by the events of 1989. To judge by the unscrupulousness with which the government-controlled media used the Communist Party's pro-Stalinist past during the 1992 election campaign, the parties of government must have been thinking that the Communist Party's successor, the so-called Democratic Party of the Left, could be stifled at birth by the judicious use of propaganda. Other political forces, notably the Northern League, the free-market, federalist movement founded and led by the iconoclastic Umberto Bossi, were not regarded as being of sufficient stature to fill the gap left by the Communist Party. The leaders of the Christian Democrats and the Socialists therefore felt authorized to ignore growing evidence that the electorate was growing increasingly scandalized at the political system's inefficiency, corruption and chaos, and disgusted by the pervasive influence of organized crime within the political process. This was despite the fact that the president of Italy, the eccentric but undeniably acute Francesco Cossiga, was warning the parties to begin reforms before it was too late. Safe in the conviction that there was no alternative to them, during the 1992 election campaign the Christian Democrats and Socialists did not even pay lip service to the idea of political and institutional reform.

The governing parties' complacency was nearly, but not quite, justified. The ex-communists' vote did collapse in the 1992 elections, but so did that of the Christian Democrats. The Northern League, by contrast, did far better than anyone had believed possible by obtaining almost 9 percent of the national vote and becoming the second party in northern Italy. The governing coalition, which included the Social Democrats and the Liberals, saw its parliamentary majority reduced to the slimmest of margins and its legitimacy reduced to similar dimensions. President Cossiga resigned and the fragile government coalition was lumbered with the delicate political task of electing a new president. It proved entirely unable to do so, and as it was giving a virtuoso display of ineptitude and indecision, events overtook it. The Mafia murdered Giovanni Falcone, the state prosecutor whose courage and skill in the fight against organized crime had made him a national hero, and other prosecutors in Milan announced that senior members of the Socialist Party close to the party leader, Bettino Craxi, were under investigation on serious corruption charges. The ice had broken, and try as the parties might to claw themselves back onto the surface, they were doomed to sink into the depths. Public support for the Christian Democrats and the Socialists plunged over the Summer of 1992, never to return to its former level.

It will be seen that this explanation for the "Italian revolution" considers that chance and contingency played a large role in the demise of the Italian party system. But this is not to say that we cannot identify a number of factors which made the recent events in Italy possible. The stifling role of the parties in every aspect of ordinary life, the growing arrogance of the Mafia, blatant fiscal injustice, the venality, waste and extravagance of the principal political parties, frustration with Italy's constitution and electoral laws, and a pervasive feeling that the collapse of communism made real reform of the political system possible, all contributed to the downfall of Europe's longest-ruling political class.

The defeat of this class, however, was not inevitable, as accounts which explain the recent upheaval in Italy purely in terms of causes and effects naturally imply. Without wishing to write history in terms of might-have-beens, I think that it is obvious that Italy's party bosses might have taken stronger action against the Mafia sooner; might have perceived that the protest of the Northern League rested upon genuine grievances; might have moderated the greed for money and power that caused politics in cities like Milan to degenerate into a sophisticated version of racketeering. They might, in short, have taken steps that would have kept them in power. Plenty of people throughout the 1980s were telling them that changes had to be made, quickly, or else the system would fall. They underestimated the wisdom of this advice, and it is not, in my view, a sufficient argument to say that the party bosses made this error because they were too closely locked into the traditional methods of governing the country to amend their conduct.

Italian politics in the 1980s was a grotesque exaggeration of traditional democracy, Italian style. Where once politicians asked millions of lire as reward for their role in approving contracts for public works, in the 1980s the ruling parties initiated pharaonic public works of little or no public utility and asked for billions of lire, or hundreds of billions, in bribes. Where once the Christian Democrats treated the Mafia as an indulgent father might treat a boisterous but picturesque son, by doling out occasional gifts of money and generally gaining a secret pleasure from his frequent excesses, in the 1980s the ruling parties sold the family silver to appease a child whose murderous tendencies had become all too evident. Where once men of talent needed to have party cards in order to take top jobs in the state holding companies, in the 1980s unqualified crooks like

Lodovico Ligato (see Chapter Three) were appointed to run major nationalized industries as a reward for their services to their bosses in the political hierarchy. Where once Italian public opinion had been content to grumble at its leaders but vote for them time and time again, in the 1990s, citizens had no patience left. The parties, especially the Christian Democrats and the Socialists, were rightly seen as the enemies of good government and were punished accordingly. To use an analogy that I think is instructive, Italy's party bosses were like an office clerk of some genuine achievement whose petty fiddling of the books was treated with reluctant complicity (and some veiled amusement) by the rest of his colleagues for many years. Business was booming and confronting the thief would have sparked off an unpleasant scene. Besides, he was doing a difficult job that no previous incumbent had managed to fulfill satisfactorily. When, however, the clerk began domineering over the rest of the office staff, looting the firm's cash-flow, consorting openly with shady characters, and swamping the business's ledgers with a flood of red ink, the decision could be put off no longer: In an impressive display of unity the thief was shown the door, though much less unity was shown over whom should assume his role.

This book is a study in the office politics that led up to this decision. If this seems a trivial topic, it should be remembered that Italy, inc., is the fifth largest economic concern in the world and one of the most innovative. Italy also has a habit of being in the forefront of political change. Mazzini, Garibaldi and Cavour ushered in the age of nationalism; Mussolini played a similar role for totalitarianism. When one looks at the growing dissatisfaction of other European peoples with the mediocrity and corruption of their leaders, who will bet against Italy not being, once more, a pace-setter for historic change?

2

Politics, Italian Style

For most of the post-war years, Italians grumbled that they were living in a society that was less a democracy than a *partitocrazia*: A political system where the principal parties ran the government in their own interests. Since 1992, it has in fact become clear that Italy was really a cleptocracy: a state whose leading political figures were running the country into the ground for their own profit.

Until their leaders were caught with their hands in the till, however, Italians showed a sneaking admiration for their political masters. The permanent boom of Italy's economy, lax tax collection and an open-handed attitude with public money bred an amused tolerance for the intrigues and palace coups of Italy's political class. For all its quarrelsome coalitions, crisis-wracked governments and occasional bribery scandals, the Italian political system was arguably the most stable of any western European democracy in the post-war years. The pro-American, center-right Christian Democrats (DC) took the helm straight after the war and administered the country in the company of the small "lay" (i.e. non-Catholic) parties of the Center until the mid-1960s. When the DC allied itself with the Republican party (PRI) or the Social Democrat Party (PSDI), these coalitions were slightly leftward leaning; when the DC allied itself to the Liberal Party (PLI), policies took on a marginally more rightist tinge. From the mid-1960s onwards the Socialist party (PSI) entered these calculations. Perennially disturbed by an identity crisis -- was it a party of government and compromise, or a leftist party with a radical program for the transformation of Italian society? -- the PSI took a prominent role in the governing coalition until 1974 and then spent an ineffectual half-decade in the wilderness of opposition.

Night and the DC, however, always returned. Every prime minister 1945-1981, and all but three presidents of the republic, was a member of the DC. The DC's grip on key ministries such as foreign affairs and defense was absolute.[1] This hegemony over the leading institutions of the state was founded on remarkably consistent levels of popular consent. Not counting the 1948 elections, which were fought in an atmosphere of anti-communist hysteria and resulted in the DC taking 48 percent of the poll, the share of the Italian electorate opting for the DC's shield and cross symbol between 1945-1979 oscillated between a high point of 42.3 percent in the 1958 elections, and lows of 38.3 percent in both 1963 and 1979. The DC's centrality was ensured by the absence of a credible opposition. Apart from the DC and the lay parties, two permanently excluded forces existed within the political system.

The first, and by far the most important, of these was the Italian Communist Party (PCI). The Communists, led by their historic leader, Palmiro Togliatti, participated in the first post-war administrations formed by the war hero Ferruccio Parri and the Christian Democrat Alcide De Gasperi.[2] The DC, however, drove the PCI from government in 1947 and thereafter the Communists represented, at any rate in the propaganda of the governing parties, a permanent anti-democratic menace to the security of Italian democracy. In 1947, this might have been true. The PCI was close to being a controlled organization of the Soviet Union, though it was never as obsequiously subservient to Moscow as the French Communist Party, and as early as the 1950s began tacking away from a narrowly pro-Soviet "line." In 1968, under the leadership of Togliatti's successor, Luigi Longo, the PCI criticized the Soviet invasion of Czechoslovakia in forthright terms -- Dubcek's "Socialism with a human face" was far more akin to the PCI's own objectives. The party remained, however, a monolithic organization run on strictly "top down" principles. Democratic discussion of policy alternatives was permitted until the leadership had made up its mind, but thereafter rigid adherence to the Leninist norms of democratic centralism ensured that the party spoke with one voice.

The other political force whose ideas never gained mainstream acceptance in Italy was the neo-fascist Italian Social Movement (MSI). This party was founded in 1946 by unrepentent supporters of the Republic of Salò, the northern Italian dictatorship constituted by Mussolini after his overthrow in July 1943 and subsequent rescue by the Germans. The early members of the MSI espoused a violently anti-capitalist, anti-American form of National Socialism which lasted until 1950 when a relatively more moderate wing of former fascists took control and attempted to make the MSI a practical alternative to the PLI on the right by supporting Italy's membership of NATO and conceding the legitimacy of Italy's democratic constitution. In 1960, the DC, during the premiership of the opportunistic Fernando Tambroni, responded to these advances by governing with the parliamentary backing of the MSI and the monarchists rather than the lay parties of the Center. Flushed with this act of legitimization, the MSI provocatively elected to hold its annual congress in the fiercely anti-fascist city of Genoa. The resulting riots and bloodshed, which spread all over Italy, chased the MSI out to the margins once more, where the party stayed despite a thought-provoking electoral triumph in the general elections of 1972. The MSI took over 8 percent of the vote in 1972, to make it easily Italy's fourth-largest party after the DC, the PCI and the PSI, and though its vote declined from this peak in subsequent elections to around 6 percent, Italian neo-fascism retained its fourth place in the polls. By the end of the 1970s, the MSI was a substantial, well-organized party that was nevertheless of little influence upon Italian public life. The DC was too wary of repeating its error of 1960 to contemplate shifting back towards the hard men in black on their right.[3]

The perpetual presence in government of a single political party was not the only distinguishing feature of Italian democracy. To a greater extent than anywhere else in democratic Europe, political power was fused with the economic power of the state. In the 1950s and 1960s, Italy's spectacular industrial growth -- its so-called "economic miracle" -- was guided by state-owned conglomerates such as IRI (the Institution for Industrial Reconstruction), or ENEL (the state electricity company).[4] Top-level appointments to such companies were invariably politically motivated. Competence, while desirable, was not enough. The DC gradually extended this blatant politicization throughout the entire state sector. Directorships of savings banks were political appointees, while a party card became a useful aid for obtaining a university chair and a crucial one for landing a job with the national broadcasting service. The heads of foundations, institutes, health authorities, the railways -- any institution dispensing public money -- were in the gift of the leading power-brokers of the DC. The main advantage of this concentration of political power, from the DC's point of view, was that it enabled the party's leaders to head off electorally disruptive decisions such as layoffs by the managers of state industry. The predictable downside to this excessive political influence was that Italy's many state holding companies rapidly became social agencies rather than internationally competitive industrial concerns. In the 1960s, when Italy's nationalized industries could sell everything they produced and did not have to face particularly intense competition in their domestic market, this did not matter. In the 1980s it did.

Institutional stagnation and the omnipresence of the main party of government had predictable consequences. By the early 1970s, the DC had evolved into a vast, corrupt bureaucracy, which owed its political staying power more to the lack of a credible alternative and to its own largesse with the tax-payers' money than to any clear vision of the kind of society Italy should be. Sitting on top of this bureaucracy (and controlling powerful factions within it) was an aging elite of power-brokers, many of whom had been in office uninterruptedly since the late 1940s. The most emblematic of these figures, the bat-eared, mandarin-like Giulio Andreotti, once remarked, in near-defiance of Acton's celebrated dictum, that "power wears out those who do not have it"[5] but by the early 1970s, a growing sector of Italian public opinion was increasingly of the opinion that too much power had stayed in the hands of the DC for too long. Radical opinion was more forthright. For critics like the Padua university professor Toni Negri, Italy was quite simply a plutocracy in which a small and unrepresentative political class, together with a handful of privileged business families and the upper ranks of the Catholic church, ran the state for its own profit.[6]

This diagnosis suffered from the left's habitual inability to take into account its opponent's intentions, but it was still essentially accurate. The radical left's solution, however, social revolution, was not one which could appeal to the mass of Italian society. Though one of the political movements formed by the radical left, *Lotta continua* (Unceasing Struggle), managed to win over many manual workers in the public sector industries and in the FIAT car plant in Turin, broad public opinion soon became frustrated by the industrial anarchy created by *Lotta continua*'s activism. Increasingly, the PCI began to look like a moderate option between the inertia of the established party system and the permanent upheaval offered by the radical left. This mood was augmented by the oil shock of 1973, which caused the first hiccough in Italy's post-war economic miracle, and by the election of Enrico Berlinguer to the leadership of the PCI in 1973. Berlinguer, whom Paul Ginsborg has justly characterized as a man of "transparent honesty and determination"[7] greeted his accession to the party secretaryship by floating the idea of a "historic compromise" between the DC and the PCI. By offering to share government with the DC, Berlinguer argued, the PCI would prevent the reactionary wing of the DC resorting to Chilean methods of dealing with the danger of a progressive government. After regional elections in June 1975, when the PCI surged to 33 percent of the national vote, just 2 percent less than the DC, Berlinguer's proposal suddenly became practical politics. Nevertheless, the general elections of 1976 were fought by the DC as an ideological war. For all Berlinguer's efforts to allay suspicions of the communists' intentions (including a promise to keep Italy in NATO), the fear that the PCI would destabilize the system by "overtaking" the DC's share of the vote and governing in coalition with the PSI, dominated the electoral campaign and enabled the DC to cling to its position as largest party. Aided by the unambiguous support of the United States and by the Italian *ceto medio* (middle class) abandoning the small center parties, the DC won nearly 39 percent of the vote, four percentage points more than the PCI, which advanced to a historic high of 34.4 percent.

Despite the DC's victory, its hegemony had been broken. Even with all three of its traditional allies, the DC's support in the country did not reach 50 percent. Short of governing with the MSI, a move which would have ignited public opinion and the organized working class, the long-standing center-right coalition was no longer able to guarantee a majority in parliament. It was thus compelled to open to the left. A government of "national solidarity" was therefore formed by Andreotti. Despite its name, this administration consisted entirely of DC ministers, with the PCI providing external support. A communist, Pietro Ingrao, became speaker of the Chamber of Deputies; the PCI and the unions became "indispensable to the management of Italy."[8] Andreotti struggled along through three years and two governments in this way. It was during these years, known to Italians as *gli anni di piombo* (literally, the "years of lead") that the Italian authorities overcame the challenge of a terrorist group, the "Red Brigades," which, between March-May 1978, succeeded in kidnapping and killing Aldo Moro, the president of the DC, a former prime minister, and the chief architect of the strategy of cooperation with the PCI.

The PCI's assistance was indispensable to the DC in these years, but Berlinguer did not receive the expected reward in progressive social legislation. In retrospect, it is difficult to see why he placed so much faith in the DC's willingness to accommodate the PCI's ideals. When, in January 1979, the government of national solidarity resigned, the PCI's historic moment had passed. Several chaotic months of political squabbling followed before elections in June. In the poll, the PCI dropped back to under 31 percent and the DC stayed steady at over 38 percent. Berlinguer announced that the PCI was abandoning the idea of a "historic compromise." From now on, the PCI would work to achieve the so-called "democratic alternative": a majority coalition of the parties of the left.

Craxi and De Mita

The leader of the PSI, however, Benedetto (Bettino) Craxi, had other ideas. Craxi had come to power in an internal party coup in 1976 and had led the party with skill, but little success, for three years. In the June 1979 elections, the PSI obtained just under 10 percent of the vote, unchanged from three years previously. Nevertheless, these years had not been without importance for the PSI. Ideologically, the PSI had moved away from its longtime subservience to the PCI under the influence of Norberto Bobbio, Italy's leading political philosopher. Bobbio's *Quale Socialismo?* was a powerful attack on the statist tendency of the Marxist left and the historical record of the PCI which eventually inspired the Socialist intelligentsia to rethink the party's dogma, projecting the PCI as the PSI's sparring partner in a "duel on the left."[9] Initially, however, this rethinking tended to lead the PSI to criticize the PCI from the left, by reaching out to Italy's extra-parliamentary movements. Craxi was even in favor of negotiating with the Red Brigades at the height of the Aldo Moro crisis in 1978. The electoral failure of 1979 proved that this strategy would not establish the PSI as a major force with public opinion. Craxi therefore made a "violent swerve"[10] in the party's political line between 1979-1981, moving the party toward social-democratic reformism and entering the governments formed by Francesco Cossiga (DC) in April 1980 and Arnaldo Forlani (DC) in October 1980. The change of the party's standpoint was confirmed at Palermo in 1981 during the first of many spectacular party conferences during the 1980s.[11]

Craxi had therefore opted to take the PSI into the system, rather than oppose it from without. One contemporary Italian writer has seen this as a fatal choice for the PSI. Craxi's decision, he argues, while it allowed the PSI to turn itself into a rival power-center to the DC and to "exploit" the "exercise of power" for electoral purposes, led to the PSI's identification with the system and prevented it from riding the "mounting wave of dissent" among the electorate later in the decade.[12] The truth of this analysis is indisputable, but it is written with the benefit of hindsight. At the time, Craxi's move seemed like a further breach in the hegemony of the DC. Forlani's short-lived administration made space for seven socialist ministers before giving way in May 1981 to the first post-war government not to be headed by a Christian Democrat, the Republican Giovanni Spadolini.

Spadolini's government was a five-party coalition, or *pentapartito*, consisting of all three of the "lay" parties of the non-Catholic center, the DC and the PSI. As such, it was both indicative of the extent to which Craxi's march to the center had depolarized Italian politics (the PLI and the PSI had never before consented to sit together around the same cabinet table) and symptomatic of the DC's malaise: For the first time, the DC had to rely on four allies to ensure a parliamentary majority. The emergence of Craxi and Spadolini as national leaders rubbed additional salt in the wound: For many in the DC, the prospect of the satellite parties establishing a permanent claim to the prime ministership seemed to loom. The mood of the DC accordingly became more open to renewal. In 1982, the party elected Ciriaco De Mita, a thoughtful lawyer from the southern province of Avellino, and the leading figure on the party's left, to the party leadership. De Mita was unusual in Italian politics in that he was identified with a precise program of reforms, being a firm believer in the necessity of incorporating the PCI into the system, so long as the process of reform begun by Berlinguer was continued, and a vocal critic of the DC's sprawling bureaucracy. De Mita's jubilant supporters promised that their man would *demitizzare* (demythologize) Craxi and restore the centrality of the DC. De Mita's strategy, however, backfired at its first electoral test. The DC, in line with De Mita's prescriptions, fought the June 1983 elections with a platform of reformist policies, promising austerity and an end to pork barrel politics. The result was an electoral disaster. The DC fell six percentage points to less than 33 percent, the PSI inched forward to more than 11 percent, the PLI, PRI and PSDI jointly arrived at 12 percent, their best result since 1953. The PCI declined below 30 percent, continuing its slither back down the electoral slope it had so painstakingly climbed.

These results left both the DC and the PCI in the unhappy position of needing the PSI to form a government. Short of a return to an alliance of the big two parties, which nobody was suggesting in 1983, Craxi was in a position to name the price of his support: His own accession to the prime minister's job. Since the choice was either Craxi or the PCI, the DC swallowed the pill. Craxi became *presidente del consiglio* in August 1983 and governed until April 1987.

By common consent, Craxi was a success as prime minister. During his time in office he propelled Italy on to the world stage, establishing a warm relationship with President Ronald Reagan and taking an active role in the United Nations. At the same time, he knew how to distance himself from American policy when necessary. Craxi's independent line during the Achille Lauro affair in October 1985 made him a national hero, though it antagonized the pro-American Republicans and almost brought his government down.[13] On the domestic front, Craxi successfully forced through the abolition of the automatic cost-of-living increase enjoyed by Italian workers, and then beat off an attempt from the trade union movement and the PCI to reverse this move by referendum. More generally, he was admired for his novel capacity to take decisions and stick by them. Cartoons caricaturing Craxi as Mussolini were not long in appearing, but most Italians appreciated having a leader who knew his own mind and acted upon it. By March 1986, the best-selling national news magazine, *L'Espresso*, was talking of the "Craxi-effect." Craxi was rated better or much better than his immediate predecessors by over 40 percent of the electorate and his government was held to be doing "well-enough" by 63 percent -- an astounding figure by Italian standards.[14]

Craxi's image was helped by the economy's success. Italy enjoyed high growth rates in the early 1980s and in 1986 overtook Britain to become the world's fifth-largest industrial nation. Inflation, the bugbear of the Italian economy during the 1970s, was brought down to just 4 percent in 1987, a figure which led the PSI's intellectual monthly, *Mondoperaio*, to claim in March of that year that Craxi's administration had defeated high prices without defeating the working class.[15] Family wealth rose sharply throughout Craxi's stay in office, consumer spending soared, the savings rate, while in decline, remained one of the highest in the industrialized world. By 1989, Italians, especially northern Italians, were visibly better off than their counterparts in almost every other major democracy, including countries, like Germany, which are often regarded as economically more successful. Their clothes, shoes, houses and lifestyles were sleeker and more expensive; their bank accounts fatter. Most (75 percent) owned their own home, millions had second houses. The emblematic FIAT mini cars of the 1960s and 1970s had been traded in for more glamorous Lancias, Alfa Romeos and BMWs. The glow of these economic triumphs caused Italy's familiar reputation for ungovernability and social chaos to be briefly forgotten. For a moment, the papers were full of what the prolific journalist Giuseppe Turani predicted would be the "second economic miracle."[16]

Craxi also opened a new dimension in the challenge to the DC's hegemony over the political process. As prime minister, he began to assert the PSI's claims to parity or near-parity with the DC in control over the main state institutions and holding companies. In particular, the PSI strove to obtain a larger share of the top jobs in the banking sector and in the RAI, the state television company. By 1985, Craxi had succeeded in turning the second RAI channel into a PSI fief, just as the DC exercised an unbroken control over RAI 1 and the PCI dominated RAI 3. The payoff here, of course, was friendly television coverage, though "friendly" is a euphemism for the gushing propaganda which passed for objective reporting of Craxi's actions from the mid-1980s onward. The "great share-out" of 1986, when hundreds of politically sensitive jobs in the media, finance, hospitals and universities were distributed after an intense behind-the-scenes battle, saw the PSI make further progress toward equality with the DC.[17]

Craxi's strategy made relations with the DC even more rancorous than before. The PSI seemed to be deliberately undermining the DC's traditional form of government. Since 1948, the DC had consciously used the state as a way of combatting the PCI's superior organization. DC politicians used their influence in the state's industrial holdings or local health committees (USL) to find jobs for the unemployed and to protect workers in those industries from layoffs. Their reward, naturally, was votes. Apart from anti-communism and a vague appeal to Catholic values and patriotism (the DC's slogan in the 1987 elections was the unimaginative but evocative appeal *Forza Italia!* "Come on Italy!"), the DC had no ideological rallying call to the faithful. Voting for the DC, especially in southern Italy, was often an explicit transaction. Clearly, therefore, any attack on the DC's patronage powers represented a potential loss of votes. Worse, it threatened the internal harmony of the DC. Internally, the DC was organized into several "currents," each of which had its own leadership, agenda and patronage networks. Relations between these *correnti* were invariably tense in any case: The PSI's demand that the DC should make room for Socialist nominees opened the prospect of a civil war within the DC as the *correnti* squabbled over the DC's diminished share of the cake. The issue was not helped by De Mita's reforming zeal. At the 1985 and 1986 party conferences of the DC, he envisaged the abolition of the *correnti* system and the transformation of the party into a more modern body with greater attractions for the entrepreneurial class. His enemies within the hierarchy would have been more convinced of his sincerity on this question if De Mita's own patronage machine had been less well oiled. Inevitably (and probably justly), it appeared that De Mita was using the rhetoric of reform to undermine the positions of his chief rivals within the DC.

The Craxi administration, therefore, was anything but stable. Its unprecedented longevity -- by the standards of post-war Italian politics -- and its noisy claims to have brought governability, were masking serious causes of discord. Craxi's biggest coalition partner was envious of his success and riven with factional strife. His parliamentary majority was under continual attack from the so-called *franchi tiratori* (literally, "snipers") on the government benches who used parliament's secret voting rules to block legislation to which factions in the DC were hostile. For much of 1984-1985, Craxi was only able to govern with the tacit support of the PCI. There existed, therefore, the remarkable situation whereby Craxi's nominal allies within the government were trying to bring him down and his nominal adversaries were sustaining him. The PCI's motive for this policy is unclear, because, as Giorgio Galli has pointed out, it undercut the the "patrimony of coherence and prestige" the Communists were acquiring by leading the fight against Craxi's policy of de-indexing workers' wages as well as much of the sympathy which Enrico Berlinguer's death in February 1984 had bestowed upon them.[18] Two possible explanations stand out. Firstly, the leadership had passed into the hands of Alessandro Natta, a bureaucratic figure who was more adept at political maneuvering than outright opposition. Secondly, the PCI had not abandoned its hope of enticing the PSI into a coalition of the left. The PCI had become the largest party in Italy in the European elections in June 1984, reaching 33.3 percent, 0.3 percent ahead of the DC, and briefly the prospect of a government of the parties of the left (PCI-PSI-PRI-PSDI, plus the fringe movement *Democrazia proletaria*) became mathematically possible. The PSI, however, would have no truck with this idea, even though PCI-PSI administrations were governing in several provinces. Craxi, to bitter communist criticism, stuck to his uncomfortable allies in the DC and had the satisfaction of seeing the PCI fall back once more in regional elections in the Spring of 1985. The PSI, by contrast, advanced to over 12 percent.

Craxi's war with De Mita burst into the open in June 1986, when DC *franchi tiratori* defeated the government on a proposal to reform local government finance. It was the 160th such defeat during Craxi's spell in office. Craxi resigned and a lengthy government crisis began. After an attempt by the inevitable Andreotti to form a new administration, Craxi and De Mita patched up a deal which allowed Craxi to return to the prime minister's job on condition that the prime ministership would be in the hands of the DC in the last year of the legislature (i.e. from May 1987). This deal, the so-called *staffetta* (relay), lasted no more than a few months. In February 1987, Craxi hinted in a television interview that he would renege on its terms. De Mita responded by pulling the plug on the administration and setting in motion a lengthy *crisi di governo* that became almost a parody of the bickering and infighting characteristic of Italian coalition politics. The two principal parties in the *pentapartito* swapped insults (one of the leading members of the PSI, Rino Formica, even cast doubt on De Mita's intelligence, though he used the studied ambiguity beloved of Italian political discourse to do so[19]) and other prominent Socialist leaders, notably Craxi's deputy and heir-apparent, Claudio Martelli, held out the prospect at the party conference of the PSI in April 1987 that Socialists and Communists would before long be calling one another "comrade."[20] After a forlorn but nevertheless historic attempt by the PCI to form a government, and after a short-lived government headed by the veteran Christian Democrat Amintore Fanfani had been brought down by a tactical vote of the DC itself (the DC's leaders feared that extending a weak DC administration excessively would strengthen Craxi's bargaining position later), President Francesco Cossiga, a Christian Democrat friendly to the PSI, opted to end the legislature early and called elections for June 1987. This decision meant postponing until November referenda on the highly complex and politically divisive issues of judges' powers and the continuance of Italy's nuclear power program, but no other solution was possible. [21]

The electoral results were hailed by the Socialist press as a historic turning point. In the elections for the Chamber of Deputies (the lower house), the PCI lost 3 percentage points relative to 1983, falling back to under 27 percent; the PSI advanced to over 14 percent, though the Communists' losses and the PSI's success were less marked in the elections to the Senate, where the PCI declined to just 28 percent and the PSI actually obtained fewer votes and seats than in 1983. Luciano Pellicano, one of the leading theorists of the PSI, oddly saw this seemingly minor transfer of electoral advantage as a sign that the PCI was becoming "a vast reservoir" of votes for the PSI and that the PSI could legitimately hold out the prospect of the Italian left being united around liberal socialist, rather than Marxist principles.[22] The perception of the PSI more generally was that the 1987 results were the first crest of a "long wave" which would eventually sweep the PSI past the PCI and enable its leaders to deal with the DC on terms of electoral parity. This perception was based less on an objective reading of the electoral evidence than a profound conviction that the two major parties of the system were moribund, a conviction which their lackluster campaigning had done nothing to dispel. To quote Pellicano again, the elections demonstrated that:

> The Italians...thought things through and liberally backed the party whose proposals and activity inside the government has contributed more than any other to the revival of the economy and to the creation of the preconditions for further steps towards the levels of civility characteristic in the countries that lead the western camp.[23]

Pellicano's remark on the significance of the 1987 poll was widely shared by observers both in Italy and outside, and in a sense represented a further slip in the position of the DC. For the first time since 1948 a non-DC politician had become the most emblematic figure of the Italian political system and a party other than the DC was being talked up as the *partito guida* of Italian democracy. This achievement, however, rested on shallow foundations. The PSI did not have enough votes to make the other parties in the system do its bidding. In retrospect, when one considers the ruthless way in which Craxi had squeezed every last drop of advantage for the PSI out of his spell as *presidente del consiglio*, the "long wave" of the PSI was of singularly feeble dimensions. Between 1979-87, the PSI had gained only 5 percent in the national standings and could still call upon no more than half of the popular support enjoyed by the PCI. Furthermore, the PSI's gains had come to a very large extent at the expense of the PCI, a fact which meant both that the alternative of the left was no nearer realization and that the PSI could not plausibly use the threat of allying with the PCI as a stick to beat concessions out of the DC, though this did not stop the PSI from brandishing the idea of a left alliance at every opportunity in the rest of 1987.[24] Craxi's position, in short, was far less comfortable than it seemed.

The Camping Van Conspiracy

In the months following the June poll, both the perception of a Socialist victory and the electoral arithmetic played a part in events. The DC, which itself had enjoyed a recovery of sorts in the June elections by gaining five seats in the Senate and nine in the Chamber of Deputies with respect to the disaster of 1983, flatly refused to allow Craxi to return to the prime minister's job. Craxi, however, was strong enough to veto De Mita's own nomination. The first post-electoral administration was consequently headed by a left-wing Christian Democrat close to De Mita, Giovanni Goria. A northern Italian technocrat who had been a success as treasury minister under Craxi, Goria rapidly showed that he lacked the experience and the political weight to be prime minister. Like Craxi before him, the unfortunate Goria soon found that the secret voting system in parliament left him at the mercy of the "snipers" within the *maggioranza*. His attempts to pass a budget which would come to terms with Italy's burgeoning public deficit were repeatedly shot down by his nominal supporters and his government ended in chaos in March 1988. At this point, De Mita himself was compelled to take center stage. To a certain extent, this elevation to the prime ministership was against the Christian Democratic leader's own wishes. De Mita felt far from sure of his position within the DC and suspected that the party old guard was hoping that he would be discredited by his handling of the difficult relationship with the PSI and would consequently be rendered vulnerable within the DC.[25]

Events were to prove De Mita's fears well-founded. De Mita's government began in distracting tragedy when Roberto Ruffilli, a Bologna university professor who was one of the DC leader's closest collaborators and advisers, was murdered by one of the remaining Red Brigade cells in April 1988. It continued in a poisonous atmosphere of inter-party bickering and spite and struggled to impose any sort of direction on government policy, despite a high-sounding program of objectives. The government quickly became bogged down in the endless struggle over the budget deficit, though De Mita himself, to the fury of the PRI and the barons of Italian industry, was even less willing than his predecessors to take any action which threatened the parties' client networks or reduced the parties' discretionary control over the public purse.

By the end of 1988, De Mita's position had become parlous. One of Italy's leading conservative newspapers, *Il Giornale*, was accusing him of having used public money designated for disaster relief after the 1980 Irpinia earthquake to strengthen his (already copious) client networks in Avellino. His coalition was in tatters and his support within the DC was ebbing away. At the party congress in February 1989, the *Andreottiani* and the "Great Center" faction led by Antonio Gava, De Mita's interior minister and the head of the DC in Naples, combined forces to replace De Mita as party secretary with Arnaldo Forlani, the warmest supporter of collaboration with the PSI in the top ranks of the party. Despite a show of unity (De Mita's faction voted for Forlani and the party emphasised its support for his premiership), De Mita's ouster plainly represented an end to his project of reform within the party and to the hope of a new opening toward the PCI. For that reason, his supporters greeted Forlani's nomination and Craxi's appearance at the congress with a storm of whistles, creating a tense atmosphere which Forlani did nothing to ameliorate in his acceptance speech by insinuating that De Mita had attempted to subvert the internal democracy of the party for his own ends.[26] After Forlani's speech, De Mita's premiership was all but over. De Mita struggled on, amid mounting criticism from the PRI for the economic policy of his government (though the PRI, with excessive regard for the comforts of ministerial office, did not consider that its objections required it to resign from the government), until May 1989, when Claudio Martelli used the party congress of the PSI as a platform to state explicitly that the Socialists believed that the government had reached its "terminus."[27]

At the same congress, Forlani held a private meeting with Craxi in the Socialist leader's headquarters, a luxury camping van. It is widely thought that the purpose of this meeting was to make an agreement for the substitution of De Mita with Andreotti after the elections to the European parliament, which were due in June. Whatever the truth of this allegation (it is unlikely that the PSI would have commited themselves before knowing the European election results[28]), the *patto del camper* signified the onset of the sinister-sounding CAF (Craxi-Andreotti-Forlani), the pact between the triumvirate of political notables which would govern Italy until June 1992. The triumvirate began its rule with a disappointment. In the European elections, the PSI's "long wave" reached no further up the beach than in 1987. The DC went backward, obtaining nearly 2,000,000 votes fewer than in 1987 and returning to their historical low of less than 33 percent. Chastened by their lack of electoral progress, the PSI accepted that Andreotti had first claim on *Palazzo Chigi* (the state residence of the Italian prime minister). Andreotti formed his sixth administration, "Giulio VI," during the summer of 1989 and embarked upon yet another stint as Italy's chief representative on the world stage. At one level, in other words, it was business as usual. At another level, however, the DC's need to make the PSI a permanent part of its power structure reflected the extent to which its electoral slide had ended the party's hegemony. With just 32-33 percent of the vote, the DC did not just need the PSI to govern, it needed to be on good terms with the PSI's leadership.

The DC's hegemony had also been eroded in another way. Just as a chronic debtor in private life complains that his life is not his own, that he works purely for the banks to whom he owes money, so the incoming Andreotti administration would discover that it no longer had control over its own financial destiny. The deficit issue, which had been beating like a metronome behind the wild improvising of Italy's political elite all decade, was pounding so loud by the summer of 1989 that even a veteran client-manager like Andreotti was briefly forced to listen. Europe's seeming progress towards greater monetary union required Italy to get its public spending in line with the other major European economies; purely domestic needs were pressing in the same direction. By the end of the 1980s, everybody recognized that high taxation and government red tape were slowing down the chief engine of Italian prosperity: its wealth of small and medium-sized companies in all sectors of light industry. The ruthlessly competitive businesses of the Po river valley are uniquely able to maintain constant increases in quality with stable prices and are exceptionally good at spotting market niches and changing customer tastes, but they were no longer able to bear the weight of the Italian state alone. Within months of the formation of the "Andreotti VI" administration, Guido Carli, the treasury minister, and Carlo Azeglio Ciampi, the governor of the Bank of Italy, had begun to shout for drastic measures.

The figures show why. In the 1980s, Italy's public debt soared from approximately 300 trillion lire (61 percent of GDP) to 1,300 trillion (101 percent) on the back of a steady annual public borrowing requirement of 10-14 percent of GDP. Apart from Belgium, this was the highest debt of any European Community country, and the rate of growth was faster than any country other than Greece. Worse, this huge expansion of the public debt had taken place

18

despite a remorseless increase in taxation in the same period. In 1981, the state took 32 percent of GDP in tax; in 1990 it was taking 40 percent, a figure that has since increased sharply. While Italians were still paying less tax, by this measure, than the Germans, the French, the Danes and some other EC nations, no other country had endured such a surge in the rate of taxation increase in the 1980s.[29] Moreover, services had not been improved by this influx of cash. If anything, they had degenerated. Hospitals, buses, universities and trains were all, in their own ways, more crowded, shabbier and inefficient than a decade previously.

This painful combination of steadily increasing taxation and steadily increasing deficits was explicitly due to the chronic reluctance of the PSI and the DC to get to grips with wasteful levels of employment in the state sector, over-generous entitlement programs, and the influence of corruption on public works spending (see Chapter Eight). The Italian state employs approximately four million people, or one person in seven of the working population, mostly in loss-making state industries or in the hugely over-staffed education system. The rational economic course would have been to slim down the state sector during the boom years of Craxi's prime ministership when the people who lost their jobs would have stood a reasonable chance of finding new employment. Instead, the parties had opted to let the efficiency issue slide, being keenly aware that their client networks within the public services could disappear if they took severe measures. The problem with this strategy was its clumsiness. Although steps had been taken from 1987 onwards to ensure that the government's current deficit was kept under some sort of control (spending being limited to 1-2 percent above incoming tax revenues), the necessity of paying interest on the debt mountain kept the budget deficit growing, despite the tightening of the tax vise on the economy. But since tax evasion is rife among professionals and the self-employed, the bulk of the new taxation needed to stave off financial disaster was levied on indirect taxes such as the duty on petroleum (gasoline reached almost $5 per gallon), sales tax (luxury goods are taxed at 19 percent or more), upon salaried workers and business overheads. By the time Andreotti took office, the injustice inherent in the government's strategy -- compelling the mass of the wage-earning population to pay more taxes to maintain a huge, inefficient, politicized state, while letting the already privileged rich escape almost scot-free (indeed, to profit via investments in high interest, tax-free government bonds) -- was a symbol of the failure of the political system as a whole.

Democracy, Italian Style

There was at least one good man in Babylon -- actually in New Haven, Connecticut -- who believed that the instability, Machiavellianism, pork-barrel politics, and fiscal irresponsibility described in this chapter were not pathological problems for Italian democracy, but colorful manifestations of the national character. In 1987, an American author and academic, Joseph LaPalombara of Yale University, published *Democracy, Italian Style*, in which he argued that despite the surface impression of chaos and factional warfare the country presented to an outsider, Italy did in fact possess a political system that was both functional and rootedly popular with its citizens. Leaving a major hostage to fortune, LaPalombara suggested that he knew of "no post-war democracy" that had a better record than Italy's.[30]

La Palombara's book was of course published at the height of the Craxi boom and the euphoria induced by Italy's entrance into the economic big leagues, but it did not depend upon a crude equation of economic with political success for its justification. LaPalombara, instead, developed a highly sophisticated account of Italian life and politics, which -- rightly -- did not shrink from generalizing about the Italian psyche. Italy, from LaPalombara's angle of vision, was an essentially divided society, with sharp regional, cultural and political differences. It was united by a certain national fondness for *furberia* (cunning or craftiness), for the dramatic gesture, and by an innate conservatism which rendered its people suspicious of far-reaching changes. The political system which had emerged in the post-war world was the reflection of these internal divisions and national characteristics. Italians admired the politician whose maneuvering brought the pork home to his electoral district, or made his position in the hierarchy more secure. They were inclined to wink at minor corruption, though they were outspoken in asserting that Italy was the most corrupt country in the world, a view which LaPalombara regarded as an exaggeration.[31] The Italians' sense of drama allowed them to enjoy the ceaseless *crisi di governo*. The endless to-ing and fro-ing of ministers and governments provided an engaging spectacle, especially as the personnel of government invariably remained the same -- a state of affairs which satisfied their conservative instincts. Underlying the nation's attitude to politics as a whole was a sense of fragility, a perception that things might fall apart. This explained the country's ambivalent approach to the PCI. On the one hand, the Italians were afraid that voting for the PCI might set in motion forces which would lead to the country's dissolution, on the other, they were concerned to ensure that the PCI was not excluded from the political process. The client networks possessed by the major parties were an indispensable part of social cohesiveness, giving practically everybody a stake in the system and providing a channel for political participation. Italy's bloated state sector, with its hundreds of thousands of people doing non-jobs, was a force for stability in a society which had seen Mussolini rise from nowhere to absolute power on the back of popular resentment at unemployment. Italian politics, in other words, while hardly a model a purist for democratic theory would recommend, nevertheless worked as well, or better, than many other long-standing democracies. Much as the Italians grumbled that they were living in a *partitocrazia*, their behavior betrayed their fundamental satisfaction with the way that they were governed. What other country in the world had voted in such numbers (participation in national elections and referenda is almost invariably 85-90 percent) for the same parties for so long?

There is much that is valuable in LaPalombara's analysis. By saying that the party system was an outgrowth of the Italian national character and that the clientelistic form of politics was deeply rooted in the nation's way of life, *Democracy, Italian Style* said something that was both unpopular and true. At the same time, the events in the 1990s have demonstrated that the Italian electorate's concern at the excesses of the *partitocrazia* was not just ritual grumbling but perfectly sincere. There was evidence even in the mid-1980s to show this was so. The same poll which started discussion of the "Craxi-effect" also revealed that 81 percent of Italians thought that their political system was in need of "profound" or "revolutionary" change.[32] The causes of this huge plurality for sweeping reform to the party system are not hard to find. They lie in the downside of party rule: Reckless management of the public purse, corruption, connivance with the Mafia and vote-rigging, features which LaPalombara mentioned almost in passing in *Democracy, Italian Style*, but which nonetheless were essential aspects of the party system he was so plausibly defending.[33]

All of these features, moreover, worsened during the 1980s. The Craxi decade was a decade of excess. Italy's party bosses (because two parties were competing, within the government, to dominate the power of the state) were more reckless with the taxpayers' money than they had ever been before. Corruption, once the oil that greased the wheels of Italy's labyrinthine bureaucracy, became endemic at all levels of the political process. The Mafia, whose influence over the political system was traditionally limited to a handful of southern cities, became a de facto government throughout much of the South, an enormous increase in its influence that took place with the tacit connivance of Italy's national political elites. Abuse of the democratic system, either through ballot fraud or through manipulative propaganda on the party-dominated state television service, became frighteningly near to being the norm.

Yet *la sbornia* (the binge) couldn't go on forever. While the quadrille of party politics danced on during the 1980s, with the political bigwigs exchanging partners and passing sly asides in time-honoured fashion, the music in the background was becoming increasingly discordant and the muttering of the servants louder and louder. The truly remarkable fact about *la rivoluzione italiana* is that none of the dancers, immersed as they were in the intricate footwork of party politics, seemed to hear.

Notes

1. There have been three non-DC Presidents of the Republic: Luigi Einaudi (PLI) 1948-55, Giuseppe Saragat (PSDI) 1964-71 and Sandro Pertini (PSI) 1978-85.

2. An excellent discussion of the political turmoil of the immediate post-war years in Italy is Antonio Gambino, *Storia della dopoguerra*, Bari (Laterza) 1980. See also Paul Ginsborg, *A History of Contemporary Italy: Society and Politics 1943-1988*, London (Penguin) 1990, Chapter 3.

3. This information on the MSI relies on Piero Ignazi, *L'Estrema destra in Europa*, Bologna (Il Mulino) 1994, pp 169-180. Ignazi's full-length study of the MSI, *Il Polo escluso. Profilo del Movimento sociale italiano*, Bologna (Il Mulino) 1989, is the standard work on the MSI.

4. A useful English language account of Italy's "economic miracle" and subsequent economic progress is the first four chapters of Donald Sassoon's informative *Contemporary Italy: Politics, Economy & Society since 1945*, London (Longman) 1986. See also Ginsborg, *A History of Contemporary Italy*, Chapters 5 and 7.

5. Andreotti's words were: "il potere logora chi non ce l'ha." His comment was in direct response to Enrico Berlinguer's accusation that the DC had been worn out by its lengthy tenure of power.

6. Negri was unjustly accused in April 1979 of being the brain behind the *Brigate Rosse* terrorist organization. Negri spent several years in prison before running as a Radical Party candidate in the 1983 elections. After his election to parliament, Negri jumped bail and fled to Paris, where he now resides, and where for several years he continued to draw much of his salary as a parliamentary deputy.

7. Paul Ginsborg, *A History of Contemporary Italy*, p 354.

8. See Giuliano Amato and Luciano Cafagna, *Duello a Sinistra*, Bologna (Il Mulino) 1982.

9. Jean-François Revel, The *Totalitarian Temptation*, London (Secker & Warburg) 1977, p 304, quoting Giovanni Agnelli, the president of FIAT. Revel has an excellent chapter on the significance of the PCI's strategy of pursuing a historic compromise with the DC, and, more generally, of the significance of Berlinguer's break with Moscow.

10. Giovanni Sabbatucci, *Il Riformismo Impossible*, Bari (Laterza) 1991, p 118. The original Italian is: "una brusca sterzata."

11. A good behind-the-scenes account of Craxi's dominance over the PSI at the beginning of the 1980s is: Elio Veltri, *Da Craxi a Craxi*, Bari (Laterza) 1993, pp 15-63 passim. An excellent English language account of the role of the PSI in the early 1980s is K. Robert Nilsson, "The Italian Socialist Party: An Indispensable Hostage," in Howard Penniman (ed), *Italy at the Polls 1983*, Durham, NC (Duke University Press) 1987, pp 78-100.

12. Sabbatucci, *Il Riformismo Impossible*, p 120.

22

13. For an English language account, see Joseph LaPalombara, "The Achille Lauro Affair: A Note on Italy and the United States," *Yale Review* 75 (1986), pp 542-63.

14. Guido Quaranta, "L'Effetto Craxi" *l'Espresso*, March 2, 1986.

15. Antonio Pedone, "Come vincere l'inflazione senza sconfiggere i lavoratori," *Mondoperaio* (40), March 1987, pp 6-10.

16. Giuseppe Turani, *Il secondo miracolo italiano 1985-95*, Milan (Sperling & Kupfer) 1986.

17. Tullio Fazzolari and Guido Quaranta, "La grande spartizione," *l'Espresso*, March 23, 1986.

18. This is the view of Giorgio Galli, *I partiti politici italiani 1943-91*, Rome (Rizzoli) 1991.

19. Formica, with a syllabine insult worthy of Andreotti, said that De Mita was not a "thinker of the *Magna Grecia* ...not just because Greek culture never reached Irpinia (De Mita's home), but because the philosophers of the ancient Greece were the expression of thought at its highest level." De Mita had once been compared to a classical philosopher by the industrialist Giovanni Agnelli. Quoted *Avanti!* April 5, 1987.

20. Martelli imagined a situation in which communists and socialists would not just be allies and fellow-travellers, but "comrades full-stop."

21. For a much fuller account of the one of the most intricate government crises in Italian history, see Enzo Balboni, "Who governs?: the crisis of the Craxi government and the role of the president of the republic" (capitalization missing in the original), in Robert Leonardi and Piergiorgio Corbetta (eds), *Italian Politics A Review*, vol 4, London (Pinter) and Bologna (Il Mulino) 1988, pp 11-24. The impact of the two referenda on the crisis is specifically dealt with in Anna Chimenti, *Storia dei referendum*, Bari (Laterza) 1993, Chapter 8.

22. Luciano Pellicano, *Mondoperaio* (40), July 1987, p 2.

23. Ibid., p 3.

24. The PSI formed a joint administration with the PCI in Milan in December 1987, to the fury of De Mita and the DC.

25. Giorgio Galli, *I partiti politici italiani*, p 315.

26. A colorful account of the dethroning of De Mita is Giampaolo Pansa, *L'Intrigo*, Milan (Sperling & Kupfer) 1990, pp 56-73.

27. The word Martelli used was "*capolinea.*"

28. Giorgio Galli, *I partiti politici italiani*, p 349.

29. All the statistics in this paragraph are from the contribution of Ignazio Musu to L'Ente Luigi Einaudi, *Il disavanzo pubblico in Italia*, vol. 1, Bologna (Il Mulino) 1991.

30. Joseph LaPalombara, *Democracy, Italian Style*, New Haven (Yale University Press) 1987, p 285.

31. Ibid., p 95. LaPalombara admits that money "changes hands" in unbelievably large amounts," but implies that bribery and corruption are part of "politics as

spectacle." The taking of money by the political parties is an understood thing, which arouses little outrage. Nevertheless, he does not describe any of the major scandals of the early 1980s in detail.

32. *L'Espresso*, March 2, 1986.

33. The entry on "mafia" in LaPalombara's index runs to just two lines.

3

The Mafia and Politics

It is a minimum precondition for the existence of civil society that citizens should feel that the state is protecting them and their families by upholding and enforcing a system of laws, is guaranteeing their economic security by sound management of the public finances, and is working for the common good, not on behalf of sectional interests. In a democracy, in addition, citizens feel that their votes and voices should have some sway in the political process and that elections should be carried out with scrupulous fairness to ensure that the people's will, so far as is possible, is the key factor in determining the political coloring of the executive.

This pedantic recital of the state's obligations to its citizens is intended to underscore the central point of this chapter. In the 1980s, the political parties in charge of the Italian state acted as if they had no notion that their governance of the country was conditional upon their meeting certain legitimate expectations. The fiscal irresponsibility of the *pentapartito* has already been noted. In three important regions of southern Italy, Sicily, Calabria and Campania, the parties' breach of the social contract was graver still. In these regions, organized crime was allowed to become a state within the state, exacting a tax on property and business (the protection racket), educating the youth of the squalid slums which surround Palermo, Catania, Naples and Reggio Calabria in violence and usurping the legitimate state's role as a dispenser of justice with arbitrary terror. Murder rates and serious crimes of all kinds soared, yet the state's response was timid. So timid, in fact, that the suspicion that the higher reaches of the legal and political hierarchies were colluding with the Mafia, the Neapolitan Camorra and the Calabrian *'Ndrangheta* had hardened into certainty by the end of the decade. Adding insult to injury, the citizens of these regions were deprived of their democratic voice. Ballot fraud reached such dimensions in southern Italy in the

1987 national elections that in many districts the final results were a work of art rather than arithmetic.

Men of Honor

The Mafia is an integral part of the culture of much of southern Italy. In three regions in particular, Sicily, Calabria and Campania, local *cosche mafiose* (mafia clans) have constituted the unofficial government for hundreds of years. Throughout the 19th century, the legal government (whether of the Bourbon Kingdom of the Two Sicilies or the Liberal administrations which followed the *Risorgimento*) was more often than not entirely lacking, existing only to collect taxes and to protect the rights of the wealthy landowners. This absence of the state bred a Hobbesian world in which personal honor was the highest of all virtues. The most respected man, the mafioso or *'ndranghetista*, was "a man of honor," a man who would fight any rival on the slightest offence and protect the name of his family and the reputation of his family's women from even the most trifling slur. In this society, justice was a question for individuals, not the state. If a man was wronged, it was expected that he would take steps to redress his wrong by killing or beating the wrongdoer. If he shrank from pursuing this *vendetta*, he and his close family could be expected to be ostracized by other members of his community. The terrific violence bred by this reliance on gun-law is illustrated in the murder rate 1880-1922. For Italy as a whole, murders averaged 12 per hundred thousand members of the population throughout this period; for the backward regions of the South, where most of these crimes of violence took place, the figures would have been much higher. The Mafia, the *'Ndrangheta* and the Camorra were the logical products of this home-made system of justice. In a world where there were no rules, only a constant prospect of danger, the mafiosi were the men who had given the highest proofs of their courage and will; the ones who had managed to instill fear in their contemporaries and who had most thoroughly rejected the norms of the absentee state.[1]

Italy's leading scholar of the Mafia, Pino Arlacchi, has emphasized, however, that mafiosi typically passed through two stages in their social development. The first, "anomic," stage applied to the period in which the would-be *uomo d'onore* was emerging from the mass of his contemporaries. In this period, he rejected all norms except his own and established his position as a man to be feared by committing one or more murders. Thereafter, the mafioso was anxious to gain respectability. He tried to "freeze" the honor structure of his community (thus preventing the emergence of rivals) by exercising governmental authority. He and his "family" of friends and relatives were responsible for three essential social functions. They provided -- at a cost --

protection for the villagers under their de facto jurisdiction, by punishing thieves and bandits. They also performed a repressive function. Delinquents, sexual deviants, petty criminals and others who offended community values were suppressed by mafiosi anxious to maintain their community's good name. Finally -- and, according to Arlacchi, by far the most important -- the mafioso was the community mediator. For a fee, the man of honor would patch up quarrels between families over property rights, seduced daughters, abandoned wives and marriage dowries. In these disputes, the mafioso acted as both arbitrator and enforcer. To dissent from his judgment was to slight his sense of personal dignity and to incur the enmity of him and his friends.[2]

The mafioso or 'ndranghetista was thus king of all he surveyed. But the territory he surveyed was essentially limited: a village, or the quarter of the small town where he lived. Within these boundaries, however, his influence was enormous, especially among the propertyless classes from which he had usually emerged. Becoming the chief of a mafia clan was, in a sense, a bloody form of social mobility; it enabled ex-shepherds, laborers and peasants to become village grandees and to live on a par with the minor nobility and professional men who formed the social elite (and the political class) of the southern regions. It also brought political influence, especially after the introduction of universal male suffrage in 1912. The mafioso commanded the votes of his immediate family, and his word could sway the choices of hundreds of others. He was thus openly courted by politicians, who attempted to build networks of friendly "dons" to support their electoral ambitions. The mafioso thus became an integral part of the power structure everywhere in southern Italy. Arlacchi states that apart from the fascist interlude (1922-43), the state authorities "substantially recognized" the parallel administration of the mafia chiefs from the *Risorgimento* to the 1960s.[3]

The most emblematic portrayal of the traditional mafia was drawn by the Sicilian writer Leonardo Sciascia in his acclaimed novel *Il giorno della civetta* (*The Day of the Owl*). The book, which deals with the vain efforts of a police officer from the North of Italy to get to the bottom of a murder of a peasant in a Sicilian village, is dominated by the local mafia *capo*, Don Mariano, and his peculiar code of honor. Humanity, Don Mariano says, can be divided into five categories. At the top, and rarest of all, are men. Next come half men, then "little men" (*ominicchi*), then cuckolds. At the bottom of the heap are the "quackers" (*quaquaraquà*), the men whose lives have no more meaning than the lives of ducks in a pond. Before asking me whether it is right to kill a man, Don Mariano tells the policeman, first you need to see if he is a man. The book ends with Don Mariano being released for lack of evidence and the policeman, whom the local clansmen had come to respect as a man, being transferred back to the North. Damiano Damiani's brilliant film version of the novel provides a memorable image of this defeat for justice. The last scene shows Don Mariano and a group of hangers-on looking across the town square at the police station.

The new police chief in the village is a plump Sicilian with a family; Don Mariano tells his cronies that they have nothing to fear from such a fellow. Yet he cannot help regretting that he no longer has an adversary worthy of his mettle, and must instead deal with a member of the despised *quaquaraquà*.

The Mafia Turns Entrepreneur

When Sciascia was writing, Don Mariano was already being replaced in the *piazze* of Sicily and Calabria by a new, more gangster-like breed of mafioso. In the 1950s, as southern Italy flourished thanks to the hectic growth of the Italian economy as a whole and the Italian state's injections of cash into the backward South, the word mafia increasingly became associated with criminal gangs operating out of the sprawling cities of southern Italy, especially Palermo and Naples. These new mafiosi were as obsessed as everyone else in Italian society with the pursuit of the new consumer goods flooding on to the market and with the acquisition of personal wealth. Social changes concurrent with the process of economic development, however, caused the prestige of the Mafia to decline. Economic growth created millions of new jobs in the industrial north, this led to mass migration from the *Mezzogiorno* and a subsequent shortage of young recruits to the Mafia's ranks. The traditional mediating role of the mafioso was usurped by the modernization of southern society. The Italian state was also less tolerant of gangsters dealing in contraband cigarettes, kidnapping and, increasingly, drugs, than it had been of the old village grandees. The Italian parliament established an anti-mafia commission in 1962 and by the end of the decade organized crime had been "pushed into a position of deviance and marginality."[4] The murder rate reflected this spike in the Mafia's influence: In 1969, it was just 2.2 per hundred thousand members of the population, the lowest in recorded history.

Only one factor enabled mafiosi to maintain a tenuous influence over the political process. All over the South in the 1960s the PCI was organizing rapidly and presenting a challenge to the hegemony over the region of the DC and other right-wing parties. The DC met this challenge with public money. Especially in Palermo, which was controlled by the faction of the DC headed by the veteran statesman Amintore Fanfani, huge sums were spent on public works and on expanding the public payroll. Men like Tommaso Buscetta, who would later become the first mafia boss to break the *omertà* (code of silence) and give testimony against organized crime in Sicily on behalf of the Italian state, were able to earn a precarious living interceding on behalf of businessmen anxious for public works contracts, but the relationship was on far less equal terms than in the past. The new kingpins in Sicilian, Calabrian and Neapolitan society were political bosses like Salvo Lima, the mayor of Palermo during the 1960s' boom; Giacomo Mancino, the Socialist leader in the province of Cosenza; and Carmelo Puija, the DC *assessore* (regional councillor with executive powers) for matters concerning "Budget, Finance, Common Land, Planning, Credit, Financing Companies, Extraordinary Intervention, Development of Internal areas" in the Calabrian regional government.[5] Much of Naples and its surroundings was Gava territory. Antonio Gava established a dominant hold on the city in the 1970s and used it as the base for his emergence as one of the DC's chief power-brokers and faction leaders in the 1980s.

All traditional areas of activity being exhausted, the *cosche mafiose* of southern Italy turned to business. They quickly prospered, especially in the road haulage, construction and tourist industries, and in the production of olive oil. This last was especially popular since it gave access to European Community farming subsidies, which were both enormously generous in themselves and easy to defraud. Mafia involvement in other food-processing industries soon followed. This rapid expansion was due to straightforward economic logic. Mafia-controlled businesses possessed four huge competitive advantages over their rivals. First, they could count on an influx of free capital from their illegal activities and thus had no need to go cap in hand to the banks. Second, when they did need bank capital, their political contacts were powerful enough to enable them to get it on favorable terms. Third, mafia labor was cheap. Mafia companies habitually hired casual, non-union labor and had a short way with anyone who tried to improve workers' rights. Fourth, and finally, the *cosche* had no qualms about using market-deforming techniques such as arson and murder to win contracts.[6] Further help was provided by the deterioration of the southern economy after the oil shock in the mid-1970s. Once more, there was a large pool of unemployed youths to be drawn into a life of crime. By the end of the 1970s, crime families such as the De Cristina, Bontade, Badalamenti, Inzerillo and Spatola in Sicily, and the De Stefano, Mamoliti and Piromalli in Calabria, were among the biggest economic concerns in their regions. Rosario Spatola had progressed from being a travelling milk salesman in the 1950s to one of Sicily's wealthiest financiers and industrialists at the time of his arrest in 1980.

With the new wealth came a return to the war of all on all. Bullets flew as the clans staked out their turf and fought over the ubiquitous *appalti pubblici* (public contracts) offered by the regional and provincial governments that gave the richest pickings on the market. The murder toll ceased its century-long decline and ticked upward. More than 700 people were killed in Sicily and Calabria in clashes between rival clans between 1970-1982. In Naples, the so-called "new Camorra" fought a bloody war of attrition against the Zaza family, which had previously reigned supreme. The extent and bloodiness of the struggle in Naples is hinted at by a brief summary of the statistics in Table 3.1.

Table 3.1. The Gang War in Naples 1977-1984

Year	Total Murders	Camorra-related murders
1977	63	50
1978	76	47
1979	96	71
1980	161	134
1981	248	193
1982	296	237
1983	320	238
1984	217	114

Source: Anti-mafia commission of the Italian Chamber of Deputies.[7]

Almost invariably, the original motive for the *faide* (blood feuds) between the rival *cosche* proved to be economic. Whenever mafia-run companies competed for, say, a contract to "maintain" a stretch of road in rural Calabria, or "collect" rubbish in Naples, the conflict took the form of a struggle between -- the metaphor is Pino Arlacchi's -- two "sovereign political communities."[8] War invariably erupted, with dozens of gang members' families, friends and dependents becoming involved in the initial clash and the subsequent *vendette*.

Palermo 1979-1986

In Sicily strife was intensified in the late 1970s and early 1980s by the emergence of the so-called *Corleonesi*, captained by Bernardo Provenzano and Salvatore "Toto" Riina. These two figures had no hesitation in ordering the execution of political and judicial opponents. The first wave of *delitti eccelenti* (supreme crimes) took place in 1979-1980. First Michele Reina, the secretary of the DC in Sicily, was assassinated in March 1979. Boris Giuliano, a Palermo policemen prominent in the battle against drug-trafficking, was killed in July 1979. In September 1979, two other law-enforcement officials, assistant DA Cesare Terranova and marshal Lenin Mancuso were also murdered. In January 1980, the political world was shaken by the murder of the president of the Sicilian regional government, Piersanti Mattarella (DC). On August 4, 1980, the chief attorney of Palermo, Gaetano Costa, ignoring nervous juniors at the *Palazzo di giustizia*, signed warrants for the arrest of more than 50 members of the Inzerillo, Spatola and Gambino clans. Two days later, he was brutally murdered. The conflict became still more ugly in 1981 when the clan chiefs of the Palermo Mafia fell out among themselves. In the Spring of 1981, Provenzano and Riina began a ruthless war of imperialism against the Palermo old guard, the Bontade and Inzerillo, killing the heads of both families. At the end of April 1982, Riina and Provenzano raised their sights still higher, murdering the Communist Party parliamentarian Pio La Torre, who was a member of the parliamentary anti-mafia commission and the author of a proposed anti-racketeering law similar to the RICO legislation in the United States. The death of La Torre compelled the Italian government to take a more active attitude. General Carlo Alberto Dalla Chiesa, the *Carabinieri* general who had successfully led the Italian state's war against the Red Brigades in the late 1970s, was sent to the prefecture of Palermo, although he was denied the special powers of arrest and detention he asked for. Dalla Chiesa's tenure lasted hardly more than a hundred days. In September 1982, he, his wife and his bodyguard were ambushed and killed.

Dalla Chiesa's death led to the passage of La Torre's proposed anti-mafia act and to the institution of a "High Commission for the Struggle against the Mafia," a body whose fine-sounding name could not disguise its limited powers. More significant was the organization of a full-time anti-mafia "pool" of prosecuting attorneys with the specific task of combating Palermo's crime families. One of these attorneys, Giovanni Falcone, issued, in July 1983, a warrant for the arrest of Riina, Provenzano and twelve other suspected members of the *Corleonesi*, including Michele "the Pope" Greco. Greco was the head of *Cosa Nostra*, which in Sicily means an alliance of about 90 crime families, grouped around the *Corleonesi*, and forming a mafia within the Mafia. The response was swift: Another Palermo prosecutor active in the fight against organized crime, Rocco Chinnici, was murdered by a car bomb on July 29, 1983.

Led by Falcone, the Palermo magistrates began to strike back. For the first time, arrested mafiosi were persuaded to break the *omertà* and reveal all they knew of the Palermo underground's workings. These *pentiti*, Tommaso Buscetta and Salvatore Contorno (who would later be joined by another remorseful mafioso, Antonio Calderone), allowed Falcone and his new chief, Antonino Caponetto, to emit several hundred arrest warrents in the Fall of 1983 and to order the arrest of Vito Ciancimino, a prominent member of the Christian Democrat party who, like Salvo Lima, had become mayor of Palermo. Buscetta's evidence, in particular, was crucial at the so-called *maxi-processo* of 475 accused mafiosi which began in a specially constructed underground court room in Palermo in February 1986 and ended in December 1987 with the imposition of 19 life sentences and hundreds of lesser penalties.[9] Ten days after the *maxi-processo* began, the Palermo authorities struck another powerful blow at organized crime by arresting Michele Greco.

The Palermo magistrates therefore appeared to have the Mafia on the ropes. By 1986, all its leaders were either in jail or on the run and the forces of law and order, thanks to the revelations of Buscetta and Contorno, had a far greater knowledge than ever before of the personalities and organization of the principal *cosche*. Yet this victory was not greeted with universal enthusiasm. On January 10, 1987, Leonardo Sciascia, whose own opposition to the Mafia was obviously beyond question, wrote a celebrated article in the *Corriere della Sera* belittling what the title of his article described as the "professional opponents of the Mafia." Sciascia singled out by name Paolo Borsellino, an attorney in the anti-mafia pool, and Leoluca Orlando (DC), the recently elected mayor of Palermo, whose left-wing Catholicism and outspoken criticism of *Cosa Nostra* had immediately made him a hero to many citizens. These two men, Sciascia insinuated, were advancing their careers under the cloak of anti-mafia rhetoric. Sciascia's critique immediately became the center of a typically Italian polemic, with intellectuals and journalists writing pieces for and against the Sicilian writer's stand. Sciascia himself both added to the row and attempted to dampen down the furore. First, he gave an interview to *Il Giornale di Sicilia* in which he implied that the PCI would be the chief beneficiaries of the current anti-mafia activity, then he wrote an article for *L'Espresso* suggesting that he had not wanted to attack Borsellino personally but had merely been concerned to underline that many figures in the legal establishment and the press seemed to regard anti-mafia zeal as the only relevant criterion for advancement within the judiciary. He did not retract his statement, however, in his original article, that power in Sicily was passing from the hands of the Mafia to the anti-Mafia, who did not permit "doubt, dissent or criticism."[10]

This notion that men like Orlando, Borsellino and Falcone were powerful was vehemently dismissed by Nando Dalla Chiesa, the son of General Carlo Alberto Dalla Chiesa, in his book *Storie di boss ministri tribunali giornali intellettuali cittadini,* which is an outstanding literary achievement as well as a passionate and penetrating account of the cultural climate of the political and intellectual world in 1980s' Italy. According to Dalla Chiesa, the sin of Sciascia's attack, (which Dalla Chiesa has elsewhere argued was a reflection of "Sicilianitude," a characteristic tendency to prefer the subtle and the ambiguous to the open and straightforward), was that it had opened the gates for the many figures in Italy's political establishment who had no wish to fight a real war against the Mafia. This was not just because they had had dealings with the clans, or relied upon *Cosa Nostra* for electoral support. Too many powerful people in Italy, Dalla Chiesa sustained, were fascinated by the crime bosses' evil-doing. Until this fascination was rooted out, the Mafia would remain a formidable enemy.[11]

The Unstable Pyramid

Dalla Chiesa's remarks introduce a vital point. Lawmen like Falcone and Borsellino, for all their successes, were fighting with one hand behind their back. The political elites did not want them to succeed. In both *Storie di boss, ministri, tribunali, giornali, intellettuali, cittadini* and in an earlier work, *Delitto imperfetto*, Dalla Chiesa recounted how his father, on being appointed to Palermo, had warned Andreotti that he would not shirk from examining the local organizations of the political parties to see if they had been contaminated by mafia influence. According to Dalla Chiesa, Andreotti (who had substituted Amintore Fanfani as the main political point of reference for the Palermo DC), "paled visibly" on hearing this news.[12]

Andreotti has always denied the veracity of this account, and indeed denied that his *corrente* in Sicily had been subject to mafia infiltration. This latter denial was certainly untrue, though Andreotti may have made it in good faith. The Palermo *Andreottiani*, like every other major DC faction in the three provinces most at risk from gangster activity, were emmeshed in a marriage of convenience with the local mafia hierarchy. Worse, whereas in the 1960s and early 1970s the politicians had been the dominant figures in this unsavory relationship, by the early 1980s the crime bosses had started calling the shots.

The root of this pollution of the political system was, like any other evil, money. Throughout the 1970s, the national leaders of the DC continued to believe that the best way of preserving their power in Sicily and elsewhere in the South was to strengthen their client networks. Craxi took the same approach after becoming *presidente del consiglio* in 1983. Vast sums were earmarked yearly for the regional and provincial governments of Sicily, Campania and Calabria, as well as for autonomous local government bodies responsible for spending on health care, transport and other functions. Most of this cash was spent wholly at the discretion of the local administrations. As the leading scholar of the Camorra, Isaia Sales, has underlined:

> The administrative economy (as we shall call the combined total of public resources and public decisions in the economic sphere) has become all-absorbing throughout the *Mezzogiorno*. In the 1970s, regions, townships, provinces, local health boards, mountain communities etc usurped the role exercised for more than 20 years by state investments, by the State Bank for the Development of Southern Italy and by the transfer of resources through the welfare and pensions system. Moreover, control over this particular "public intervention" moved away from the "mediators" at the heart of the state and toward local political bosses.[13]

The results of this system from a purely economic point of view were absurd. Hundreds of thousands of people were employed in non-jobs, the most notorious case being the Calabrian forestry service which had almost 30,000 employees by the mid-1980s, even though Calabria is almost barren of trees.[14] The post offices, railways and hospitals were similarly over-staffed. Yet because these jobs were mostly low-paid and unproductive, they did little to stimulate the southern economy. The list of Italy's richest provinces in terms of per capita income invariably showed the towns of the industrial north -- Milan, Bologna, Pavia, Varese, Bergamo -- at the top of the list, and the provinces of Sicily and Calabria -- Catania, Reggio Calabria, Cosenza, Caltanisetta -- at the bottom.[15]

This system also had immense consequences for the political process. Every elected official was transformed into a potential distributor of largesse, a fact which enormously intensified the political struggle within the governing political parties. Would-be politicians knew that if they could only get elected they would exercise almost unsupervised control over substantial budgets and would thus enjoy remarkable opportunities for personal enrichment. To get elected, however, they needed votes. Consequently, they tended to turn to the organizations that could, in one way or another, guarantee these votes: The *cosche mafiose*. The Mafia, however, did not do this favor for free. Regional and provincial deputies were expected to repay their elevation to office by steering *appalti pubblici* toward mafia-owned enterprises and by closing an eye to breaches of the law by mafia companies, especially in the construction industry. The visitor to southern Italian towns like Reggio Calabria, Palermo and Catania cannot but be amazed at the huge numbers of unfinished homes dotted all around the outskirts. These houses, which are often unconnected to mains water or sewerage, were usually hastily built by mafia-dominated building firms in defiance of the zoning laws and with the tacit acquiescence of the local political elite. To quote Pino Arlacchi, by the early 1980s:

> The distribution of subsidies, of pensions, of public sector jobs -- the management of the "assisted economy" of southern Italy -- has been gradually falling under the control of mafia politicians, or mafia bosses *tout court*, at the expense of the traditional political elite, which is no longer able to match (the Mafia's) competition.[16]

The national leaderships of the government parties acquiesced in the establishment of this new political elite. No other explanation will cover the behavior of the governing coalition from 1986 onward. At the very moment that the *capi* of the Palermo *cosche* were on trial in the *maxi-processo*, the Rome government was busy restoking the mafia conflagration with the hot coals of government money. The so-called *legge 64* of 1986 provided about 80 billion dollars of public investment for a nine-year plan of "extraordinary aid" for the

South. These funds were dispensed by the usual methods and by 1990, the minister in charge of the development of the *Mezzogiorno*, Riccardo Misasi, a Calabrian whose own patronage network was second to none, was back in parliament pleading for another 40 billion. Misasi claimed that the money had mostly been spent on completing projects contracted by the government in the past, on paying "social duties" and on "financing a series of particular laws and projects."[17] Others gave a more specific account of the money's destination. A special report on the future of the *Mezzogiorno* published by *Mondoperaio* in August 1990 alleged that the money had been frittered away in "myriad minor interventions solicited by local and personal interests."[18] What is certain is that gangland violence flared in the late 1980s, especially in Calabria, as the *'Ndrangheta* clans fought for control over this new influx of government cash.

A still more blatant example of state aid for the mob was the Irpinia earthquake disaster relief fund, which probably deserves to be called the financial fraud of the century. The earthquake, which left more than 3,000 people dead and hundreds of thousands of people homeless in November 1980, was one of the worst natural disasters in the history of modern Italy. Reconstruction, however, turned into a bonanza for anyone with political connections and, above all, for the Camorra (Irpinia is the mountainous area to the north east of Naples). The number of villages originally estimated to have suffered serious damage was 339. Over the next seven years this figure -- in one of the most remarkable post-seismic shifts on record -- rose to 687, as national and local political bosses anxious to strengthen their client networks added further townships to the list. In particular, the city of Naples itself became the destination of colossal sums of reconstruction money, as Naples' able party bosses, notably Antonio Gava and Paolo Cirino Pomincino, the head of the local *Andreottiani*, struggled to grab a "fair" share of the money being handed out. Naples would eventually receive billions of dollars in disaster aid, despite the fact that it had suffered hardly any earthquake damage.

Priority in the reconstruction in Irpinia was given to prestige projects such as roads, acquaducts and sewers, all of which were built at astronomic prices, or not built at all, despite the payment of substantial cash advances. Local entrepreneurs and businessmen from the North of Italy meanwhile competed to present schemes to build new factories and create jobs -- at a price. Some of these ideas were manifestly absurd: One successful proposal led to the partial construction of a boat factory in a mountain-top village badly served with roads. In dozens of cases, entrepreneurs took the state's money, inflated costs with the connivance of the local politicians responsible for seeing that the project was completed, and then left the work unfinished when the funds ran out. In the meantime, tens of thousands of people were still living in tents and pre-fabricated homes. In all, expenditure on the Irpinia disaster rose from an initial estimate of approximately 6 billion dollars to more than 30 billion dollars by

1988, though the final figures are impossible to state with any certainty since all spending took place "off-budget." What is certain is that almost all of this expenditure was of no benefit whatever to the victims of the earthquake. Camorra-controlled construction firms, local politicians, architects (who made a fortune designing houses and factories which were destined never to be used) and a flock of vulture-like entrepreneurs from northern Italy had swallowed at least half of the funds.[19] Yet when, in 1991, a parliamentary commission of inquiry headed by Oscar Luigi Scalfaro, the current president of Italy, presented a huge and detailed report on the extent of the Irpinia fraud to parliament, the DC and the PSI united to block any attempt to apportion blame. Too many important politicians risked being found with their hands in the jar. Ciriaco De Mita, whose political power base was the province of Avellino, at the heart of the disaster area, was a natural suspect. De Mita was accused in December 1988 of having enriched himself with funds destined for the post-quake reconstruction. This suspicion arose from the enormous influx of funds into a bank partly owned by the De Mita family in the aftermath of the tremor. Though De Mita was cleared of any personal wrongdoing, he should not be exonerated from a more general moral culpability. He and the other leading politicians of the zone cannot escape the charge of aquiescence in the face of blatant fraud.

The reason for this acquiescence is clear. The local *camorristi* and village politicians who were doing so well from the disaster relief fund were the very people upon whom national figures like De Mita relied to get out their vote at election time. By the early and mid-1980s, the political system had become -- if this does not sound ridiculous -- an unstable pyramid. Major political figures at the top funnelled public funds to hand-picked cronies or temporary allies at regional and provincial level, who did the same to their cronies and allies in township and village administrations. The bottom and middle layers of this pyramid were closely controlled by organized crime in many parts of the South; it has since been alleged (see Chapter Eight) that many first-rank members of the DC, in particular, were working hand in glove with the Mafia too. Yet even those politicians who were not explicitly connected to crime families felt obliged to keep the subsidies flowing southward. The clans controlled thousands of floating voters and were able to rig the vote during national elections. A politician, even one of national standing, who showed too much zeal in anti-mafia activity, or who voted to reduce extraordinary aid to the *Mezzogiorno*, stamped himself an enemy of the "friends" and put his electoral support on the line. Thousands of votes might mysteriously slither away to other candidates, weakening his position within his party, or, in extreme cases, the offending politician could be killed. The murder of Giuseppe Insalaco, an ex-mayor of Palermo, in January 1988, was almost certainly due to this cause. Insalaco, while hardly a knight in shining armor, had made some effort to clean up the process for awarding public works contracts in the Sicilian capital, and at the time of his death was rumored to be talking to the police about the Mafia's political connections. His reward for this breach of the unwritten code governing the relations of local politicians with the clans was chilling. Two gunmen shot him to death inside his car before escaping on a motor scooter.

How to Win Votes and Influence People

These comments on the Mafia's hold over the electoral process may seem exaggerated. They are not. Arlacchi estimates that mafia clans command as much as 30 percent of the vote in the small towns of Calabria and Sicily and 15 percent of the electorate in larger cities.[20] Throw in ballot fraud and the ability of criminal gangs to influence electoral results is considerable. The results of the national elections of 1987 should certainly have been annulled in much of Campania, but the parties decided to take almost no action, despite the discovery of ballot fraud on a massive scale. Fraud in Sicily or Calabria was probably as bad, but remained undiscovered.

The fraudsters were helped by the arcane complexity of Italy's system of proportional representation for elections to the Chamber of Deputies. The country was divided into 32 electoral colleges, each of which was allocated a certain number of parliamentary seats. These colleges were not equal in size. The smallest of them, Trieste, had just three seats; the largest, Rome-Viterbo-Latino-Frosinone, included more than 3,000,000 voters and sent over 50 deputies to Montecitorio, as the palace housing the Italian Chamber of Deputies is known. To obtain a seat in an electoral college, a party had to surpass a fixed quota ascertained by dividing the number of people who voted by the number of available seats plus two. Thus, in a college with 600,000 electors and ten deputies, the quota of votes required to obtain a seat would be 600,000 divided by twelve -- 50,000. A party which obtained, say, 162,000 votes in this college would immediately receive three deputies. The remaining 12,000 votes (known as the *resti*, the remainders) would then be transferred to a national pool of unrepresented votes, though only parties that had obtained at least one seat in an electoral college, and at least 300,000 votes nationwide, could participate in this so-called *collegio unico nazionale* (single national constituency). The seats that had not been directly allocated in the colleges were then distributed in accordance with the number of "remainders" totalled by each of the parties admitted to the CUN. Usually, the big beneficiaries of this system were the smaller "lay" parties, which won relatively few seats in the direct election but consequently amassed a large number of unrepresented votes. To conclude the electoral process, the seats awarded in the CUN were then reallocated to the electoral colleges, with each party list choosing the "remainders" which in percentage terms most closely approached the quota.

In theory, the choice of the candidates elected was entirely in the hands of the electorate. In each college, the parties would present a numbered list of approved candidates. The voter, having indicated the party of his choice, could then select up to four of the numbers on the list as his or her personal preferences, and the ones obtaining the most preferences were automatically elected. It was in fact here that the criminal bosses intervened in the process. The system ensured that a candidate who could mobilize a hard core of the electorate to vote for him personally stood a very good chance of getting elected. The Mafia specialized in ensuring that, one way or another, "favored" candidates did succeed in reaching an imposing number of personal preferences. At regional and provincial level, where an essentially similar electoral system prevailed, except on a smaller scale, the results were even easier to influence.

The Mafia had a number of techniques to "place" their favored candidates. One of the most widely used was the so-called "the number that's not there." Voters would be assigned the numbers of the Mafia's preferred candidates, plus a number higher than the highest number on the party list. When they voted, they wrote all four numbers down. The high number would be discarded when the votes were counted, but the men in charge of the count would be able to keep a record of how everyone had voted. Few voters were willing to risk that none of the scrutineers was affiliated with the local *cosche*. Another technique was the revolving ballot. Of brilliant simplicity, all this trick required was the provision of a legally validated ballot paper by a friendly (or intimidated) polling station scrutineer. Once the ballot was obtained, everything became easy. The first of the Mafia's voters would fill out the ballot paper according to directions, enter the polling station, where he would receive a blank ballot form from the election committee, and switch the forms in the privacy of the voting booth. He would then cast the pre-prepared vote and leave the polling station with the new blank form as proof of his faithfulness. The blank was then filled out in appropriate fashion and recycled. Once the first paper had been stolen, this process could obviously go on for as long as the Mafia had voters. And to get voters, all the Mafia had to do was make them an offer they couldn't refuse.

One can be sure that both of these techniques were used in the Naples-Caserta electoral college in 1987. The vote in Naples, however, showed that even after the vote was over, a vast range of other fraudulent techniques were at the Camorra's disposal. The "greatest fraud in Italian history" began in June 1987, when four leading politicians in the Naples area launched an appeal against the electoral results.[21] All four felt that preferences had been manipulated to their disadvantage; the worst case was the provincial secretary of the DC, Giovanni Piccirillo, who had thousands of preferences inexplicably disqualified, allowing his nearest rival on the party list, Gaetano Vairo, to overtake him. An independent parliamentary commission of inquiry was formed, headed by the neo-fascist Enzo Trantino and by a Green deputy, Giancarlo Savoldi. The commission undertook a detailed investigation of a representative sample (10 percent) of the ballots cast in the Naples-Caserta college. It did not take long for the commission to find out that Piccirillo's complaints were merely the tip of a huge iceberg of voting abuses. All of the most prominent political figures named on the ballot paper for Naples-Caserta, including men of national standing such as Bettino Craxi, Antonio Gava, Giorgio Napolitano (PCI) and Enzo Scotti (DC), were found to have had their individual tallies of preferences inflated by fraud. Gava, in particular, was suspected of having been a major beneficiary. His 110,000 personal preferences in 1983 had more than doubled to 225,000, while an anonymous ally of Gava's, Alfredo Vito, had scored more than 150,000. In certain sections of the electoral college, mathematically impossible numbers of preferences had been cast; in others, records had not been kept, or were destroyed by fire during the investigation; in others still, voting slips had clearly been altered. In some areas no spoilt or blank ballots were recorded, the obvious suspicion being that all such votes had been replaced by positive votes in favor of certain candidates. Ballot boxes had been illegally carried off to unknown locations and had been missing for several hours before being returned to the central counting office. In Torre del Greco, a coastal town in the shadow of Vesuvius, mysterious thieves stole electoral archives and ballot papers before the commission could examine them. Still more mysteriously, only the votes awarded to the DC and the PSI went missing. All in all, it could be taken as certain that tens of thousands of votes, perhaps more, had been deliberately falsified. At the end of the inquiry, Trantino did not mince his words. The frauds, he asserted, had been so large as to constitute a "disguised coup d'etat" and had altered the "genetic code of consensus which is the basis of democracy."[22]

In his final report, Savoldi proposed -- obviously -- that the elections should be annulled for all Naples-Caserta, though a consensus was soon reached that only the results for Torre del Greco and another town, Marcianise (where the ballot papers were said to have been torched in a huge bonfire at the local magistrates' office by unknown hands), should be definitively wiped clean. Yet even this compromise was too bold for the DC and the PSI. The parliamentary committee responsible for the affair, led by its chair, Nicola Quarta (DC), incredibly claimed that any abuses had been "marginal and in any event irrelevant" and hinted that Savoldi's report had been politically motivated.[23] Quarta proposed that a handful of minor changes be made to the preferences obtained in a handful of contaminated sections, but that nothing otherwise should be done. The committee voted by 12-10 in favor of this solution (the DC and the PSI were joined by the PRI and the PSDI, both of which stood to lose a deputy in the event of a rectification of the results). This whitewash was too much even for the Chamber of Deputies, which sent this solution back to the committee. A third report, by Trantino, met with more favor. Trantino argued that the votes of some 45 sections, mostly in Torre del Greco and its surrounds, should be annulled, and that the preferences of leading figures should be appropriately trimmed. This solution was the one adopted. Gava lost almost 2,500 preferences, Scotti 1,700, Craxi 2,157. The electoral results, however, were left fundamentally unchanged; nobody lost a post in parliament, nobody finished in jail.

Prisoners of the Mafia

By 1989, when Trantino's compromise was accepted by the Italian parliament, organized crime had made a comeback from the defeats of 1984-1987. The anti-mafia professionals denounced by Sciascia were in disarray: The anti-mafia pool of attorneys was being dissuaded from its desire to press ahead with new mass trials by Antonio Meli, the recently appointed chief attorney in Palermo, who preferred a more traditional, case by case approach. Before long, the *Palazzo di giustizia* in Palermo was a battlefield of conflicting groups and factions. In July 1988, Borsellino denounced what he regarded as an attempt by Meli to dismantle the anti-mafia pool. Falcone spoke out too. On July 31, 1988, he deplored the situation in Palermo in a secret deposition before the *Consiglio superiore della magistratura* (the governing body of the Italian judiciary), arguing that the attorneys of the pool were being swamped with trivial cases which had no connection to their primary duties and were being denied the opportunity to investigate other cases which might have shed light on the Mafia's internal organization and workings.[24]

Meanwhile, the *Palazzo di giustizia* in Palermo continued to live up to its reputation as "the palace of poison": In June 1989 an anonymous letter-writer known as "the crow" calumnied Falcone and some of his closest colleagues with the accusation that they were blocking investigations into Leoluca Orlando's handling of public works contracts. The "crow" was eventually discovered to be a fellow attorney, Alberto Di Pisa, who was condemned for slander in February 1992 and sentenced to eighteen months' imprisonment. (Di Pisa, who was convicted mainly on the basis of fingerprint evidence, continues to insist that he was innocent of the charges.) Also in June 1989, *Cosa Nostra* made an unsuccessful bomb attack on Falcone. Some of the victories of the *maxi-processo* also began to unravel on appeal. The High Court of Appeal, chaired by Judge Corrado Carnevale, reduced the number of life sentences from 19 to 12 in December 1990. Carnevale would become known as "Judge Sentence-killer" for his extraordinary leniency and his willingness to use minor procedural slips on the part of the prosecutors as grounds for ordering trials to be repeated or evidence dismissed, at any rate in cases where the Mafia was involved. In March 1991, a frustrated Falcone decided to take a senior post in the ministry of justice in Rome.

In politics, it was the same story. Leoluca Orlando's position in Palermo came under increasing attack inside the DC after the fall of De Mita and the institution of the CAF. In January 1990, the national leadership of the DC decided to end the anomaly of Palermo (where Orlando was governing with the support of the leftist parties and without the PSI) by insisting on the formation of a *giunta comunale* that included the party's national allies. Orlando resigned after a furious polemical exchange with Forlani, and despite heading the DC's list in the May 1990 regional elections, shortly afterward left the DC to found his own political party, *La Rete* (The Network).[25] The newspaper *La Repubblica*, which was itself in 1990 fighting a bitter takeover battle against the media empire of the pro-government entrepreneur Silvio Berlusconi, was inclined to see a common thread in the downfall of the anti-mafia pool in Palermo, in Orlando's defeat in Palermo, and in its own travails. The "plotters of the camper," the paper contended, were trying to ensure that dissenting opinion was squashed and traditional politics returned to its pedestal.[26]

Italy is always pullulating with conspiracy theories, some, like this one, being more convincing than others. Even if Craxi, Andreotti and Forlani are cleared of this accusation, however, there is no doubt that the upper reaches of the DC and the PSI were more concerned with maintaining their grip on power than getting to the roots of southern Italy's problems. The continuing flood of government funds to the mafia-affected regions and the refusal to get to the bottom of either the Irpinia or the Naples-Caserta scandals are proof enough of this. One is tempted to resort to irony and suggest a utilitarian rationale for the DC and the PSI's policy toward the Camorra and the Mafia. Perhaps the politicians hoped that pumping public money into the affected areas would spark off a bloody war between the clans and lead to the main mafia families killing each other off.

If so, their policy nearly succeeded. The late 1980s was characterized by renewed lawlessness throughout southern Italy, as the gangs fought turf wars for the control of public contracts. Murders in Sicily, Calabria and Campania rose from (the already high) total of 550 in 1984 to almost 700 in 1986 and to well above 800 in 1989. Calabria, in particular, saw its murder rates double from around 100 in 1984 to more than 200 in 1989. The province of Reggio Calabria, in particular, endured New York City levels of murderous violence. In the first six months of 1989, the boiling point of a very hot war, there were fourteen homicides per 100,000 members of the population. In the whole period 1986-1990, 773 people were killed, almost invariably as a result of 'ndrangheta activity. The most deadly place of all was the little Calabrian town of Taurianova, which was marked by nineteen murders and nine attempted murders in the single year May 1990-1991. In a township of just 16,000 people, this meant -- as is easily calculable -- a murder rate of more than 100 per 100,000 inhabitants. Taurianova is in fact a good example of the phenomenon described by Arlacchi and Sales: A town which is the fief of a local political boss who controls, unchecked by the central government, a major source of public revenue. In Taurianova, the local political and criminal boss, Don Francesco "Ciccio Mazzetta" Macrì (DC), used the local health authority as his cash cow. More than 2,000 people worked for a health authority "serving" no more than 50,000 people and 20 percent of Taurianova's small population enjoyed state disability payments. Don Francesco did not run as a candidate in the May 1990 local elections, but his sister Olga did, obtaining 55 percent of the votes.

In addition to murder, other serious crimes rose dramatically. Armed robberies, extortion, dynamite attacks on shopkeepers all showed huge increases, though in these fields Sicily led the way. There were 113 armed robberies per 100,000 of the population in both Palermo and Catania in 1989; Naples trailed in third with 60. Gangland violence also began to spread to parts of the *Mezzogiorno* which had previously been almost untouched by organized crime. Apulia (the heel of the Italian boot) provided the most alarming instance of this trend. A delegation of the parliamentary anti-mafia committee which visited the region in 1989 recorded an "absolutely abnormal increase in the crime rate" and in the capacity of organized crime to "condition productive activity." Another alarming sign was the formation of a criminal association on the lines of *Cosa Nostra*, known as the *Sacra Corona Unita*. These sinister developments were reflected in the crime rates: Apulia passed from 43 murders in 1984 to more than 100 in 1989 and from 250 serious robberies to over 800.[27]

Among the grim lists of victims there were numerous *delitti eccelenti*. The killing of Giuseppe Insalaco in January 1988 has already been mentioned; in September of the same year the sentencer of Michele Greco, Judge Antonino Saetta, and a 1960s radical turned anti-mafia TV personality, Mauro Rostagno, also perished. The most emblematic killings, however, were of Lodovico Ligato and Rosario Livatino.

Lodovico Ligato was shot in August 1989 at his seaside villa in the province of Reggio Calabria. He was the first politician of national standing to be murdered in Calabria. Ligato had begun his career as a journalist, but then hitched himself to the star of Riccardo Misasi, whose *portaborse* (personal aide) he became. Ligato became first a deputy in the Calabrian regional government, then, in 1979, a parliamentary deputy, obtaining 86,000 personal preferences. In 1983, however, Ligato's tally of preferences fell off to just 64,000, signifying that he had reached his political ceiling. Consequently, he did not wait until the next elections in 1987; instead, he left mid-term to become chairman of the Italian national railways. Naturally, he knew nothing about railways, nor had he any experience of running a major corporation (the *Ferrovia nazionale* employs more than 200,000 people). What he did know about was image-making and fraud. Amid much fanfare, Ligato promised change and innovation, but was soon disgraced, along with the entire board of directors, for involvement in a complex scheme to defraud the state by overcharging for bed linen on overnight trains. Bowed but not beaten (nor imprisoned), Ligato returned to Reggio where he seemingly tried to play a part in the share-out of government investment for the "reconstruction" of Reggio Calabria. Ligato was no longer as powerful as he thought, however. His position in the local political-criminal hierarchy had weakened since the end of the 1970s and his intervention annoyed both prominent members of the local DC (three leading figures were accused of ordering Ligato's murder in December 1992, and though they have since been found not guilty of this specific crime, they are still suspected of association with the Mafia) and the gang leaders who had once slipped Ligato their votes.[28]

The significance of his death, however, was obvious. The DC greeted it with a long, profoundly embarrassed silence, broken only by Arnaldo Forlani's ludicrous remark that Ligato had merely been "a simple card-carrying member." Italy's leading journalists were less coy. Giorgio Bocca of *La Repubblica* spoke for many when he declared that Ligato's death was indicative of a "Colombia syndrome" in Italian politics. As in South America, politicians who had played with the fire of organized crime were now being burned. Bocca argued explicitly:

> The death of Ligato means precisely this: Gentlemen of the political parties, don't think you can pull out now, the joint venture that you've been running with the mob in recent years is not one that you can wash your hands of easily. The price you pledge for the votes we bring you is one you have to pay.[29]

The justice minister, Giuliano Vassalli (PSI), had reached a similar conclusion. In April 1990, he publicly warned that "entire regions" were "prisoners of the Mafia" and that "too little" was being done to combat organized crime. Vassalli's words were echoed in September 1990 by a Calabrian DA, Agostino Cordova, who lamented the abysmal facilities at his disposal for combating the 'Ndrangheta and claimed that the judiciary were "in hostage to the Mafia."[30] The same complaint was heard even more strongly later that month when a 38-year-old assistant DA in the Sicilian town of Agrigento, Rosario Livatino, was brutally killed by a gang of killers who followed his unescorted car, forced him off the highway, chased him down the road embankment and shot him, at close range, in the face.

The murder of this superbly professional and dedicated young man sent a shock of revulsion through Italy, foreshadowing the later, even stronger, public reaction to the murders of Falcone and Borsellino in 1992. Andreotti's seventh government, formed in April 1991, finally gave the key posts of minister for the interior and minister of justice to two politicians determined to fight organized crime seriously, Enzo Scotti and Claudio Martelli. These two, helped by the knowledge and advice of Giovanni Falcone, forced through a law against money-laundering in July 1991, instituted a witness protection program, and presided over the creation of the *Direzione nazionale anti-mafia*, the Italian FBI, in November 1991.

Yet for public opinion this was too little, too late. Giorgio Bocca caught the general mood in his brilliant, best-selling pamphlet, *La Disunità d' Italia*, which was published in the Fall of 1990. For Bocca, democracy in southern Italy was in a "coma."[31] The question of southern under-development, which for years had seemed a technical matter to be resolved by economic experts, now presented itself as a threat to national unity. With the complicity and encouragement of the political class, much of the *Mezzogiorno* had been allowed to deteriorate into a banana republic, while the industrial and industrious North was expected to pay the bills. This could not go on, Bocca warned. The Italian state had broken its contract with its citizens too crudely. Millions of southerners, such as the tradesmen and shop-owners of Capo d'Orlando in the province of Messina, who organized an anti-racket association in December 1990, certainly agreed.[32] And by the time Bocca was writing, protest had already taken political form in the North.

Notes

1. This description of the social and cultural background of the Mafia is largely taken from Pino Arlacchi, *La Mafia Imprenditrice*, Bologna (Il Mulino) 1983 chapter one. Arlacchi's book has been translated into English under the title *Mafia Business: The Mafia Ethic and the Spirit of Capitalism*, New York (Verso) 1989. The structure and analysis of pages 26-29 of this chapter owe an enormous amount to this remarkable book, which, in my view, deserves to be regarded as one of the finest pieces of historical sociology written in recent years. An English language description of the social history of the Mafia is A Blok, *The Mafia of a Sicilian Village 1860-1960*, New York (Harpers & Row) 1974. Several of Leonardo Sciascia's novels deal with the Mafia: *The Day of the Owl*, Boston (Godine) 1984, is the most famous of these. A history of the *'Ndrangheta* is to be found in Enzo Ciconte, *'Ndrangheta dall'unita a oggi*, Bari (Laterza) 1992. On the Camorra, the reader is directed to Isaia Sales, *La Camorra, le camorre*, Rome (Riuniti) 1988. As an editorial note, I would like to add that I have capitalized the word "mafia" when talking in general terms, but left it in lower case when it is being used as an adjective. I have not italicized "Mafia," "mafioso" and "Camorra," since they are words that have passed into the English language.

2. The portrayal of the mafioso's mediating functions is from Arlacchi, *La Mafia Imprenditrice*, Chapter Two.

3. Arlacchi, *La Mafia Imprenditrice*, p 57.

4. Arlacchi, *La Mafia Imprenditrice*, p 83.

44

5. An English language account of Puija's career is to be found in James Walston, *The Mafia and Clientelism*, London (Routledge) 1988, pp 125-127.

6. This paragraph closely follows Arlacchi, *La Mafia Imprenditrice*, Chapter Four, "Gli anni 70 e l'impresa mafiosa."

7 The original version of this table is to be found in Nicola Tranfaglia (ed), *Mafia, politica e affari 1943-91*, Bari (Laterza) 1992, p 310. This book is an invaluable collection of parliamentary reports and other documents on the mafia phenomenon.

8. Arlacchi, *La Mafia Imprenditrice*, p 183.

9. Buscetta recounted his life story and philosophy to the Italian journalist Enzo Biagi in *Il Boss è solo*, Milan (Mondadori) 1986.

10. See Leonardo Sciascia, "Io ho difeso il diritto e la dignità" *L'Espresso*, January 25, 1987. See also P. Calderone, "Peccati di antimafia" in the same issue.

11. Nando Dalla Chiesa, *Storie di Boss, ministri, tribunali, giornali, intellettuali, cittadini*, Turin (Einaudi) 1990, especially Chapter Five, "Operazione Voltaire." Dalla Chiesa provides several moving portraits of the loneliness of anti-mafia activists in Sicily and elsewhere, and in particular describes the travails of the small independent magazine *I Siciliani*, which made a speciality of investigating the Mafia in the large Sicilian town of Catania. The editor of this magazine, Giuseppe Fava, was murdered by the clans in 1984. For Fava's ideas on the Mafia see Giuseppe Fava, *Mafia*, Catania (Siciliani) and Rome (Riuniti) 1986. This book was published posthumously with an afterword by the editorial staff of *I Siciliani*, including Fava's son, Claudio.

12. Nando Dalla Chiesa, *Storie di Boss, ministri*, pp 106-108. The original Italian is "si è sbiancato in volto."

13. Isaia Sales, *La Camorra, le camorre*, p 181.

14. James Walston, *The Mafia and Clientelism*, p 125. The peak number was reached in December 1982 when 28,686 people were "working" as forestry guards. It was reported that many of these state employees were mafiosi who were using their standard issue two-way radios to warn their colleagues of the approach of the police. By 1987, after this brazen misuse of public funds had been exposed, the numbers fell somewhat, but still totalled more than 22,000.

15. In July 1990, a survey carried out at the behest of the Italian Chamber of Commerce revealed this clearly. All the richest 15 provinces came from north of the river Po; all the poorest, in terms of per capita income, from below Naples. The gap between richest and poorest was enormous. The wealthiest province, Milan, had a per capita income of 24m lire; the poorest, Agrigento, just 9m. The average Milanese, in other words, was nearly 300 percent better off in monetary (though arguably not purchasing power) terms. For a full account of the survey's findings, see *La Repubblica* July 15/16, 1990.

16. Arlacchi, *La Mafia Imprenditrice*, p 205.

17. Riccardo Misasi, interview in *La Repubblica* July 15/16, 1990.

18. Luigi di Majo, "La beffa numero 64," *Mondoperaio* (43), August/September 1990, p 44.

19. A sometimes hilarious, though somewhat fragmented account of the Irpinia fraud is Goffredo Locatelli, *Irpiniagate*, Rome (Newton Compton) 1988, which despite the title and the publisher is written in Italian. An English language account is Ada Becchi, "The difficult reconstruction in Irpinia," in S. Hellman and G. Pasquino (eds), *Italian Politics, A Review*, (vol 7), London (Pinter), Bologna (Il Mulino) 1992, pp 110-129.

20. Arlacchi, *La Mafia Imprenditrice*, p 193.

21. Sebastiano Messina, *Nomenklatura: Come sopravvive in Italia la specie politica più antica nel mondo*, Milan (Mondadori) 1992, p 66. Messina is an outstanding journalist and writer and I am indebted to his chapter "Storie di truffe e imbroglioni" for much of my material on the voting scandal in Naples-Caserta.

22. Messina, *Nomenklatura*, p 72.

23. Messina, *Nomenklatura*, p 73.

24. Falcone's words were leaked to *L'Espresso* and published September 18, 1988.

25. For an account of the downfall of Orlando's Palermo giunta see Alfio Mastropaolo, "Machine Politics and Mass Mobilization in Palermo: Epitaph for a failed Revolt," in Robert Leonardi and Fausto Anderlini (eds), *Italian Politics: A Review*, London (Pinter) and Bologna (Il Mulino) vol 6, 1992, pp 123-142.

26. See Giovanni Ferrara, "La resistible ascesa dei congiurati del camper" *La Repubblica*, January 24, 1990.

27. All statistics and quotations are from Nicola Tranfaglia, *Mafia, politica e affari*, pp 333-341. The discussion of Taurianova relies on Franco Giustoli, "Cosca nostra," *L'Espresso*, May 19, 1991.

28. A brief English language account of Ligato's life can be found in James Walston, *The Mafia and Clientelism*, pp 225-226. See also Sandra Bonsanti, "Presto parleranno le mie memorie..." *La Repubblica*, August 29, 1989. The fullest account of Ligato's life, times and ambitions, however, is a lengthy recent essay by Enzo Ciconte in Nicola Tranfaglia (ed), *Cirillo, Ligato e Lima: Tre storie di mafia e politica*, Bari (Laterza) 1994, pp 101-183.

29. Giorgio Bocca, "La sindrome columbiana," *La Repubblica*, August 29, 1989. The quotation from Forlani was carried by every national newspaper on the same day.

30. Agostino Cordova, "Noi giudici calabresi ostaggi della mafia," *La Repubblica*, September 11, 1990. Vassalli's comments were widely reported in the press on April 14, 1990.

31. Giorgio Bocca, *La Disunità d'Italia*, Milan (Garzanti) 1990. The book's subtitle read: "For 20m Italians democracy is in a coma and Europe is slipping farther away."

32. The leader of this revolt, Libero Grassi, a small factory owner, was murdered by the Mafia in 1991.

4

The Lega Nord

The abuses described in the previous chapter were bound to provoke a political reaction. This reaction, however, came not from the southern poor, but from the rich North of the country. The long-smoldering frustration of the working and lower-middle classes in Lombardy, Italy's commercial and industrial heartland, at the waste, rank folly and outright criminality of the party system was about to explode. The outlook of these classes was summed up by a poster published by an obscure party of Lombard nationalists called the *Lega Lombarda* in the mid-1980s. Under the heading *Così No!* (Not like this!), the poster showed a strained-looking Milanese hen filling the basket of a plump, vaguely porcine, Roman matron with shiny gold eggs. The *Lega Lombarda*'s leader, an iconoclastic ex-medical student called Umberto Bossi, would shortly become a national figure. Better than anyone in the entrenched ranks of the traditional parties, he would prove able to articulate the economic and regional grievances of a vital section of the Italian electorate. Between the spring of 1987 and the autumn of 1991, Bossi's much-derided movement for regional autonomy was propelled by the rising swell of northern discontent to the status of Italy's fourth largest political party.

Umberto Bossi

Bossi's career is a fascinating one. Born into a working-class peasant family from Varese in 1943, Bossi was to a certain extent brought up in hardship. He tried a series of odd jobs (he was, among other things, a dance-band guitarist, a laborer and a private tutor in mathematics) while working toward his degree in medicine. He had almost finished his degree, and was in his mid-thirties, when he discovered politics thanks to a chance meeting in Pavia in 1979. The politics he discovered, however, were not those of the traditional parties, with their prediliction for seeing Italy as a single people and state, but the federalism of the *Union Valdotaine* and its leading intellectual, Bruno Salvadori. The *Union Valdotaine* has long been the political voice of the small province of the (French dialect speaking) Aosta valley, which like Trentino-Alto Adige, Sardinia, Friuli-Venezia Giulia and Sicily, is a special region, enjoying more autonomy from Rome than the rest of Italy's 20 regions. Salvadori introduced Bossi to the notion that Italy was less a unified state than a hodge-podge of local cultures, languages and identities which could and should be governed federally, within the context of a wider European federal state.[1] Bossi was convinced. He became the publisher and editor of a small local newspaper, *Nord-Ovest*, and the founder of a short-lived political movement called UNOLPA, the North-West Lombardy Union for Autonomy. In the course of this political activity, Bossi also ran up debts of 20 million lire. In June 1980 Salvadori was killed in a car crash and Bossi became personally liable for the full amount, a crushing sum for a laboratory technician (his job at that time) with a wife and young son to support. Bossi was obliged to spend more than a year working at any and every odd job he could find to pay off his backload of debt. In the meantime, his marriage collapsed and his medical studies were cut short when he was just four credits away from taking his degree.

Bossi therefore had good reasons for abandoning politics. Instead he found his interest strengthened. By his own account, he spent much of 1981-1982 educating himself in political theory and Lombard culture and language, a period of study which only confirmed his view that Italy should be decentralized, with each of its local cultures having the right to considerable local autonomy.[2]

Accordingly, in March 1982, Bossi formed the Lombard League, the *Lega Autonoma Lombarda*, (the word *autonoma* was dropped in 1986) attracting an oddball membership consisting mainly of devotees of Lombard dialect poetry and culture. Yet from the very beginning, two features which have distinguished the League's activities ever since were apparent. First, the League was tightly organized, with the leadership keeping an eye on every detail of the movement's activities and restricting advancement within the movement only to those whose commitment was unquestioned. Great emphasis was placed upon propaganda: Bossi moved heaven and earth to ensure that the League's newspaper, *Lombardia Autonoma*, managed to stay in sporadic print. Bossi's determination to win a mass following for Lombard autonomy, while remaining selective toward the individual Lombards who would be allowed influence in the movement, irresistibly recalls *Mein Kampf*, in which Hitler states that a nascent political movement must build up a following for its ideas among the public at large by agitation and propaganda, but must ensure that the party itself remains a trusted elite. This comparison, however, should not be misinterpreted. The League -- and this is the second feature which has remained constant from the movement's beginnings -- has invariably articulated an ideology which for want of a better term might be described as liberal-conservative localism. This ideology has its crude side and can be reasonably accused of possessing a xenophobic edge (the kind of hostility toward outsiders many of the Swiss cantons are notorious for; Switzerland, after all, is only a few miles from Varese), but it is not in any sense fascist. The very word fascist is derived from the Roman *fascio littorale*: A bundle of sticks bound together and thus unbreakably strong. The crucial point to understand about the League's platform is that it wants to unbind Italy, to restore government as far as possible to local political entities. A favorite quotation of Bossi's is Rousseau's remark that democracy is only possible in relatively small communities. The best way of verifying this argument is to look in detail at the League's first manifesto, "Introducing the League." The starting point of this document is a classic assertion of nationalist rhetoric:

> Lombards! It does not matter how old you are, what job you do, or what your political views are: what matters is that you are -- and we are -- all Lombards ... and as Lombards ... we have a fundamental common interest to which our division into parties of every political hue must be subordinated.

The nature of this "common interest" is then explained frankly:

> This fundamental interest of ours is the liberation of Lombardy from the insatiable and suffocating hegemony of the centralist government in Rome, via Lombard autonomy within the far wider context of northern Italian autonomy.

The manifesto then lists a number of grievances to be laid at Rome's door. Lombardy has been reduced to a "geographic expression of no political value," its people have been reduced to "a crowd, without political identity ... incorporated anonymously into a bankrupt state." State sector jobs and public housing are being taken over by "outsiders," which is alleged to be no coincidence but part of "a deliberate plan of the Roman government" to "cancel Lombardy's ethnic identity." Above all, Lombardy has economic grievances against Rome. Without the misrule and corruption of the parties in Rome, "the Lombards and other north Italian peoples ... would be capable of living without crises and of being on a par with European levels." Rome, it is asserted, thinks of Lombardy as "a milch cow." In so doing, the manifesto states flatly (and prophetically), it is making a serious mistake:

> Lombardy is not an idiot who will pay other people's debts. Lombardy is not going to follow Rome passively into bankruptcy because it has no

intention of sacrificing the rights of its citiziens, the sweat of its sons, the diligence of its people and the personality of its people on the altar of Roman misgovernment.[3]

This declaration of principles was accompanied by a fifteen-point program of specific political goals, which was later amended into a "definitive" twelve-point agenda the following year (1983). In this latter document, the League stated that it was:

-- For the self-government of Lombardy, and the superceding of the centralized state with a modern Federal State that respects all of the peoples which constitute it (in the longer, fifteen-point program, it was stressed that "decision-making power should be decentralized from the regions to the provinces and the communes).
-- For the precedence of Lombards in the assignation of jobs, houses, welfare and financial contributions....
-- For the (regional) control and management of the fruits of the Lombards' labour and their taxes....
-- For a schools system and public administration in the hands of Lombards, not "denaturized" ones...
-- Against the opportunistic mentality of the Roman parties ....
-- For the construction of a Europe founded on autonomy, federalism, and mutual solidarity and respect between peoples, and thus between the Lombards and all other peoples.... [4]

Much of this manifesto and program was self-pitying and false. The notion that Lombardy was little more than a geographic entity which counted for nothing in political terms, for instance, was simply ridiculous. Lombardy was not ignored when government pork was distributed: As the most populous region in the country, and the richest, none of the political parties could possibly afford not to take public opinion in Lombardy into their calculations. In certain regards, too, the League's policy was downright unpleasant. The insistence on "Lombards first" in public service jobs was a not so veiled way of saying that many hundreds of thousands of southern Italians working in Lombardy should go home and leave their jobs to people from the local community. By including this demand in his program, Bossi was cynically pandering (as he candidly admits in his autobiography, *Vento dal Nord*[5]), to the widespread view in northern Italy that southerners are less competent and hard-working than northerners. As long ago as 1927, Gramsci complained that northern Italians were inclined to see the *meridionali* as "inferior beings" and to blame the industrial and commercial backwardness of the South on the "laziness, ineptness and criminal nature" of its inhabitants.[6] The League's policy can be seen as a deliberate incitement of this same narrow-minded and ignorant attitude.

Yet Bossi's program and ideas should not be simply dismissed. It has since become the fashion to explain the League's subsequent electoral success on revulsion at the misgovernment of the *partitocrazia* and to portray it as a vulgar protest party which has succeeded by virtue of the fact that it was in the right place at the right time. This idea is far too simplistic. The views expressed in the League's early statements of intent were shared by millions of people in northern Italy; to this extent they were consistent with the mood of public opinion. Furthermore -- and this is the vital point -- in substance they gave a plausible critique of the state of the Italian nation. The North of Italy and Lombardy in particular was supporting the South of Italy by its labors; the parties were leading the country to bankruptcy; the North was carrying an undue share of the national taxation burden. The Italian state, initially for the purpose of equalizing socio-economic differences between the North and the South, invested one trillion lire of taxpayers' money in the South between 1945-1991 without altering the relative economic status of the two regions one jot. Throughout the 1980s, southern Italy's per capita production was 55-57 percent of the North's, but consumption levels were 68-70 percent.[7] This variation, which was repeated year after year in the 1980s, was almost entirely due to the effect of government transfers and gave substance to the claim that the North was being asked to maintain the southern standard of living. There was even some justice in the League's complaints about the *meridionali* in public service in the North. Southerners, in part because state jobs were their only source of employment, in part because they were usually better connected with the client networks of the political parties, did represent a disproportionate portion of public employees in the North. Moreover, many tended, perfectly naturally, to regard employment in the northern provinces as a temporary hiatus before their transfer back to their home towns. This situation led to a constant coming and going of state employees, especially in the schools, which inevitably aroused resentment. Bossi, who would soon prove himself a skilled and unscrupulous leader, was in the enviable position for a populist politician of being able to exploit genuine grievances.

Warriors of the New Pontida

In 1982-1983, however, nobody thought it worthwhile to discuss the merits or demerits of the League's policies. It was regarded, insofar as its existence was recognized at all, as a handful of cranks led by a man who believed he was the new Alberto di Giussano, the medieval knight who had led a twelfth-century coalition of twenty northern Italian city-states against the invading armies of Frederick Barbarossa. One of Bossi's earliest (and most astute) acts was to make this ancient attempt at northern unity into a powerful foundation myth. The party emblem is a stylised image of Di Giussano standing with legs athwart and sword held aloft, which Bossi himself designed. The party's electoral symbol is the same image superimposed upon the red and white flag of Lombardy. Every year since 1989, the League's members have gathered at Pontida, the site of the original *giuramento* (oath-taking) of the twenty city-states, to swear to liberate Lombardy from Roman oppression.

For several years, however, Bossi was a general without an army. He and a nucleus of committed activists spent several years in the political wilderness, speaking to semi-deserted school halls and social clubs and engaging in occasional brawls with supporters of the marxist *Democrazia proletaria* party and of the nationalist MSI. In the 1985 local elections, the infant movement scored its first, pitifully small, success, electing a town councillor in Varese and obtaining 13,000 votes. In Lombardy as a whole, however, they captured a mere 0.5 percent of the electorate. As the movement's first historian rightly states, at this stage the League was little more than a "club of friends."[8] A club, however, which Bossi was at pains to organize with a certain ruthlessness. The League's inner party of "founder members" was purged in 1986, as Bossi maneuvered to rid himself of a clique of rivals who did not share his vision of the movement's future direction.[9] Also in 1986, Bossi invented the category of *soci ordinari* (ordinary members). Despite their name, these party members possess extraordinary privileges: They alone have the right to vote at all levels of the League's decision-making process, are the leaders of the local sections and act as the movement's candidates at election time. Bossi centralized the creation of new *soci ordinari* in the hands of the party secretariat -- in his own hands, in other words -- and was thus able to build up an inner elite whose dedication to Bossi personally and the movement more generally is remarkable.

This reorganization improved the movement's efficiency, and soon started bringing results. Gradually, a crude understanding of the League's ideas began to diffuse itself among the voters of northern Lombardy (the movement's popularity spread to Milan and the commercial centers of the Po river valley only later). The movement was identified with anti-southerner feeling and with opposition to North African immigration, as well as growing discontent with the parties' inability to reform the political system. In the national elections of 1987, this constituency of disgruntled voters brought the League to national attention when almost 200,000 of them, 3 percent of the Lombard electorate, voted for the League's candidates. Bossi was elected to the Senate and his friend and fellow founder member Giuseppe·Leoni, an architect from Varese, was elected to the Chamber of Deputies.

Electoral success brought media attention, most of it sneering in tone, as well as public funds to help the movement's expenses and publicity. Bossi and Leoni, setting a precedent for all future League parliamentarians, also pledged a substantial part of their income from political sources to party funds. All of a sudden, the League, which already had a network of activists who were prepared to give their services for free, had cash to spend on the party newspaper and on posters and handbills. This additional publicity was soon translated into votes. In the European elections in June 1989, the movement registered a huge leap in its electoral share, moving to over 8 percent of the regional vote (470,000 preferences) and becoming the fourth largest party in Lombardy behind the DC, PCI and PSI. Even more significantly, perhaps, voters from all over Lombardy were becoming attracted to its stance. The League took 11-12 percent of the vote in Sondrio, Varese and Como, the three north Lombard provinces where the movement had been founded, but also gained over 9 percent in Cremona, a prosperous southern Lombardy province, and 14 percent in industrial Bergamo. In both provinces, these results were obtained almost without trying: The League's organization was scarce in Bergamo and almost non-existent in Cremona. Only in Milan (5.3 percent) and Mantua (3.3 percent) was the result in any sense disappointing, and here, too, lack of organization was responsible. For the first time, moreover, the contagion of the *Lega Lombarda*'s ideas was detected outside the Lombardy region. In Piedmont, 55,000 voters (2.1 percent) supported northern autonomy candidates; in Venetia, 50,000 (1.9 percent). Extraordinarily, votes were cast for the League even in the South, including more than 3,000 in Sicily. Two League deputies, Francesco Speroni and Luigi Moretti, were elected to the European parliament in Strasbourg.

Bossi's next moves were, in retrospect, crucial for the development of the movement. At the "national congress" of the *Lega Lombarda* in December 1989, Bossi stressed the League's federalist goals and persuaded the movement's militants to broaden their horizons to encompass the whole of the North down to Tuscany. The previous month, the *Lega Lombarda* had formally joined with two already existing regional autonomy parties, *La Liga Veneta* and *Piemont Autonomista* and three new movements, the *Lega Emiliano-Romagnolo*, *L'Union Ligure* and *L'Alleanza Toscana*, to form the *Lega Nord*. The new umbrella organization was initially confederal in organization, with the *Liga Veneta* in particular retaining a very high degree of autonomy. Indeed, until the *Lega Nord*'s "constituent assembly" in February 1991, it is purely a matter of convenience to talk of the regional leagues as a single party at all. At the same congress, the anti-southern rhetoric of the past was dropped. In compensation, activity against the growing wave of third world immigration was stepped up. Anti-immigration rhetoric would be the staple of the League's propaganda throughout 1990-1991.

Voicing concern over immigration kept the *Lega Nord* at the forefront of the most contentious issue in Italian politics in these two years. The decision to form the Northern League, however, was the more significant for the Italian political system. Bossi was self-consciously trying to break away from traditional regionalist politics in Italy, from the vision of regionalism as the protection of local rights, customs, dialects and cultures. Instead he was gambling on being able to build a new political force which could break the stranglehold of the DC and force consent for its platform by dint of its electoral strength.[10] There was a sense, therefore, in which his objective was similar to that of the Socialist Party. But whereas Craxi's PSI was integrated into the system and offered no real alternative to it, Bossi was an outsider with an entirely new vocabulary of ideas. Events would show that his was the stronger position.

In the run-up to the regional elections of May 1990, the parties showed some concern at the *Lega Lombarda*'s potential to disrupt the balance of forces in the regional assembly. The "L-factor" weighed heavily upon both the local and national leaderships of the PSI and the DC. Attempts were made by the major parties to steal the League's clothes, most notably by Craxi, who symbolically chose Pontida to launch a ten-point plan for greater regional autonomy in March 1990. Yet worried though the *partitocrazia* was, it is unlikely that any politician, national or regional, quite expected the electoral calamity which resulted. As Daniele Vimercati has written: "A tremor was expected, instead there was an earthquake. The epicenter was in Lombardy, but shock waves spread all over the north and shook the rest of Italy."[11]

A few weeks before the poll, Bossi had predicted that the *Lega Lombarda* would get 20 percent in Lombardy and had been greeted with derision. When the poll was counted, it emerged that Bossi had been all but right. The League had obtained almost 1,200,000 votes in Lombardy (19 percent) and had surged past the PSI and the PCI to become the second largest party in the region. In Milan alone, the *Lega* had secured more than 400,000 votes (13 percent); in the provinces of Brescia, Bergamo, Como and Varese more than 20 percent of the electorate had opted for northern autonomy. Fifteen regional deputies were awarded to the League, reducing the DC and its allies to the slenderest of margins and ending the possibility of a PSI - PCI administration. Elsewhere in the North results were encouraging, with the *Lega Nord* arriving fourth in Liguria and obtaining more than 150,000 votes in Piedmont. Even in the South, the *Lega Sud*, an independent movement founded with Bossi's approval and encouragement, succeeded in obtaining almost 5,000 votes in Naples and 2,000 in Salerno. Bossi's reaction was to state unequivocally, "The 1990s will be characterized by the explosion of federalism in the South. We Lombards are not alone in feeling that we've had about as much as we will stand from Rome."[12]

A Movement Under Scrutiny

The League's dramatic victory in the regional elections brought an unprecedented wave of publicity and analysis in its wake. Journalists and academics began looking at Bossi's movement with greater interest. By and large, they did not like what they saw. The League was routinely condemned as a mere protest party, which was thriving like "fungus" on the rotting log of the political system and which lacked coherent ideas for the reform of the political system.[13] Nevertheless, few denied the significance of the Northern League's victory. Giorgio Bocca warned that the League's triumph showed that "a growing number of Lombards and other Italians are profoundly deluded by a democracy which in some regions has ceased to be a democracy"; the editor of *La Repubblica*, Eugenio Scalfari, said the League's victory was the *partitocrazia*'s "last warning." Yet nobody suggested that the *Lega Nord* was destined to endure. Bocca gloomily opined that the partitocratic "python" would swallow the *Lega Nord* "toad" in the same way that it had devoured other protests in the past.[14] The general consensus was that the League was a "straw fire" which would swiftly burn out, but which testified to the tinderbox mood of public opinion.

Yet before jumping to this conclusion, pundits should have looked carefully at the emerging profile of the *Lega Nord*'s electorate. By and large, most Northern League voters were coming from the DC and hailed from the section of the traditional middle class which was bearing the brunt of increased taxation. The same portion of the population had also been the mainstay of anti-communist sentiment in Italy, and arguably felt liberated by the fall of the Berlin Wall from their pact of convenience with the political old guard. Yet factory workers and professionals were also beginning to vote for Bossi's movement by 1990, enabling the League to eat away at the vote of the Republicans, Socialists and Communists. The *Lega* was, in other words, a broad-based movement whose appeal crossed party boundaries. The *Lega Nord* was, moreover, a grass-roots movement. Local League candidates and organizers tended to be people of no particular academic or social distinction -- bar-room philosophers -- who were nevertheless well-known in their communities and who could count on a considerable personal vote. Sometimes these people were lacking in political skills, but that hardly mattered: the important thing was their participation.[15] *Lega Nord* activists believe very strongly, as anyone who has talked to them will testify, that they are part of something worthwhile; a patriotic crusade to make the country a better place to live in. It was therefore unlikely that the League's support would melt away while the quality of Italian life was in their view visibly deteriorating.

This concern for the quality of life was one reason why Bossi decided to make immigration a major issue. Massive unplanned immigration from the Maghreb countries and eastern Europe had had predictable social consequences by 1990. Many immigrants were living in conditions of extreme poverty, a state of affairs that posed major problems for the health authorities and the police in the outskirts of Italy's largest cities, especially Milan. The thrust of the League's public pronouncements on this issue was to emphasize that a continuance of these conditions was unfair both to the local communities obliged to endure increases in crime, disease and prostitution, and to the immigrants themselves.

The League's anti-immigration rhetoric ("bringing blacks here is slavery") and actions gave the mainstream parties a handle for critical propaganda. Bossi seemed to spend most of 1990-1991 replying to accusations from immigrant organizations, concerned journalists, and opportunistic politicians that the League was kindling the emotions of hate against Italy's growing non-native community. Gradually, however, the campaign died away. In part, this was because the League's stand on immigration was quite simply popular with the lower-middle class voters who made up the bulk of the League's electoral base. A more important reason, however, was the convergence of the governing parties' attitude toward immigration with Bossi's. Particularly after the collapse of the Albanian economy in 1990, when Italy was suddenly threatened with the arrival of huge numbers of economic migrants, Italy began getting tough with immigrants, especially unauthorized ones. Bossi and the government found themselves in rare agreement in August 1991, when Andreotti's administration ruthlessly turned back the makeshift armada of vessels transporting Albanian refugees towards the ports of Apulia. It was difficult for a government which had herded several hundred desperate economic migrants into a soccer stadium in temperatures of over 90 degrees fahrenheit, kept them there for several days without adequate toilet facilities or water and then tricked them into believing that they would be allowed to stay in Italy before using the military to deport them, to condemn anyone else as intolerant of racial or cultural diversity.

Bossi's own repeated assertions that the *Lega Nord* was not racist may also have had some effect. In his best-selling biography cum manifesto *Vento dal Nord*, he makes the League's justification for opposing mass immigration in what it is not absurd to describe as philosophical terms:

> Not even the Christian Democrats believe we are racists any longer. Federalism is a democratic and liberal theory, nothing else. I myself am not capable of racial or any other kind of hatred. For me, all men are equal, in the sense that they have the same dignity. The blackest man on earth has the same rights as my next door neighbour. Mind you, he also has the same duties. He should therefore contribute to the common wealth, before obtaining the right to a house, to unemployment benefit and health care... Rights like these don't grow on trees, they are not guaranteed to all human beings in the way that the rebels of 1968 believed, with their idiot slogan "Everything now". Resources are necessarily inferior to needs ... even in an industrialized country like Italy ... We are not super-rich, or even well-off, despite appearances. Certain economic rights cannot be guaranteed to everyone who walks about in Italian territory. To benefit from them, in my view, one should already have contributed to the wealth of all. I emphasize the economic dimension because we are not talking here about the

inalienable rights every man possesses such as freedom of person or speech.

Bossi then meets the objection that the "haves" have a moral obligation to show social solidarity toward those who have nothing:

Don't come to me mouthing the word "solidarity". This word is a hypocritical slogan which means everything and nothing. It is a word behind which the most sordid trickery and glib demagogery are hidden. What does "solidarity" mean? The word itself means nothing, it is just the worst kind of philanthropic drivel, if it is not backed up with action. We can't be "solidary" with everyone. Unfortunately, as I was saying, resources are not sufficient. You have to direct your efforts, sacrificing some to the benefit of others. For this reason, the League retains that we should first show solidarity towards our own people, towards people like us.[16]

The stern economic liberalism of these two passages illustrate better than any summary what the *Lega Nord* stands for and explain its appeal to the thrifty burghers of northern Italy. Bossi, in addition to importing the hostility to central government most cogently expressed in the *Federalist Papers*, was also associating the League with the hard-boiled Social Darwinism of Malthus, Spencer, Sumner and -- at a more popular level -- Samuel Smiles. The attraction of Social Darwinism for the diligent, tax-paying individuals who social policy-makers tend to discount in their theories has always been apparent in Anglo-Saxon democracies. Bossi was gambling that such ideas would strike a chord in Italy too. It wasn't too risky a bet. As one perceptive Italian writer who has since become associated with the League has remarked:

I think the first and fundamental ability of the leader of the *Lega Nord* is his skill at perceiving and expressing the convictions and aspirations of the popular classes of his home area; where by "popular" I don't just mean the least well educated people of the population, but everybody who is used (despite being socially qualified) to brushing aside sophistries and doubts and opting for straightforward diagnoses based on fundamental values.[17]

This point is a vital adjunct to the common conviction after the May 1990 elections, that the League was nothing more than a protest party. The League's vote was a protest, but it was not an unthinking, knee-jerk act of repulsion toward the parties. Had the electorate of Lombardy wanted simply to punish the parties of government, they could have voted for the traditional right-wing opposition: the MSI. Or else, they could have supported the Greens, another anti-party par excellence. Within the government itself, the Republicans, under the leadership of the mild-mannered but determined Giorgio La Malfa, were making many sensible and pertinent comments about the necessity of both political and economic renewal: Voters could have turned to them. Instead, the northern electorate chose to vote *Lega Nord.* The reason, surely, was the League's outspoken Social Darwinist belief that the individual only has a right to what he has earned. By saying this clearly -- actually, by shouting it from the street corners -- the League was able to act as the focal point for a conscious revolt against what northern Italians see as decades of compulsory charity to the South and near-banditry on the part of the parties. Beneath the superficial triviality and vulgarity of many of its activities, the *Lega Nord* is a movement founded on a clear ideological position about the extent to which (and the way in which) the state may redistribute its citizens' wealth. Scholars and journalists, who have both a more sophisticated understanding of rights and obligations than the average *Lega Nord* supporter and (often) a snobbish tendency to believe that the ordinary man doesn't think theoretically about politics, have usually missed this aspect of the League's doctrine, and have thus missed the chief reason why the partitocratic python found Bossi's movement hard to ingest.

Another point needs to be made about the motives of the League's supporters. And this is that the protest against Rome and the parties was far more responsible than any supposed racial hostility towards the *meridionali* or North Africans for its success in the period 1987-1990. A comprehensive survey of voters in the Milan region made by Italy's leading political sociologist, Renato Mannheimer, in 1990-1991 proved this point beyond question. Mannheimer found that huge majorities of those questioned identified "Opposition to the bureaucracy and inefficiency of Rome," "A Protest against the *partitocrazia*," "Wanting an autonomous Lombardy," "Protesting the disparity of treatment between the North and the South" as the principal causes of the *Lega Lombarda*'s popularity. Moreover, the percentages giving these explanations by and large rose in tandem with political sympathy for the League. Eighty percent of committed League supporters gave the first of these motives in one poll. Seventy-one percent chose the desire for Lombard autonomy in another. Among ordinary voters hostility to southerners and immigrants was perceived as a major motive for voting for the League: By contrast, less than 5 percent of *Lega Lombarda* supporters would admit that their political activity was driven by ill-will towards southerners. In one poll at least, moreover, none -- 0 percent -- would admit to possessing racial feeling against immigrants. [18] While these figures were no doubt deflated by a desire not to appear bigoted, the general picture is open to only one interpretation. In this connection, it is also worth pointing out that the only hiatus in the League's electoral growth came between the May 1990 elections and local elections in Brescia in November 1991. During this period, the League stayed steady at approximately 20 percent of the Lombard electorate. Many potential voters were undoubtedly repelled rather than attracted by the *Lega Nord*'s close association with the anti-immigrant campaign. The League, in other words, was perceived to be missing its vocation in these months: Voters arguably wanted it to condemn the injustice of the central state and the parties which controlled it, not waste its energies on other, peripheral issues.

The Republic of the North

Bossi was as aware as any of the League's critics, however, that it was not enough to voice the northern Italians' commonsense interpretation of their social contract with the Italian state. The movement needed to have a wider, more constructive, ideological apparatus. Bossi realized that the *Lega Nord* had to flesh out its manifesto with a corpus of more sophisticated policies if it was going to retain its momentum and become a political force of national importance. His crucial step in this direction came in September 1990 when he told the assembly of the *Lega Lombarda* that the logical end of the movement's federalism was the division of Italy into three "macro-regions" or "Republics" for the North, Center and South. This move was greeted with disdain by the government, with dismay by many journalists, who saw it as another sign that Italy's social fabric was unravelling,[19] and with incomprehension by public opinion. It also provided the parties with a handle for propaganda: The League were immediately accused of being a movement which allied Mussolini-style demagogic leadership and rhetoric with a threat to national unity. It was nevertheless a move which gave Bossi's federalism enhanced credibility. By espousing the idea of macro-regions, Bossi was aligning himself with the views of one of Italy's most controversial constitutionalists and political philosophers, Gianfranco Miglio of Milan's Cattolica University.

Miglio had been watching the growth of federalist ideas in northern Italy with interest and sympathy and had defended Bossi's movement from some of the criticism levelled against it. In Miglio's view, the birth of the *Lega Nord* was the political expression of the fact that the Italians "do not constitute an ethnic and cultural entity sufficiently homogeneous to sustain a centralized unitary state."[20] Those nineteenth-century political thinkers like Carlo Cattaneo and Vincenzo Gioberti who had argued that Italy should be united in a federal state, not in the national state wanted by Giuseppe Mazzini, had belatedly been proved right, Miglio asserted. The economic and cultural differences between North and South were too great to bear. The North was now piloting itself toward Mitteleuropa; the South toward the Mediterranean. A more elastic constitutional form than the unitary national state was urgently needed to take this unstoppable historical development into account. Macroregions, Miglio believed, were the answer. They were an intermediate form between outdated "Great Nations" and the fragmentation of pure regionalism. They are also the most appropriate political form for the current era. In Miglio's view, the historical epoch of the nation state is definitely ending. People all over Europe are discovering that their sense of communal feeling -- and hence their perception of political obligation -- is restricted to smaller units than at any time since the seventeenth century. Miglio believes that Europe is likely to see an enormous dispersal of sovereignty in the coming decades, with the authority of nation states being gradually blurred and the power of voluntary territorial associations of all kinds being greatly increased. Europe might (in Miglio's view, should) develop into the old Hanseatic League writ large. It may become a web of small, independent trading states which, remaining fiercely proud of their local cultures and traditions, acknowledge the necessity of European integration and supra-national co-operation to ensure mutual prosperity.[21]

Ideas of this kind began to pepper Bossi's speeches (he will often address three public meetings in a single day) and were probably more responsible than any other single factor for moderating the League's public image. Italians warm instinctively to the notion of European integration. Italian politicians and political thinkers such as Altiero Spinelli were among the earliest and most active proponents of European union during and after World War Two and Bossi's emphasis of such themes made the League look much less threatening. This is not to imply that Bossi's articulation of these views was in any sense dictated by propaganda considerations. The sincerity of his commitment to democracy on a small scale cannot be disputed:

> The new Europe, in the League's view, must be a federation of free peoples governed by strong sovereign regional institutions ... European man, as the sociologist Alberto Gasperini says, enjoys a "multiplicity of belongings." He belongs to a family, to a local community, to a city or region, to a nation or ethnic group, to a professional group, to the culture of the social group and so on. This sociological fact is the ideal starting point for federal institutions based on the principle of subsidiarity, of sovereignty from below, of capillary democracy inserted into a great continental confederation, which will guarantee constitutional rights and individual liberties.[22]

At the first "federal" conference of the *Lega Nord* in February 1991, Bossi drove this point home, emphasizing in his speeches that the League favored that decisions should be taken as far as possible by those most affected by them and that the decentralization of power within the proposed Republic of the North should be delegated to local institutions. This emphasis on the devolution of powers was an important one, because the main event of the conference was the centralization of the confederation of leagues into a single party under his leadership. He did not get his way without grumbling -- and even some muttering against his personal hegemony -- within the *Lega Nord*. Some extremist regionalists, including his sister, who now regards him as a traitor to the cause of Lombard nationalism, considered that he was sacrificing the original goals of the movement on the altar of political ambition. Other critics argued that Lombardy would dominate the new formation if Bossi maintained a dual role as head of the federation of northern leagues and as chief of the *Lega Lombarda*. Bossi scotched the views of these dissident voices by saying that if he was compelled to choose between the leadership of the *Lega Nord* and the *Lega Lombarda*, he would choose to retain his position at the head of the Lombardy movement. Since the *Lega Lombarda* was the "locomotive" of the federalist movement, providing the other regions with financial and logistical aid, Bossi was essentially threatening to go it alone. Bossi had the bulk of the delegates behind him, moreover. In general, the view that there is a basic "ethno-cultural affinity" and common political interest between the "peoples" of northern Italy prevailed among the broad membership of the *Lega Nord*. Bossi's opponents knew that they would have to confront their own membership if they opposed the planned centralization. A compromise was reached whereby Franco Rocchetta, the leader of the *Liga Veneta*, became president of the new movement, but it is fair to say that the scars left by this conference have never completely healed. A ranking member of the League's hierarchy, Franco Castellazzi, noisily left the *Lega Nord* within months of the conference, and relations between Bossi and Rocchetta have been far from idyllic ever since.[23]

At the same congress, senior members of the League also put flesh on the bones of the economic strategy they favoured for Italy and for the future "Republic of the North." Like the proposal for the federation of the Italian state, the League's economic policy breached a number of taboos. Papers presented by Marco Formentini, Luigi Roveda and Giuseppe Sarogni outlined a homemade economic strategy of thought-provoking subtlety and rigor.

The central concern of this strategy was transferring economic power from the public sector to the private, from the large corporation to the small business. It was, in other words, designed to reflect the same "small is beautiful" approach as the movement's constitutional policies. In practical terms, this meant that the *Lega* stood for privatization of the RAI networks, all public housing and all of the state's industrial and financial holdings. The League's economists, Formentini to the fore, argued that market-deforming subsidies should be slashed to zero and aid to the *Mezzogiorno* should be channeled through tax breaks and incentives, rather than through direct state aid to the southern regional governments. Italy's heavily protected markets for automobiles and banking services should be opened to foreign competition even sooner and further than EC trade policy was demanding. In general, the state's share of the economy (and the share possessed by large corporations) should be cut back, giving space to the small and mid-sized businesses of Lombardy, Venetia and Piedmont which are the main strengths of the Italian economy (and the *Lega*'s main source of votes).[24]

This strongly free-market approach was of unheard-of radicalism by Italian standards. Whatever its rights and wrongs as a recipe for the Italian economy (it would require an upheaval of far greater dimensions than the Thatcherite interlude brought to 1980s Britain), it was not the work of a party of unsophisticated flagwaving hicks. One prominent Italian economist, Marco Vitale of the Bocconi University in Milan, has openly said that the League's economic ideas are "concrete, coherent, detailed, and aimed at improving the economy's productivity."[25] As a coda to this section, it is worth commenting that Bossi's *leghismo* is much closer to Thatcherism than to any more sinister political ideology. Like early Thatcherism, it is a plain-spoken combination of populism and economic Social Darwinism which causes "liberals" -- in the American sense of the word -- to recoil with distaste. Like Thatcherism again, its most enthusiastic supporters are the lower and middle-middle classes and the self-employed. And just as within ten years the language of Thatcherism -- privatization, people's capitalism, individualism -- formed the core vocabulary of British politics, so the themes articulated by Bossi's raucous, nicotine-stained voice in the early 1990s have since become fixtures in Italian political discourse.

The Ruins of Brescia

It should be obvious by this stage in the narrative that the rise of the *Lega Nord* owed very little to accident. The League was a vocal exponent for an outlook on the relationship between the state and the citizen which was widespread in northern Italy; it was organized more tightly and efficiently than any other party and was headed by a leader who realized that in order to reshape the state on federalist lines the League had to establish itself as the hegemonic political force throughout the northern regions. By the end of 1990, the crudities of the *Lega Lombarda*'s early program had been surmounted by a batch of policies which -- whether one agrees with them or not -- courageously addressed the two real issues facing the Italian state: the accelerating gap between the North and South and the economic lunacy of the central government.

The only question mark over the League's progress by February 1991 was its perceived extremism. But this question mark was a big one, not least because Bossi did little in public to enhance the moderate side of the movement's rhetoric and image. At the end of his concluding address to the Constituent Assembly of the *Lega Nord*, he famously vaunted the superior masculinity of the League over the other parties by asserting that "The League has a hard-on." At Pontida in May 1991, to the strains of the triumphal march from Aida and before 15,000 gathered *leghisti*, he announced the formal foundation of the Republic of the

North, in a guarded speech which took pains to avoid any accusation of sedition. Once the announcement was over, however, he threw caution to the winds and treated the crowd to a vintage performance of rhetoric, culminating in a firework display of insults that spared nobody: Andreotti, Occhetto, Craxi, the MSI and Orlando were all flayed with equal vigor. On other occasions, he hinted at secession and the possibility of street violence if the League's federalist demands were not taken seriously. He also made the serious tactical error of refusing to support the June 1991 referendum on electoral reform (see Chapter Six), saying that he would be spending referendum Sunday on the beach. When northern voters turned out *en masse* to back the referendum's supporters (whom Bossi had accused of being the *partitocrazia*'s under-the-counter allies), the *Lega* leader was left with egg on his face.[26] This was especially damaging since Bossi was the personification of the movement. None of the League's other senior figures was at this stage widely known to the public. Beginning in 1991, in fact, the League did its best to dispel the belief that it was a one-man band. Figures such as the astringent Euro-deputy Francesco Speroni and the emollient Marco Formentini, who is Dr Jekyll to Bossi's Mr Hyde, as well as being an accomplished debater, were given more prominence. Progress was slow, however. Much of the media and the party-controlled state television service were intent on persuading the public that the Northern League was a semi-fascist movement of egoists and tax evaders led by a half-crazed demagogue and were therefore reluctant to to give either Bossi or anybody else a platform to air the League's real views.

The press campaign against it and the genuine public disquiet about Bossi's unorthodox rhetoric made local elections in the Lombardy town of Brescia in November 1991 a test that the League had to overcome. Brescia, a prosperous industrial city, was the fief of one of the leading lights of the Christian Democratic hierarchy, Gianni Prandini. Prandini's ability to bring home the pork to Brescia was notorious, as was the size of his electoral war chest. Brescia was also the power base of the one DC politician for whom Bossi has any respect, Mino Martinazzoli, a prominent member of the DC's left who is renowned for his personal integrity. The two DC factions were squabbling bitterly, but Martinazzoli's reputation meant that the DC retained some credibility. Prandini had also once been quoted as saying that the League "would not pass" in Brescia.[27] The stakes were thus high, and became higher still for the League after the public defection of Castellazzi and his clique of supporters on the eve of the poll. Early predictions showed the League slipping back from the 20 percent share of the vote that it had obtained in May 1990, though these poll findings did not square with the tumultuous reception accorded to Bossi when he canvassed the terraces of the local second division football team. All uncertainty was dispelled when the votes were counted on November 25. Bossi could celebrate a narrow victory for the League, the national hierarchies of the two chief government parties were left glum in the face of a disaster for the DC and, to a lesser extent, the PSI. The share of the vote of the two main parties of the government declined by over 10 percentage points, from 45 percent to 34 percent, with votes trickling away to a pensioner's party and a "List for Brescia" as well as to the League. The League, with 24.4 percent of the vote, had inched ahead of the DC (24.3 percent) to become the largest party. The *Carroccio* (chariot), as the *Lega Nord* is popularly known, had squeezed through Prandini's vaunted defences, though its performance had been far from spectacular.

The papers the next day sounded the death knell for the *partitocrazia* which was alleged to have perished in the "Ruins of Brescia."[28] On November 26, *La Repubblica* printed an acidic leading article by the well-known journalist Mino Fuccillo. Fuccillo's theme was that the election of Brescia was a "war bulletin" for Italian democracy. The first Italian republic was disintegrating in the face of the "stormy winds" of a blind hostility toward democratic values. Infuriated by the DC's smug belief that governing was synonmous with "a shrewd share out of public privileges and money" and the PSI's craven identification with the system, the voters had elected to reward Bossi's "mass egoism" and "age-old xenophobia."[29] The problem with this analysis was that Fuccillo was mistaking progressive thinking for democracy. Democracy is arguably a mere system for choosing society's leaders, not a normative system of values. The League's win in Brescia, like its triumph in the May 1990 elections, was quintessentially democratic. Better than any other party, the League had articulated the growing impatience and despair of a substantial segment of public opinion toward a system of government which was rapidly losing all legitimacy. As such, its victory was deserved. It was also crucial. Winning at Brescia enabled the League to go into 1992 on a high note, as the most visible and successful opponent of a political class that was increasingly referred to as the "regime." And 1992 would be the year in which the "regime" would crumble, leaving Bossi to pick up the pieces.

The eruption of the Northern League on to the political scene would shortly prove to be a crippling blow for the traditional parties. It is a measure of the turbulence within Italian politics at the start of this decade, however, that Bossi's triumphal electoral progress was overshadowed between 1989-1991 by two other major events: the drawn-out death of Italian communism and a popular revolt for electoral reform. At the same time that the League's federalist vocabulary was challenging the unitary assumptions of the Italian state, the PCI was questioning and rejecting its own assumption of the necessity of a communist alternative in Italy and millions of voters were starting to wonder whether the electoral system should prize representation or governability. Instead of formulating answers of their own to these questions, the party leaderships, especially the Socialist, smugly assumed their own position to be immune to this debate. Few political classes have ever made a more glaring error.

Notes

1. An English language account of the *Union Valdotaine* is Michéal Thompson, "From Chanoux to Bossi: The Roots of Northern Italian Regionalist Politics," *Italian Politics and Society* (no. 39), Spring 1993, pp 8-15.

2. For Bossi's early life, see: Daniele Vimercati, *I Lombardi alla nuova crociata*, Milan (Mursia) 1990, pp 3-35. Also: Umberto Bossi (with Daniele Vimercati), *Vento dal Nord*, Milan (Sperling & Kupfer) 1992, pp 3-49.

3 "La Lega Si Presenta" Appendix to Vimercati, *I Lombardi alla nuova crociata* , pp 148-50.'

4. "Il programma definitiva della Lega Lombarda," *I Lombardi alla nuova crociata*, ibid., p 153.

5. Bossi, p 174.

6. Antonio Gramsci, *La Questione Meridionale*, Rome (Riuniti) 1990, p 9.

7. Giulio Savelli, *Che Cosa Vuole La Lega*, Milan (Longanesi & Co) 1992, p 127, quoting the 1990 report of SVIMEZ (Association for the Industrial Development of the *Mezzogiorno*).

8. Vimercati, *I Lombardi alla nuova crociata* , p 34.

9. Ibid., pp 32-33.

10. In *Vento dal Nord*, Bossi says, p 173: "The League started its fortunes in the mountains and valleys of Lombardy. But it couldn't, and didn't wish to, stop there. From the very beginning, we understood that the federalist revolution would have to be realized in Italy as a whole or not at all."

11. Vimercati, *I Lombardi alla nuova crociata*, p 126.

12. Bossi, quoted in Vimercati, *I Lombardi alla nuova crociata*, p 127.

13. Carlo Galli, "Un paradosso di cattiva Lega," *Il Mulino* (39), no. 4 (July-August 1990), p 572. Galli's view was: "The Leagues are less worrying for what they propose than for what they implicitly and explicitly denounce... the degeneration of our state."

14. Giorgio Bocca, "Attenti, Milano non è uno scherzo" and Eugenio Scalfari, "L'Ultimo avviso per i partiti," both in *La Repubblica* , May 8, 1990.

15. The League's electoral success in May 1990 provoked a series of analyses on the composition of the *Lega Lombarda*'s vote. A good piece of journalism on this subject is Renzo Di Rienzo, "Una Lega in bianco," *L'Espresso*, June 10, 1990. See also, Renato Mannheimer, "Chi vota Lega e perchè" and Ilvo Diamanti, "Un tipologia dei simpatizzanti della Lega" in Renato Mannheimer (ed), *La Lega Lombarda*, Milan (Feltrinelli) 1991. An interesting recent article on the *Lega*'s electorate is Luca Ricolfi, "Politica senza fede: l'estremismo di centro dei piccoli leghisti," *Il Mulino* (42), January - February 1993, pp 53-69.

16. Bossi, *Vento dal Nord*, pp 143-144.

17. Gianfranco Miglio, introduction to *Vento dal Nord*, p viii.

18. Roberto Mannheimer, *La Lega Lombarda*, p 144-145.

19. Gianni Rocca, "E lo stivale va in pezzi," *La Repubblica* , September 4, 1990.

20. Gianfranco Miglio, "Toward a Federal Italy," *Telos* (90), Winter 1991-1992, p19. This edition of *Telos* also contains useful articles on the *Lega Nord* by Bernard Poche and Roberto Biorcio, among others. A good English language discussion of the League's federalism is Tom Gallagher, "The Challenge of the Northern League to the Italian State," *Government & Opposition* (27), 4/92. Readers of Italian should also see Daniele Vimercati (ed), *Stati Uniti d'Italia*, Milan (Sugarco) 1991, and Bossi's own thoughtful essay "I piccoli grandi popoli" in Umberto Bossi and Daniele Vimercati, *La Rivoluzione: La Lega storie e idee*, Milan (Sperling & Kupfer) 1993, pp 127-143.

21. Ibid., pp 41-42.

22. Bossi, *Vento dal Nord*, p 202.

23. The debate at the assembly of the *Lega Nord* is collected as *Le tesi congressuali della Lega Nord* and is a font of great importance for the understanding of the movement's ideology. I drew largely on this source in my own "Warriors of the New Pontida: The Challenge of the Lega Nord to the Italian Party System," *Political Quarterly* (64), January-March 1993, pp 99-106. The quotation in this paragraph is an allusion to a paper presented by Mario Borghezio, "L'Affinità etno-culturale dei popoli del nord." Background -- albeit slightly self-serving background -- to the politicking that accompanied the first federal conference of the *Lega Nord* is to be found in *Vento dal Nord*, Chapter 7, "Il difficile trionfo."

24. See Formentini, Sarogni and Roveda's contributions to the *Tesi congressuali*, as well as Giulio Savelli, *Che cosa vuole la Lega*, especially the last chapter "Proposte e calunnie."

25. Marco Vitale, quoted Toni Visentini, *La Lega*, Bolzano (Raetia) 1993, p 48.

26. Bossi admits this error in *Vento dal Nord*, p 118.

27. Quoted Vimercati, p 128.

28. "Le macerie di Brescia," *La Repubblica* , November 26, 1991.

29. Mino Fuccillo, accompanying comment to ibid.

5

The End of Italian Communism

On November 9-10, 1989, hundreds of thousands of East Berliners pulled down the wall separating them from their fellow Germans in the West. The following day, *L'Unità*, the official newspaper of the Italian Communist Party, declared that the end of the communist dictatorship in the DDR heralded "Europe's happiest day." A front-page editorial added the hope that East Germany would not be the last bastion of totalitarianism to fall: The "old guard" in Bulgaria and Czechoslovakia, and the "disgraceful" regime in Rumania, should share the same fate.[1]

These sentiments were, of course, echoed in a thousand leading articles all over the world. Their novelty lay in the fact that they meant that the PCI was unambiguously washing its hands of the eastern bloc. Ever since the crushing of the Prague spring in 1968, to which the PCI had been vocally opposed, Italian communists had been sharply critical of the denial of democracy in the Soviet Union and its puppet regimes. Nevertheless, it is also fair to say that many in the PCI had never given the Soviet bloc up for lost. The repressive character of the communist state was routinely attributed in PCI publications to the West's encirclement of the socialist states, rather than to inherent flaws in communism itself; the notion that the USSR was -- or even could be -- an imperialist power was invariably rejected (though the USSR was described as a great power that resorted to *realpolitik* like everyone else[2]); Italian writers and intellectuals who had admitted that communism was the "god that failed" were ignored and in some cases denigrated in the PCI-controlled press until the early 1980s, though the PCI never put the same Stalinist premium on orthodoxy as did the French communists. The most blatant victim of this intellectual self-censorship was Ignazio Silone, arguably Italy's greatest political novelist, who was an unperson with the communist *literati* until 1991. The emergence of Gorbachev, moreover, had, if anything, stimulated this belief in the Soviet bloc's ability to swim out of the stagnation of the Brezhnev-Andropov-Chernenko period. Perestroika and glasnost were seen as signs that the Soviet system, while ailing, was not yet moribund, and this led to an almost embarrassing cult of Gorbachev in the party press.

The PCI's plaudits for Gorbachev's program of renewal, however, masked the fact that, by 1989, much of the party leadership had long since ceased to believe in the economic and social superiority of the Soviet bloc to the social democracies of western Europe and no longer regarded Marxism as a useful guide to political action. Like the congregations of sexually deviant TV evangelists, the leaders of the PCI continued to profess their faith in public while privately whispering behind their hands that perhaps -- just perhaps -- the Soviet system was too rotten to be reformed. But once this private thought was uttered publicly, there was nothing to prevent the PCI from cutting the cord binding it to the rotting hulk of communist theory and practice and setting a new course as a socially progressive party of the independent left. And within days of the wall coming down, this is precisely what Achille Occhetto, the party secretary, suggested that the PCI should do. Speaking at a dramatic meeting of the executive committee of the PCI on November 14, 1989, Occhetto proposed that the PCI should "bring into being" a leftist political force "new even in name."[3]

A Rare and Curious Animal

There is a sense in which Occhetto's announcement can be seen as the logical culmination of a lengthy historical process. Beginning in the first post-war decade, when the PCI's longtime leader, the gelid-featured Palmiro Togliatti, had elevated the unorthodox Marxism of Antonio Gramsci to the status of the party's official ideology, the PCI had charted a steady course away from both Marxist dogmatics and narrow adhesion to a pro-Moscow line. The PCI's outspoken criticism, under the leadership of Togliatti's successor, Luigi Longo, of the suppression of Dubcek's "communism with a human face," marked the second rest camp on this intellectual trek; Enrico Berlinguer's willingness to moot continued Italian membership of NATO during the 1976 election campaign was a third stopping point. In 1979, the 15th Congress of the PCI, after the failure of the government of national solidarity, declared that the party would find a "third way" to socialism, accepting neither the narrow dogmatism of the Soviet bloc, nor the social democratic compromise with the market economy. In 1981, after the imposition of martial law in Poland, Berlinguer argued that the countries of the Soviet bloc had exhausted the "propulsive force of the October revolution."

Berlinguer's death in 1984 left the party wallowing in the "middle of the ford" between Soviet-style socialism and adhesion to the norms of social democracy.[4] Berlinguer's successor, Alessandro Natta, an able apparatchik and functionary, at times seemed distinctly nostalgic for the party's pro-Soviet past. Nonetheless, during Natta's stewardship the party shifted, in 1986, toward a more explicitly social democratic stance. It also embraced a number of causes, such as the struggle for greater sexual equality, which did not form part of the traditional communist repertoire. Natta, however, made heavy weather of turning these ideological innovations into a coherent political policy. In the mid-1980s, Natta, like Berlinguer before him, vacillated between appealing to the PSI for a vague policy of "leftist unity" and flirting with Ciriaco De Mita's relatively progressive wing of the DC. This ambiguous stance caused the party to lose credibility in the eyes of the electorate, especially the young, and led directly to a series of electoral setbacks. The PCI did badly in the 1985 regional elections, and was embarrassingly defeated in the referendum on wage indexing (see Chapter One). Then, in 1987, came the party's major defeat in the general elections.

As Piero Ignazi has shown in *Dal PCI al PDS*, his outstanding account of the travails of the PCI in the 1980s, the PCI's defeat in the 1987 elections was the "decisive element in beginning the transformation of the PCI."[5] The party's electoral loss was hardly devastating in numerical terms (in the ballot for the Chamber of Deputies, the party's share of the vote slipped from 29.9 percent to 26.6 percent, while in the Senate, it retained over 28 percent), but psychologically the results were very damaging. Since the near-triumph of the 1976 election, the 1987 poll was the PCI's third successive defeat in a general election. The party's share of the vote had, moreover, slithered back to its pre-Berlinguer levels of consent. As a result, the tone of the debate within the party in the aftermath of the elections was, to quote Ignazi once more, of "unprecedented dramatic intensity."[6] The PCI's right wing, the so-called *miglioristi*, urged the party to cast itself as a responsible party of government able to join with the PSI in an explicitly social democratic "alternative." The left, by contrast, lamented the failure of the party to portray itself as an aggressively campaigning force for social justice.

For the first time, moreover, the party's notoriously top-down internal discipline began to fail it. Throughout the country, the grass-roots membership, for once without waiting for orders from the party chiefs, began asking what the PCI was in politics to do. The consequences of this debate were immediate; Natta and a core group of senior members of the party hierarchy, with some dissension from the crustier members of the party's Central Committee, bowed to the "wave of dissatisfaction and criticism from the party periphery" and appointed a relatively youthful reformist, Achille Occhetto, to the post of Vice Secretary.[7] In June 1988, following Natta's hospitalization with a heart attack, his resignation, and a second disaster in local elections held in May 1988, Occhetto was advanced into the top job after a tense internal debate among the party's grandees.

He faced a daunting prospect. Broadly speaking, Occhetto had become leader of a party that knew it wanted to modernize, but was bitterly divided over the form of modernization it should choose; that had already modernized its ideology significantly, but often pretended it hadn't; that had been held together by rigid discipline, but was now tolerating unprecedented internal democracy. The party's most active members, moreover, embodied a fundamental contradiction. Militant communists all over Italy knew that the party was losing its leading role among the organized working class (one of the most interesting developments in Italian trade unionism in the mid-1980s was the rise of the so-called COBAS, spontaneous workers' organizations which by-passed the mostly communist-led official unions in industrial disputes in the schools, railways and air transport), with young people, with professionals and skilled workers. They also knew that this development was due to a widespread perception that the PCI was an anachronism. At the same time, however, these same militants were usually more hidebound in their attachment to traditional communist ideals and shibboleths than the party leadership. To give just one example: A poll of delegates at the 17th party congress in 1986 revealed the startling and telling fact that more than 30 percent of those questioned regarded the USSR as the society "which most closely approaches the ideal." China and Yugoslavia were next; Sweden, the only western society to attract much support, was cited by just 8 percent of the delegates quizzed.[8]

The party was also riven by now with open, though not formally recognized, factions. Historically, the PCI had followed a Leninist "democratic centralist" model of party organization, whereby discussion of policy was free and open until the party had made up its mind. At that point, all discussion of the party line stopped and any formal attempt to modify policy became an act of deviationism, to be penalized by expulsion. Naturally, this had not prevented the evolution of different tendencies within the party; the *miglioristi*, whose main political point of reference was the party spokesman on foreign affairs, Giorgio Napolitano, would not have looked out of place in any western European social democratic party. At the other end of the spectrum, however, lay a tiny but vocal faction of Leninist zealots, headed by the Milanese machine politician Armando Cossutta, and a slightly more moderate faction centered around the party's weekly magazine *Rinascita*: This faction's leading lights were the literary critic Alberto Asor Rosa and the philosopher Mario Tronti. A further leftist faction, led by a veteran figure of granite-like integrity, Pietro Ingrao, married forceful criticism of the Soviet bloc to a radical defense of workers' rights. Ingrao wanted the party to emphasize its roots in working class organizations and trade union issues, but also to take a leading role in emerging social movements. The heart of the party, and most of its leadership, oscillated between the positions of Ingrao and Napolitano, with the balance tipping more rightwards than leftwards. Occhetto himself, however, hailed from a left-center background: Originally an

Ingraiano, he had "migrated" toward the party's ideological middle-ground in the 1980s.

Holding together a political movement boasting this breadth of opinion was obviously not going to be easy. Occhetto solved the problem by a twofold strategy. On the one hand, he made much of the common ideological and historical bond between the PCI and the PSI; on the other hand, he stressed that a joint platform would have to be on the basis of a socially progressive policies that addressed the real problems of Italian society and politics. In particular, Occhetto emphasized patronage politics, corruption, the empowerment of ordinary citizens at the expense of the party hierarchies as areas in which urgent reforms were necessary. Internationally, Occhetto claimed the PCI was part of the "Euroleft," a vague expression that too often seemed to amount to chanting hosannas to Gorbachev and to making empty pronouncements about the importance of the environment. Nevertheless, after a visit by Occhetto to Gorbachev in March 1989, there emerged a clearer picture of what the PCI stood for. The PCI supported the democratization of the regimes of eastern Europe; it was not yet prepared to join the principal institution of European social democracy, the Socialist International. After the European elections in May 1989, the PCI decided that it would no longer remain part of the Communist group in the European parliament: The party did not, however, join the Socialist group, but preferred to set up a new faction inside the Parliament, the "European Unitary Left," along with a handful of fellow travellers from other countries.

The sum of these new policies was a portfolio that had something for everyone within the PCI. Occhetto's opening to the PSI satisfied the *miglioristi*, while adding conditions that implied an end of Bettino Craxi's thorny but profitable relationship with the DC enabled Occhetto to keep the respect of the PCI's mass membership, which regarded Craxi as dishonest and as a traitor to socialism. At the same time, the PCI's genuine warmth toward perestroika, and the new radicalism implied by Occhetto's attacks on the party system, succeeded in keeping the left on board. This twin approach owed much to the ideas of a non-communist thinker, the independent left philosopher Paolo Flores d'Arcais, who from 1986 onward regularly used his column in the intellectual bi-monthly *Micromega* to press the PCI to transform itself into a "mass Radical Party," and took the lead in organizing an independent network of discussion clubs with the same purpose.[9] Italy's Radical Party, which is presided over by a Gandhi with a taste for high living, the ebullient, chain-smoking, white-haired Marco Pannella, has won itself a stable niche in public affections by the consistency with which it has campaigned for fundamental social reforms, especially abortion and electoral reform.[10] Flores d'Arcais' insight was that the ills of the party system were such that the political force that made their reform the cardinal point of its program stood to harvest a heavy crop of votes from what Flores D'Arcais called the "submerged left."[11] It would also give the PCI a leftist substitute for Marxism in the post-modern, post-class warfare world. Occhetto seemed to find this reasoning compelling. In an interview with *L'Espresso* shortly after the party's 18th Congress (March 19-23, 1989), Occhetto did not entirely disdain the "Mass Radical Party" label; he merely affirmed that the PCI was and should remain a party of government, and not be seen as a protest party. To underline the PCI's vision of itself as a future power of government, Occhetto had earlier borrowed the English idea of assembling a *governo ombra* (shadow cabinet) whose members were given specific areas of competence and were encouraged to develop the PCI's new policy initiatives. In an upbeat mood, Occhetto described the PCI as a "rare and curious animal" that was reinventing the European left. The PCI, Occhetto implied, was the left's future.[12]

One Step Forward, Two Steps Back

Occhetto's confident mood in the wake of the 18th Congress reflected his success at imposing his new course at the party assembly. The 18th Congress approved momentous changes in three crucial areas: party discipline, its communist identity, and the composition of the party leadership. Democratic centralism was abolished (though the formation of factions remained outlawed) and a long-suppressed explosion of amendments and motions criticising the leadership testified to the sincerity of this change. The party's communist identity was all but dismantled: the PCI described itself as a "non-ideological" movement and removed all references to Marx, Lenin and Togliatti from the new party statute. This change, which might be compared to the British Labour Party finally summoning up the courage to abolish the notorious "Clause Four" of its party statutes, was marred by a symptomatic refusal on the part of the active membership to abolish other, emotionally important, symbols of the party's communist past: the hammer and sickle and the ritual singing of the *Internazionale*.

The Congress also put its seal on Occhetto's leadership. The 18th Congress overwhelmingly confirmed Occhetto as the party's political secretary, voting, in the first secret ballot ever for the party leader, by 235 votes to 2, with 6 abstentions, to keep their reform-minded new leader. In addition, Occhetto managed to place "young colonels" into the party's key governing bodies: the Central Committee, the *Direzione* and the Secretariat. This transition was partly achieved by resignations among the old guard -- Pietro Ingrao retired from the *Direzione* after a speech in which he warmly praised the direction Occhetto was taking -- but it mostly relied on a substantial expansion of all three institutions. The Central Committee, the movement's parliament, increased from 215 members to an unwieldy 300; the *Direzione*, or Cabinet, from 39 to 49; the

Secretariat, or inner Cabinet, from five to six. This influx of new leaders had one immediate effect: a shifting of the party's internal balance of power from the center-right to the center-left. When the Central Committee met to elect the *Direzione* and Secretariat the two weeks after the Congress, the *miglioristi* were all but excluded from the PCI's top tables.[13]

Whatever the views of the *miglioristi*, Italian public opinion seemed to approve of Occhetto's renewal of the PCI. The rate of decline in party membership slowed in 1989, and in the May 1989 elections to the European Parliament the PCI reversed its downward spiral. 27.6 percent of the electorate voted Communist, 1 percent more than the 1987 national elections and 6 percent more than in the 1988 local elections.

Events in eastern Europe in the summer of 1989, however, shattered the mood of optimism induced by the European elections. The PCI was caught off balance by the speed of changes in Hungary and Poland, and was unable to form a coherent response to the fact that the eastern Europeans were abandoning communism, not just democratizing gradually. The same tendency was seen in domestic Italian politics. On August 6, 1989, the twenty-fifth anniversary of Togliatti's death, one of Occhetto's young colonels, Biagio De Giovanni, published an article in *L'Unità* entitled "Once upon a time there was Togliatti and Really Existing Socialism," which argued that there was no place in the renewed PCI for Togliatti's Stalinist legacy. This article sparked off a huge row within the party and the open opposition of influential figures like Natta and Ingrao. Biagio De Giovanni, in good Stalinist style, was compelled to admit that his views were merely personal and did not reflect the ideas of the reformers in the party, an explanation which convinced nobody but did allow the dust to settle. The PCI was not allowed to get away with this open display of disunity so easily, however. The PSI, which after initially hesitating over how to respond to Occhetto's innovations, had by now decided upon a policy of sniping hostility, gleefully made the most of the PCI's failure to shrug off its pro-Soviet past and to take the logical last step of changing its name. The internal opposition, moreover, led by Armando Cossutta, claimed that the party's historical role was being subverted and demanded the right to organize to better express its views. Other factions insisted that they should have the same right. The party, in short, by the Autumn of 1989 was in danger of falling to pieces. Thus, as Martin Bull has argued, Occhetto's *svolta* (sudden change of direction) in November 1989 did not so much plunge the PCI into crisis (since the party was wracked with crisis already) as prevent the party from slipping back into the no-man's land between democratic socialism and communism.[14] Occhetto was not about to see the good work of eighteen months undermined by a sentimental attachment to the PCI's historic legacy, though one criticism which may be fairly levelled at the PCI's leader in the months following the November *svolta* is that he persistently underestimated the strength of the emotional loyalty within the party rank and file to the trappings of the old PCI. The PCI's membership were to prove much less willing to give up the communist name, the hammer and sickle and the symbols of communist ideology than they had been to revolutionize the ideology itself.[15]

This fact became obvious in the immediate reaction to Occhetto's proposal. The party's left argued strongly both that the PCI's history, unlike the history of eastern European communism, was nothing to be ashamed of and that Occhetto, by shunning consultation with the party's membership and senior figures, had acted with the traditional authoritarian disregard for party democracy displayed in the past by the party leadership. These two complaints were arguably contradictory, but they carried tremendous weight with the PCI's most militant members and ensured that Occhetto's move provoked a febrile atmosphere within the party. Fear that the party would split was so great that voices urging a compromise began to swirl around the corridors of the PCI's Rome headquarters. Occhetto, like a gambler who sees his debts mounting up, chose to stake his future on the turn of a single political card. Having obtained the support of the *Direzione* for his policy, he boldly demanded that a meeting of the Central Committee should back his initiative and decide upon a method to implement it.

This meeting of the Central Committee was held between November 20-24, 1989. Occhetto's speeches to this assembly of senior party faithful constitute a summary of his reasons for the *svolta* and an assessment of his expectations for the Italian Left's future.[16] At times repetitive and jargon-filled, they were nevertheless a subtle attempt to show the sentimentalists within the PCI that the proposal to found a new party was the logical conclusion of the PCI's history; that it was precisely because the PCI had never been akin to Soviet-style socialism that it had to be with the avant-garde in 1989. Occhetto was at pains to stress that abandoning the word communist was merely an act of historical acknowledgment, not a skid to the "right" and a concession that the capitalist enemy had won. So long as there were nations wracked with hunger and ignorance; so long as rapacious capital could deplete the world's environmental resources at will; so long as there were huge stockpiles of arms; so long as the ideals of human solidarity were appealing as a basis for social policy, so there would be socialists. Indeed, the struggle for justice in all these fields could only be held back by those who did not have the courage to "go beyond old ideological barriers" and remained attached to the "fallen idols" of the party's communist tradition.

Occhetto further contended that Italy itself was crying out for the solutions that only a revitalized left could bring. The political system was beginning to "suffocate civil society," the institutions of the state were "falling prey" to corruption and illegality. In the face of this rapid and disastrous degeneration of Italian democracy, Occhetto alleged that the left was failing in its social and political duty to unite and "put its renewed force at the service of Italy." The changing PCI, Occhetto affirmed, wanted dialogue with all those, be they "lay" or Catholic, who rejected the idea that "this is the best possible of all worlds" to establish a common program for radical reform. As such, it was launching a "challenge" to the PSI. Occhetto called upon the PSI to follow the example of the PCI by initiating a radical revision of its policy and ideology. In a phrase that was clearly aimed at Craxi, Occhetto argued that now the Cold War was over and the PCI had unequivocally moved into the democratic camp, "all alibis are destined to fall." The PSI's comfortable cohabitation with the DC, Occhetto implied, could no longer continue without the suspicion growing that the PSI was no longer part of the left. Occhetto's ascetic and notoriously anti-Socialist deputy, Massimo D'Alema, had put the same thought more explicitly on November 15, in a front page leading article in *L'Unità*:

> We want to assure the leaders of the PSI calmly and firmly that the root of the division between our two parties is not the distinction between democracy and totalitarianism. What keeps us apart is the political, ideological and programmatic choices made by the PSI and which have entangled that party in an alliance with the conservative forces of our country. [17]

The leftist rhetoric of Occhetto's speech and the Socialist bashing in D'Alema's article, while doubtless sincere, were clearly also designed to appease the left wing of the party. Occhetto also added a concession on the question of the new party's name. In his speech to the Central Committee, Occhetto conceded that "First comes the thing (*la cosa*), then comes the name."[18] He was willing to accept, in other words, that the party should transform itself in principle, without getting bogged down in a heated debate over its new name. Nevertheless, even with these enticements, Occhetto did not get all his own way. The Central Committee voted by 219 votes to 73, with 34 abstainers, to accept Occhetto's initiative, but contradicted the party secretary on procedure. Against Occhetto's preferences, the Central Committee passed the buck by arguing that an extraordinary Congress (so-called because it would be specially convened and would interrupt the usual two-year cycle between meetings of the party's "parliament") of the PCI had to ratify their decision before the constituent period of the new party could begin. The PCI would remain the PCI until its entire membership had been consulted and had had the chance to say it should become something else.

The extraordinary Congress was scheduled for the beginning of March 1990 in Bologna. In the meantime, the party splintered into three major factions, each of which presented lengthy motions stating its philosophical and political understanding of the role of the left in the post-Cold War world. Occhetto's motion, which was supported by the *miglioristi* and left-modernizers like

Occhetto himself and D'Alema, took up four broadsheet pages in *L'Unità* and outlined a nine point program for change. The motion's title, "Launching the founding phase of a new political formation" unambiguously stated its sponsors' intentions. The nature of the new political formation itself was outlined less vaguely than in Occhetto's Central Committee speech. Occhetto's faction wished to found "a new democratic, popular and reforming political movement that is open to progressive elements from both the lay and the Catholic communities." It should be able to "interpret new questions being raised in the world of work, and of culture, as well as by youth movements, environmentalists, women's groups and pacifists and proponents of non-violent resistance."[19] The second motion made a strong case for the retention of a communist identity in Italian politics and had as its principal sponsors Natta and Ingrao; the third motion was presented by Cossutta's extremist wing of the party. In keeping with the party's new democratic calling, all three motions were debated and vote upon in PCI sections and federations throughout the country. Frank Belloni has called this procedure "the Italian communist equivalent of a large-scale exercise in town-hall democracy."[20] It swiftly became clear that the motion of the Central Committee *maggioranza* was destined to prevail. Occhetto's proposal was supported by nearly 66 percent of the PCI membership who voted: Ingrao's motion took a respectable 31 percent. Cossutta's hardliners trailed in last with just 3 percent.

Nevertheless, Occhetto's overall victory was more marked in some regions rather than others. In the PCI's heartland, Emilia-Romagna, Tuscany and Umbria, where the PCI had long been accustomed to govern and where the pressure for reform was strongest, Occhetto's motion took nearly 80 percent of the votes. In more Catholic regions where the PCI had long been in opposition, the first motion's majority was less striking. In Trentino-Alto Adige, for instance, Occhetto's proposal received only 51 percent; Ingrao received 38 percent and Cossutta 11 percent. In Campania, Occhetto took just 58 percent and Ingrao 39 percent. Delegates to the extraordinary Congress were parcelled out proportionately among the different motions: Motion 1 received 730 votes, Motion 2 received 324 votes and Motion 3 received just 37 votes. Occhetto thus went into the Congress knowing that he had a sure majority for his platform.

La Cosa

The delegates meeting at the extraordinary Congress in Bologna were engaged in the truly extraordinary task of putting an end to an old political formation without instituting a new party in its place. Ingrao's strongest argument during the consultation process had always been that the leadership was asking the party membership to step into the unknown. Nevertheless, with impressive discipline, the delegates did just that: At the Congress, Occhetto's motion received 726 votes, Ingrao's 322 and Cossutta's 37. Occhetto, in tears, was embraced by an emotional Pietro Ingrao, setting a tone of reconciliation and unity that was reflected in the Congress's other decisions. A new, once more expanded, Central Committee was elected with the two minority factions being guaranteed representation proportional to their strength within the party. The new Central Committee thus consisted of 236 supporters of Occhetto's motion, 105 supporters of Ingrao's and 12 of Cossuta's. Holding out an additional olive branch, the majority allowed the Presidency of the Central Committee to go to Aldo Tortorella, one of Ingrao's most prominent followers and one of the most vociferous critics of the Occhetto's new approach. The left reciprocated. Occhetto was re-elected party leader by 213 Central Committee votes to 23, with 71 abstainers among Ingrao's followers. As the historian Nicola Tranfaglia argued in *L'Unità* on March 11, 1990, the ship of the new movement had "set sail."[21] It had departed, moreover, with a crew that, for all their "profound differences" were united in wanting to change the political balance of power in Italy. In Occhetto's own words, the Congress had shown that there were not "two PCIs," there was just one united movement that had made a "net" choice to turn itself into a "mass laboratory" for an experiment of vital importance for Italy.[22] Even the PSI seemed impressed. At the party conference of the PSI, which met the following week in the seaside resort of Rimini, D'Alema met with Craxi and Giuliano Amato, the former deputy prime minister during the Goria administration and treasury minister under De Mita. The meeting, which was carried on with unusual cordiality, seemed to indicate a "thaw" in the two parties' relations.

The optimism and unity on show at the 19th Congress in Bologna faded away quickly. External events swiftly highlighted the internal divisions and weaknesses of *la Cosa*. The first such event was the election of regional governments in May 1990, the first electoral test of any significance since the collapse of the Berlin Wall and Occhetto's intensification of the process of change within the PCI. The results were a disaster for the *Cosa*. The PCI's share of the vote collapsed by 6 percent relative to the previous poll in 1985; compared to the previous year's European elections, the PCI lost 3.5 percent, declining to a little over 24 percent. The PSI, meanwhile, gained 2 percent, arriving at over 15 percent, just 9 percent behind. This relative setback, which was compounded by steadily mounting evidence that the party's membership figures were dropping dramatically as disillusioned militants failed to renew their party cards, was seized upon by the left as evidence that the PCI had been demoralized by Occhetto's changes and had consequently lost the campaigning zeal that had long made it the central opposition force to the *partitocrazia*. Occhetto and D'Alema, by contrast, argued that the local elections confirmed the validity of the new course. Their argument was that the elections, more than a defeat for the PCI, were a monumental rejection of the existing political system.[23] The dramatic success of the *Lega Lombarda* and (by Italian standards) the colossal number of abstentions, blank ballots and spoilt ballot papers were proof of this. *L'Unità* pointed out on May 9, 1990, that the sum of votes not directly cast for a party was 8,784,268: This was more than the PCI, the second largest political formation, had managed to obtain.[24] The voters, in other words, were now crying out for an alternative to the political system which had squandered the wealth generated by Italian industry and had allowed the *Mezzogiorno* to deteriorate into a battlefield. Occhetto and D'Alema's point was that the PCI had to present itself plausibly as this alternative, something that could only be done by an intensification of the modernizing process.

The truth lay somewhere between these two poles. The left inside the PCI were correct to say that Occhetto's innovations had alienated a great many of the party's most active workers. The PCI's campaign had been lackluster and introspective at local level. The leadership's analysis, however, in retrospect seems prescient. May 1990 was the harbinger of things to come. Despite some growth of the DC's vote in the South and the national advance of the PSI (which also owed much to a client vote in the South), there is no doubt that these regional elections were the first major sign of a deep-seated change in the public mood. It is almost certainly true that by observing this and by insisting on the process of renewal, Occhetto and D'Alema ensured the existence of a major leftist force in Italy. An unreformed PCI, for all its deep roots in the Italian working class, would have seemed an unbearable anachronism in the feverish atmosphere of the "Italian revolution" 1992-1994.

The summer of 1990 confirmed that the various *anime* (souls) of the PCI were increasingly incompatible. In August 1990, a large part of the parliamentary party's left-wing voted against the Italian government's decision to send aircraft and naval forces to Saudi Arabia following the invasion of Kuwait, instead of abstaining as the party leadership wanted. The decision touched a nerve: The *miglioristi*, in particular Napolitano, had long been trying to emphasize that the modernization of the PCI would require an increased realism in foreign policy matters. Abstention had at least been a gesture in this direction.[25]

Foreign policy, however, was, to translate an Italian idiom, a difficult cat for the PCI to skin. Neither Occhetto nor D'Alema was prepared to push their modernizing impulses so far as to give unqualified support to military action by a coalition of First World powers against a Third World power, even when the Third World power was Saddam Hussein's Iraq. Operation Desert Shield smacked too much of imperialism to even right-wing members of the PCI. Besides, the *Cosa* was supposed to be appealing to pacifist movements and to progressive Catholics. Moreover, as in other movements of the European left, disillusionment with the Soviet bloc had not been greeted with a concomitant softening of position toward the United States. If anything, the opposite was true. The fourth chapter of Piero Ignazi's *Dal PCI al PDS* consists of an analysis of the political attitudes of the delegates to the extraordinary 19th Congress in Bologna, and is a mine of useful data, especially with respect to the delegates' understanding of international relations. The typical PCI activist emerges as an uncritical supporter of Third World governments, anti-American, pacifist, anti-capitalist and anti-Israeli. Nearly 97 percent of the delegates polled believed that Third World poverty was due to exploitation by the industrialized nations; 93 percent concurred with the proposition that the United States was an imperialist power. Almost 80 percent argued that membership of NATO had been of no relevance for the growth of democracy in Italy; 74 percent doubted Israel's democratic credentials. Seventy percent denied that Italy had been protected by the American nuclear umbrella. There was also strong pacifist sentiment among the delegates. More than 90 percent disagreed with the affirmation "Military service does at least give useful experience for later life," while 72 percent declared their belief that "non-violence is the only practicable form of political action." The delegates' discussion of capitalism and the free market was distinguished by suspicion and hostility. Eighty-one percent believed that "the essence of capitalism" was the "exploitation of man by man" (though 65 percent did believe that private enterprise was an essential part of a just society). Asked, moreover, to place themselves on a left/right scale where "1" was an extreme left standpoint and "10" a standpoint of the extreme right, 93 percent categorized themselves between 1 and 3. Occhetto's new political formation, for all its abandonment of communism, was not a conventional centrist social democratic party.[26]

It is in part this feeling among both the militants and leadership of the *Cosa* that they were *duri e puri* (hard and pure) in their left-wing beliefs that explains the failure of the post-Congress "thaw" in relations with the PSI to wash away all the uncomfortable debris hampering a political alliance between the two parties. Only the *miglioristi* within the PCI were willing to turn the PCI into an outright social democratic force on the German or Scandinavian model. The other main factions in the *Cosa* -- Occhetto's left-modernizers, Ingrao's working class radicals and Cossutta's neo-Stalinists, were really divided over how steeped in the traditional symbolism of Italian communism the nascent movement's radical leftism should be.

This endless agonizing over the soul of the PCI was no use to Craxi. Craxi might have been prepared to discuss a power alliance: An agreement with the PCI which would liberate him of his entanglement with the DC and create an alternative parliamentary axis to the *pentapartito* coalition (though it is doubtful in the extreme whether Craxi would have risked such a move while the PCI remained numerically far stronger than the PSI). Occhetto, however, was not prepared to compromise the vocal radicalism of his new political formation. He and his colleagues in the reforming wing of the PCI were in politics to bring about large-scale social change, not just to occupy ministerial chairs. The two parties' positions were wholly incompatible, and, not surprisingly, once this fact became clear the "thaw" swiftly froze over again. This point is very important. It is all too easy, reading the PCI and PSI press, to imagine that the gulf between the two parties was essentially intellectual. *Mondoperaio*, especially, printed dozens of articles in the aftermath of the fall of the Berlin wall that contended that the unity of the Italian Left was attendant on the PCI conducting a thorough examination of its conscience. If the PCI could face its past, if it could look squarely at the horrors of the Gulag, and the servility of its own leaders to the Stalinist form of totalitarianism, then the PSI would be ready to embrace Italy's ex-communists with the good-fellowship of social democracy. The *miglioristi* certainly appeared to believe that ideological differences were all that obstructed an alliance of the left. Their intellectual review, *Il Ponte*, strove to break down differing perceptions of contemporary history and to establish intellectual common ground between the PCI and the PSI. Yet somehow, despite all the heart-searching in the ranks of the PCI over the party's past, the two sides never seemed to get closer. Writing just after Occhetto's *svolta*, *Mondoperaio*'s editor Luciano Pellicano claimed that "the communist mentality, whatever it chooses to call itself, will not melt away like snow in the sun."[27] Despite exploratory talks between Craxi and Occhetto in September 1990 and a meeting between Craxi and Napolitano in November 1990, this attitude of suspicion was the mainstay of the PSI's often savage criticism of the new *Partito Democratico della Sinistra* (PDS) from the autumn of 1990 to the April 1992 elections. In the case of Pellicano and others among the Socialist intelligentsia, this conviction that the PCI was still beguiled by the sins of its past was probably sincere. For the party leadership, accusing the Communists of being stuck fast in an undemocratic political culture was merely a convenient way of avoiding an alliance that would have brought a decade of feeding at democracy's trough to an end. The *miglioristi*, Italy's most genuine social democrats, were wrong and the mass of the party membership -- which *loathed* Craxi -- was right. The gulf between the PCI and the leadership of the PSI was not ideological: It was a question of different political styles. Craxi and the PSI were too closely identified with the worst features of the old regime by 1990 to be compatible with the progressive impulse guiding the renewal of the old PCI.

The Birth of the PDS

Occhetto introduced the name and emblem (an oak tree with a minature version of the PCI's old hammer and sickle symbol at the tree's roots) of the Democratic Party of the Left at a press conference on October 10 1990. The new name was warmly welcomed by the movement's militants and also received the dubious blessing of influential figures such as President Cossiga.[28] Occhetto did not escape without polemic, however. Both the left and the right of the party used the unveiling of the new symbol as a pretext to froth internal disagreements into life. The *miglioristi*, already infuriated by the way that the party leadership was co-operating with pacifist groups and progressive Catholics in organizing street demonstrations against the use of force in the Gulf, were upset that the word 'socialist' did not appear in the new movement's name (though Craxi had cynically rendered this impossible for Occhetto by adding the words 'Socialist Unity' to the PSI symbol only shortly before). The far left-wing of the party, while appeased by the retention of the old communist emblem, was increasingly prepared to push its differences with the leadership to the point of secession. Cossutta's faction made no bones about their intention of leaving the new PDS if there was no mention of the word 'communist' in the party name; Ingrao and his supporters also wanted to retain the PCI's comunist inheritance but were not prepared to leave and start a new party. (Had Ingrao and his supporters been willing to accept that the character of Occhetto's innovations -- with which they strongly concurred -- also required the party to alter its name and some of its mythology, the whole process of modernizing the party would have been less excruciatingly slow.) To complicate matters still further, a new leftist faction headed by Antonio Bassolino, a longtime ally of Ingrao's who had nevertheless voted with the *maggioranza* at the 19th Congress, had also emerged at the end of October 1990. Bassolino's view of the party's future, which had been outlined as early as September in *Rinascita* (whose editorial staff became his warmest supporters), can perhaps best be described as souped-up Occhettoism. Bassolino, like Occhetto, placed the emphasis of his program on women's issues, environmental concerns, the struggle for peace and a "sustainable society," but the tone was diverse. Bassolino argued that the "new European socialism" that he was proposing should eventually fulfil an ominous-sounding "hegemonic function" in European society and that any new party should have an "antagonistic" role in Italian society.[29]

The center of gravity of the PDS lay on the left; the majority within the leadership that had won the battle to abolish the old PCI was rightward-leaning; the chief political issue of the moment, the Gulf War, tended to drive the left together in their common opposition to militarism and the use of armed force by the United States. In this straightforward list of elementary facts about the PCI as it approached its 20th and last Congress in January 1991 lies the clue to why the birth of the PDS was such an arduous and fraught affair.

The Congress was preceded by the same exhaustive consultations of the membership that had prefaced the 19th Congress. The leadership's motion, recommending the adoption of the PDS's new name and symbol, once more received about two-thirds of the membership's votes and delegates to the Congress, far more than Cossutta and Ingrao, who presented a joint motion urging the party to become a "democratic communist" formation, or Bassolino, whose individual motion scored just under 6 percent, his votes mostly coming at the expense of the left rather than the center-right majority. The foundation of the new party, however, was overshadowed by the predictable walkout of Cossuta's hardliners, by a major split in the nascent party over the Gulf War and, most sensationally of all, by the failure of Achille Occhetto to obtain a convincing mandate for his leadership in the post-congressional vote of the National Council, the body that had replaced the old Central Committee.

Feelings were running strongly over the Gulf War, where bombing had now begun. At the Congress, the *miglioristi* found themselves repudiated for their ambivalent attitude toward the American use of force. Napolitano was booed when he urged the delegates to adopt a more pragmatic approach to the United States. Occhetto's own position to the Gulf crisis was spelled out in his introductory speech to the Congress. The PDS, he argued, did not deny Saddam Hussein's responsibility for the crisis; the Iraqi dictator's "criminal and odious behavior" was not to be condoned for a moment. The real issue, however, was means and ends. Occhetto insisted that the Italian left had "long rejected the idea that war can be an acceptable way of resolving international disputes." The "merciless character" of modern technology and the damage that modern weaponry was able to inflict on human life and the environment impelled the international community to "draw a fixed line at the use of force" since, if it did not (and here Occhetto, as he might once have thrown in a quotation from Marx, explicitly called upon the authority of the Pope, whose pacifism during Desert Shield had already won him unprecedented praise from Italian progressives), "humanity would embark on an adventure without return, the decline of the entire human species." The PDS's position, therefore, was to favor an international embargo of Iraq and to promote every diplomatic attempt to make the Iraqi leader see sense. So long as Saddam Hussein's "aberrant logic" drove him to reject every offer held out to him for a peaceful resolution to the Kuwait crisis, the PDS would have no choice but to appeal for a withdrawal of Italian forces in the Gulf and to throw its resources into opposition of the use of military action.[30]

This uncritically pacifist position, which amounted to saying that the more intransigent Saddam Hussein was, the more ethically unacceptable the use of military force by the Western powers must be, was not satisfactory for either the left or the right of the party. The *miglioristi* had by this stage decided that they were opposed to the withdrawal of the Italian forces, even though it was party policy; the left regarded Occhetto's line as all but sanctioning a new Vietnam on the part of the American military-industrial complex. In the event, after some astute maneuvering by D'Alema, the issue of the party line towards the Gulf War was voted upon separately from the motion establishing the PDS. Occhetto's "self-sufficient" center grouping won 60 percent support, with both the left and the right abstaining.

Earlier on the same day, February 3, 1991, the PDS had officially come into being by an overwhelming vote of the Congress. 807 delegates voted in favor; only 75 voted against, along with 49 abstentions. Despite the massive majority for unity, the new PDS was unable to avoid a split. Cossutta and a handful of other senior members of the party announced at a gloomy and tearful press conference that they would be forming a new political formation, *Rifondazione comunista* (Communist Refoundation). Free of the hard left, but with Ingrao's faction seemingly on board, Occhetto felt able to distance himself from Craxi in his concluding speech (asking with heavy irony, "Craxi? Who's that?") and to set out the PDS's store as an independent leftist party that needed nobody's help to fight for "peace, work and the rights of the people."[31] He did not even promise to lead the new formation into the Socialist International. Occhetto knew that this abrasive line would not help his relations with the *miglioristi*, but presumably calculated that he could do without them when the National Council, the body which had replaced the old Central Committee, came to select the new leader. On February 4, 1991, everything was set for Occhetto's triumphant coronation as leader of the new PDS.

Instead, Occhetto received a monumental slap in the face. The PDS's regulations, drafted and redrafted in the early morning of February 3 and unread by most of the National Council's members, required the party leader to obtain an actual majority (274 votes) of the membership of the National Council, not just a majority of those voting. When Occhetto's nomination was proposed, more than a hundred members of the National Council had slipped away from the Congress. Occhetto was thus exposed to the revenge of the *miglioristi*, who took the chance, despite later denials, with gusto. Just over 100 delegates voted against Occhetto and 41 abstained; only 264 voted in his favor, ten short of the quorum. Achille Occhetto, after dragging the party out of the ford and on to dry land, albeit farther upstream than the party's moderates might have liked, now found himself thrust back into the water.

Occhetto gave way to blind fury. His first reaction was to say "get yourself another party secretary" and to retire into political purdah in his Tuscan cottage. The new PDS, however, did not want to contemplate the immediate future in his absence. As a leading article in *L'Unità* argued, when one looked at the arduous gestation of the PDS, it was hard not to conclude that Occhetto was "condemned" to be its first leader. He had been, after all, its "principal architect."[32] By the end of the week, Occhetto had been prevailed upon to present himself once more before the National Council. On February 8, 1991, after D'Alema had mounted an urgent series of consultations with the leaders of the *miglioristi*, and Occhetto had been persuaded to backtrack embarrassingly on the leftist tone of his Congress speech, Occhetto was confirmed, by 376 votes to 127, with 17 abstentions, as the new leader of the PDS. The assembly burst into what *L'Unità* called a "liberating, joyous and emotional" round of applause.[33]

Occhetto must have enjoyed the moment, but must equally have been aware that his new job was likely to be a crown of thorns. The process of renewal in the PCI, after promising so well in both 1989 and 1990, had turned sour. As the PDS lay panting and exhausted on the democratic bank of the river, it was beginning to dawn upon its leadership that the new movement now had to set off on a hard trek into an unknown interior. Vultures, moreover, were circling. Craxi had sneeringly described the PDS as "born badly and finished worse" and had plainly decided upon a policy of aggression. *Rifondazione comunista*, meanwhile, was poaching huge numbers of former PCI militants (it boasted 100,000 members within a few weeks of its foundation) from the PDS, which thus lost much of its grassroots expertise and workforce.

Occhetto's solution to this uncomfortable dilemma, in retrospect, was a brilliant one. Between February and June 1991, the PDS threw its main efforts into the campaign for electoral reform. Two years before, a handful of academics, constitutionalists and reform-minded politicians, led by the Christian Democrat Mario Segni, had embarked upon a quixotic attempt to alter Italy's longstanding system of narrowly proportional representation, which they believed was largely responsible for the immobility of the political system. To this end they had proposed three referenda; the first (and least important) to reduce the number of preferences a voter could give to candidates on the party lists in elections to the Chamber of Deputies; the second, to introduce direct voting for mayors in all towns of over 5,000 population; the third, and most important, to alter the system of election to the Senate to a mixed "first past the post' and proportional one. On January 18, 1991, Italy's Constitutional Court ruled that though the latter two referenda were inappropriate subjects for a referendum, the first, more technical change, could go ahead. Occhetto, who at the end of 1990 had already outlined the PDS's own ideas on the form institutional reform should take, gave the referendum committee the backing of the new party. As Patrick McCarthy has argued, this decision allowed the PDS to "re-establish a connection with civil society."[34] New life was pumped back into the debilitated and divided PDS as it became obvious that the referendum was turning into a poll, not of Italy's electoral system, but of Italy's governing class. The groundswell of public opinion which had sent a tremor through the political system in May 1990 was about to send a further shock wave: The PDS, to stretch the metaphor, would be riding that wave. The June 1991 referendum, in Occhetto's words, was the "real birth of the PDS."[35] The new party faced off against the PSI, which condemned itself irretrievably as a party of the establishment during the referendum campaign, and won a striking victory.

84

Notes

0

1. Renzo Foa, "È così cambia tutto il continente," *L'Unità* , November 11, 1989. "Europe's happiest day" is my (free) translation of "il giorno più bello di Europa."

2. I owe this particular insight to Stephen Hellman, who kindly read an earlier version of this chapter and made numerous suggestions that have significantly improved the piece as a whole. Martin Bull also most kindly read the first version of this chapter and identified a number of slips of fact or style that I consequently corrected.

3. Quoted, *L'Unità*, November 15, 1989. Occhetto's actual words were "far vivere una forza politica che, in quanto nuovo, cambia anche il nome."

4. "In the middle of the ford" is the literal translation of the Italian phrase "in mezzo al guado." It was also the title of an influential book by Giorgio Napolitano (Rome, Riuniti 1979). Articles discussing the state of the PCI in the mid-1980s are Philip Daniels, "In the Middle of the Ford": The Italian Communist party in the Mid-1980s," *Journal of Communist Studies* (1), (March 1985); Stephen Hellman, "The Italian Communist Party between Berlinguer and the Seventeenth Congress," in Robert Leonardi and Raffaela Nanetti (eds) *Italian Politics: A Review*, London (Pinter) and Bologna (Il Mulino) 1986.

5. Piero Ignazi, *Dal PCI al PDS*, Bologna (Il Mulino) 1992, p 60.

6. Ibid., p 61.

7. Ibid., p 63.

8. Ibid., p 59

9. See especially, Paolo Flores D'Arcais, "Il club dei riformisti," *Micromega* 2/87, pp 7-14 and the same author's "Se il PCI diventa superfluo e subalterno," *Micromega* 1/88, pp 7-13.

10 The Radical party has since dissipated much of this patrimony of respect among the electorate. Since 1992, Pannella has undertaken an eccentric defense of the politicians involved in the bribery scandal known as *tangentopoli* (see Chapter Eight) and has lent his support to such discredited figures as Bettino Craxi and to the new right of Silvio Berlusconi. Pannella's chief motive for this perplexing move seems to be distaste for the spectacle (as he sees it) of the guilty (the legal system that turned a blind eye to the doings of the political class for years) condemning the guilty.

11. Paolo Flores D'Arcais, "Lettera aperta al Congresso del PCI," *Micromega* 1/89, pp 7-30.

12. Achille Occhetto, interviewed *L'Espresso*, May 14, 1989. For a much more sceptical view of the "culture" of the PCI and the possibility of its managing democratic change, see Salvatore Sechi, "L'autunno del PCI," *Il Mulino* (38), 1/89, pp 114-133.

13. An excellent English language account of the Eighteenth Congress and its aftermath is: Martin J. Bull, "The Unremarkable death of the Italian Communist

Party", in Filippo Sabetti and Raimondo Catanzaro (eds), *Italian Politics: A Review*, vol. 5, London (Pinter) and Bologna (Il Mulino) 1991, pp 23-40. See also the same author's "Whatever happened to Italian Communism?", *West European Politics* (14) October 1991, pp 96-120.

14. Bull, "The Unremarkable death," p 35.

15. For a good description of the importance of symbolism to the PCI see: David I. Kertzer, "The 19th Congress of the PCI: the role of symbolism in the Communist crisis," in Robert Leonardi and Fausto Anderlini (eds), *Italian Politics: A Review*, vol 6, London (Pinter) and Bologna (Il Mulino) 1992, pp 69-83.

16. Achille Occhetto, *Una costituente per aprire una nuova prospettiva a sinistra*, Rome (Propaganda section of the PCI) 1989. Quotations in the subsequent two paragraphs all derive from this pamphlet.

17. Massimo D'Alema, "L'Orgoglio delle nostre idee," *L'Unità*, November 15, 1989.

18. Occhetto, *Una Costituente*, p 17.

19. "Dare vita alla fase costituente di una nuova formazione politica", Motion of the Majority faction of the Central Committee, published as an insert in *L'Unità*, December 24, 1989, p 3.

20. Frank Belloni, "The Italian Communist Party: Towards Dissolution and the Unknown," in *Italian Politics: A Review*, (vol 6), p 88.

21. Nicola Tranfaglia, "La nave è salpata," *L'Unità*, March 11, 1990.

22. Quoted in *L'Unità*, March 11, 1990.

23. See Massimo D'Alema, L'Allarme suona per tutti", *L'Unità*, May 8, 1990.

24. *L'Unità*, May 8, 1990.

25. Giorgio Napolitano collected his thoughts on foreign policy in a short book entitled *Europa e America dopo l'89*, Bari (Laterza) 1992.

26. Piero Ignazi, *Dal PCI al PDS*, pp 154-57.

27. Luciano Pellicano, "Lo strappo di Occhetto," *Mondoperaio* (43), January 1990, p 2.

28. "Il PDS ci piace cosi." Results of an opinion poll among delegates to the 18th Congress of the PCI , Supplement to *L'Unità*, October 19, 1990, pp 3-6. Seventy-five percent of those quizzed approved of the new name.

29 Antonio Bassolino, *Rinascita*, September 16, 1990, pp 36-49.

30. Opening speech of Achille Occhetto to the 20th Congress of the PCI, published in *L'Unità*, February 1, 1991. When the ground war broke out, Occhetto stuck rigidly to the line outlined in his Congress speech. On February 25, as the battle for Kuwait city began, Occhetto stated the PDS's attitude to the war in an article on the front page of *L'Unità*. The line he took was purely pacifist and tinged with anti-Americanism. Thus, Occhetto "reproved and condemned" the United States for its "rigidity," in imposing a deadline to all attempts at mediation; he raised the suspicion that the war might now become "qualitatively diverse" with the Americans following "objectives other than the liberation of Kuwait city." Stopping the war, he

86

concluded, had become the PDS's "watchword." War could only lead to a "tragic spiral of destruction" that would make the already complex situation in the Middle East still worse. The membership of the PDS was even more anti-war than its leadership. One of Italy's best-selling books on politics in 1991-1992 was Alberto Asor Rosa's *Fuori Dall'Occidente*, Torino (Einaudi), 1992. Asor Rosa argued that the Gulf War was a symbolic affirmation of the West's will to power. When the government of Iraq committed what Asor Rosa called (p 24) a "minor infraction" of international law by invading Kuwait, it also made a direct challenge to the world order established by the industrialized nations. These, faced with this unprecedented act of daring, banded together to crush the upstart with all the might at their disposal. By so doing, the West created the conditions for a worldwide "government of evil" (p 13) and ensured that the western nations would act as "policeman and hangman" (p 25) in all future world conflicts. Quite apart from the fact that this prediction is already looking fairly lame in the light of events in Bosnia, there is no question that this nonsensical understanding of the causes of the Gulf War was widely believed among members of the PDS.

31. Concluding speech of Achille Occhetto to the 20th Congress of the PCI, published in *L'Unità*, February 4, 1991.

32. Renzo Foa, "C'è un rimedio a questo pasticcio," *L'Unità*, February 5, 1991.

33. *L'Unità*, February 9, 1991.

34. Patrick McCarthy, "The Referendum of June 9," in S. Hellman and G. Pasquino (eds), *Italian Politics: A Review* , (vol 7), London (Pinter) and Bologna (Il Mulino) 1992, p 15.

35. Quoted ibid.

6

The June 1991 Referendum

On Tuesday June 11, 1991, the Italian people awoke to news of the most remarkable election upset in post-war Italian history. On June 9 and 10, the voters had gone to the polls and voted "Yes" by plebiscite-like margins in the referendum for electoral reform sponsored by the Christian Democrat deputy Mario Segni's Committee for Electoral Reform and the PDS. The referendum's supporters were jubilant. *L' Unità* bellowed from its normally demure front page that a "reformist landslide" had triumphed;[1] *La Repubblica* shrilled that "Clean Italy has won" and claimed that June 9 was a "day of rejoicing" for Italian democracy.[2] *L'Espresso*, which had waged a propaganda war on behalf of the referendum for several months, crowed that the June 9 poll had been "the victory of clean, honest, dutiful Italy" over what the paper's editor, Giovanni Valentini, described as "the invasiveness and overbearing power" of the *partitocrazia*. The referendum, Valentini asserted, was a request for greater "openness" in Italian politics. There would be "trouble" if the parties ignored the people's message.[3]

The victorious reformists could be forgiven for their rhetoric. Only a few days before, it had seemed likely that less than 50 percent of the electorate would vote, thus rendering the poll's results invalid. Instead, the June 9 referendum was the first in Italian history to secure the favorable vote of more than half of all registered voters. 95.6 percent of those voting were in favor of the proposed change; 62.5 percent of all adults actually cast a ballot. This colossal margin of victory, moreover, was reflected all over the country. Traditionally Christian Democrat areas such as Venetia and Campania voted in the same way as traditionally communist regions like Emilia Romagna and Umbria; the North and the South were for once united politically, though, as usual, turnout was lower in the *Mezzogiorno*. The region warmest in support of the referendum was Liguria, in NW Italy, where 96.9 percent voted in favor. The most enthusiastic participants were from Venetia, where 73.8 percent voted. The least enthusiastic, by both measures, was the center-south region of the Molise, where only 50 percent voted and "only" 92.8 percent approved. The South was by no means a laggard, however: Campania and Calabria, the two regions where the party bosses held firmest command, voted "Sì" by huge margins. 97 percent approved in the province of Naples; 95 percent in Reggio Calabria (though '*ndrangheta* dominated rural villages in Calabria recorded lows of as little as 20 percent participation). Accumulating the region-by-region data into a simplified chart according to the standard three "macroregions" used by Italian political scientists gives the following results:

Table 6.1: Results of the June 1991 Referendum on Electoral Reform

Macroregion	Percentage "Yes"	Percentage "No"	Percentage Voting
North	95.7	4.3	68.3
Center	95.8	4.2	64.4
South & Islands	94.7	5.3	55.3
Overall	95.6	4.4	62.5

Source: *La Repubblica* , June 11, 1991.

The outburst of joy that greeted the results may seem excessive for what was, after all, merely a technical change of limited scope to the rules governing the election of individual candidates from the party lists to the Chamber of Deputies. Instead of choosing up to four names from the party lists, the voters could now only choose one preference vote, and that name had to be written out in full. The referendum victory was of tremendous symbolic importance, however. Ever since the 1979 elections, when the shortcomings of the political system had been exposed by the collapse of the government of national solidarity and the subsequent two-year delay in achieving a stable government coalition, a reform of Italy's proportional system of representation to allow for greater governability had been a constant topic for debate. *L'Unità* published a front-page editorial by Professor Gianfranco Pasquino of the University of Bologna on June 11, 1991, pleading "in the name of the sovereign people" for further electoral reforms.[4]

The referendum result was also widely regarded as a poll on the Italians' level of satisfaction with their leaders. The main parties of government, the DC and the PSI, made the elementary mistake of resisting the referendum with all the power at their command. Politicians who had once been partisans of electoral reform, notably Bettino Craxi and Ciriaco De Mita, came out openly against Segni's proposed reform. The state TV channels, with the Socialist-controlled

Channel Two to the fore, gave endless airtime to the party bosses as they explained that the referendum would not achieve its goals and was thus a huge waste of money. The referendum's goals, however, were the public's goals. Reducing the number of preferences to one fully inscribed choice, the referendum's promoters explained, would make ballot fraud harder (since it would no longer be possible to manipulate the numbers on the party list) and would make the ubiquitous *caccia alla preferenza* (hunt for personal preferences) less harmful (since most voters would simply choose the most able and well-known people on the list, thus leaving less space for the party hacks reliant on client votes). The power of the Mafia and the party bosses to influence the will of the people would be reduced. The Italian electorate understood these arguments, and reasoned -- rightly -- that influential people within the party hierarchies were opposed to the referendum for precisely this motive. The referendum therefore became an opportunity to vote against all the practices which the ordinary voter most disliked about the rule of the DC-PSI axis. Giorgio Bocca expressed their sentiments most pithily in *L'Espresso*, shortly after the June 9 triumph. The voters, he argued, had not been rejecting the entire Italian constitution: Italy's parliamentary system, while flawed, was "no worse" than those of other civil societies in Europe. With splendid scorn Bocca insisted that what the electorate was objecting to was the usurpation of civil society itself by the parties. They were sending a message that parties should "stay out and keep out" of "banks, state holding companies, televisions, newspapers" and "everywhere else that they have dug in their claws." They should also stop wasting trillions of lire on cultural visits, congresses, bureaucracy, public relations, free hospitality, and lavish living. Individual politicians should stop extorting bribes and consorting with known gangsters. The June 9 vote had not been "thoughtless populism," Bocca concluded, it had been a reasoned rejection of an entire political class.[5]

A Question of Proportion

The debate over Italy's method of electing its parliament was almost as old as the Republic itself. Apart from lending itself to fraud (see Chapter Three), the electoral system used to choose the members of the Chamber of Deputies also worked to ensure that all currents of political opinion were represented in strict proportion to the votes they garnered at the ballot box. Only very tiny parties, which had obtained less than 300,000 votes nationwide and which had failed to win a seat directly in a single electoral college, were denied a place in parliament. This extreme attention to the needs of minority views had been prompted by the sheer ideological diversity of post-war Italy and by the need to ensure, in the volatile atmosphere of the early Cold War years, that all strains of opinion were included in the national debate. As early as 1953, however, it was recognized that the system lent itself to paralysis. In that year, the DC, taking advantage of the narrow absolute majority it had won in the ideologically charged 1948 elections, passed, with Republican, Social Democrat and Liberal support, an electoral law that seemed to have been designed to allow it to govern in perpetuity. This law, the so-called *legge truffa* (swindle law), gave two-thirds of the seats in parliament to any coalition that succeeded in winning more than 50 percent of the vote. The DC, obviously, stood to gain from an election held with these rules. Had the DC and its allies obtained 50 percent in the 1953 general elections, the DC, contributing nearly 90 percent of the center-right coalition's vote, would have stood to gain 55-60 percent of the seats in the Chamber. Sensing that this was less a swindle than a backdoor *coup d'etat*, the electorate rallied to the parties opposing the law and inflicted the heaviest defeat that the DC would have to endure until the dramatic events of 1992-1994. The DC's share of the vote fell by over 8 percent to hardly more than 40 percent, and even with the support of its center party allies, the total still did not reach the crucial 50 percent threshold. Bowing to the inevitable, the law was repealed by the new parliament and normality returned. The DC's defense, however, was straightforward: Without some such mechanism to reward the largest party, there could be no stable government in Italy.

Subsequent events proved this hypothesis. Throughout the 1960s and early 1970s, governments rose and fell with bewildering frequency, and the DC changed its partners with a flirtatiousness born of desperation. Italy won the reputation of being a "republic without government."[6] The advance of Berlinguer's more moderate PCI compounded the problem, which was eased only by Bettino Craxi's decision to invade the political center. By abandoning the PSI's traditional leftism in favor of a resolute determination to play the game of place-hunting as well as the DC, Craxi created all kinds of new tensions within the party system, but he did at least ensure that a numerical majority for a DC-led coalition did exist. At least to begin with, however, he was widely regarded as a breath of fresh air by the many parliamentarians and scholars who had come to the conclusion that Italy was in urgent need of a new electoral system prizing governability rather than proportionality. In September 1979, Craxi had spoken of the necessity for what he called a "great reform" to the electoral process. While his speech did not go into detail, it was generally believed that the Socialist leader would use his leverage inside the *pentapartito* to press for institutional change.[7]

In this regard, as in so many others, Craxi deluded his more discerning followers. Once in power, the PSI found that it had become the pivot of the system, able to extort a disproportionate share of the spoils of government from its nominally more powerful senior partner. Its enthusiasm for change consequently diminished. Electoral reform, while it was not abandoned, was entrusted to a parliamentary commission presided over by the PLI deputy Aldo

Bozzi. The first major initiative for reform presented to the Bozzi commission, however, came not from the PSI, but from Ciriaco De Mita and the progressive wing of the DC. De Mita proposed in February 1984, following the principles of the *legge truffa*, that a *premio di maggioranza* (winner's prize) should be awarded to a victorious coalition (even if this coalition did not obtain 50 percent of the votes), but with the prize being distributed largely to the minor parties of the coalition. In this way, De Mita hoped to avoid the accusation of manipulating the process to the advantage of the DC. Predictably, he failed. De Mita's proposal was widely seen as a maneuver to restore the DC's ascendancy inside the government, and another of his proposals, substantial reductions in the number of deputies and senators, was greeted with gelid hostility. Neither the PSI or even the majority of his own party was willing to go along with De Mita's ideas: In September 1984, the National Council of the DC (its internal "parliament") bluntly refused to affirm that De Mita's ideas constituted party policy.

By the summer of 1984, it was already clear that institutional and electoral reform, if left to the parties, would be a long time coming. This prompted Gianfranco Pasquino, who had been elected to the Italian Senate in 1983 as a member of the "independent left" with the assistance of the PCI, to put forward a plan of his own. Pasquino's chief concern was to restore the scepter of sovereignty to the people.[8] In his view, the most destructive weakness of the Italian system was that it prevented the electorate from choosing its governors. The electorate voted and the parties bosses patched up a deal once the votes had been counted. The people had no idea who the prime minister would be; nor did they know for certain what the governing coalition would be, or even if there would be a majority able to govern. Pasquino, accordingly, in July 1984 advanced an ingenious plan that combined the existing system's respect for proportionality with an improved version of De Mita's notion of a "prize" for a winning coalition. In addition, Pasquino proposed a series of clever measures to extend the voting public's control over their representatives and rulers.

Pasquino suggested that there should be two rounds of voting. The first round would be by an amended system of proportional representation that ironed out some of the most notable weaknesses of the existing system. Instead of 32 electoral colleges of disparate size and the convoluted process of redistributing remainders via the *Collegio unico nazionale*, Pasquino proposed that there should be 40 electoral colleges, each of which would elect ten deputies by the D'Hondt formula used in elections to the Italian Senate. Pasquino's choice of the D'Hondt formula, which establishes a series of "quotas" by dividing the vote obtained by the individual parties in a given electoral college by a numerical progression 1,2,3,4,5, was intended to reduce the representation of minor parties in the Chamber, since the D'Hondt system, unlike the similar Sainte Laguë method preferred in Scandinavia, notoriously gives disproportional representation to the parties that obtained the most votes.[9] Pasquino dealt with the problem of the *caccia alla preferenza*, meanwhile, by abolishing preference voting. Instead of offering lengthy lists of party hacks, Pasquino proposed that the parties should put forward a fixed list of ten names in each electoral college. These names would be elected in strict numerical order. The higher one was on the list, therefore, the better the chance of becoming a deputy.

Out of interest, the Bozzi commission calculated the composition of a 400 seat Chamber of Deputies, using both Pasquino's formula and the existing formula of proportional representation on the basis of the 1983 election results. The results underline the effect Pasquino's plan would theoretically have had on the small parties, which are squeezed down to a third or a quarter of their former size by the three biggest parties. Broadly speaking, the bigger the party, the more representation it would gain: The PSI, as the third party in the system, hardly alters its contingent at Montecitorio at all:

Table 6.2: Simulated Distribution of Seats in a 400- Seat Chamber of Deputies

Party	Existing System	Pasquino Plan
DC	148	179
PCI	130	153
PSI	47	49
MSI	25	9
PRI	17	4
PLI	9	1
Radicals	7	0
Other	17	5

Source: Sebastiano Messina, *La Grande Riforma*, Bari (Laterza) 1992, p 103.

Nevertheless, despite the simplification offered by Pasquino's plan, in all probability neither of the big parties could have obtained a clear majority. Pasquino thus envisaged a second round of balloting, two weeks after the first vote. In this second ballot 100 seats would have been at stake, 75 of which were destined for the largest party, or coalition of parties, 25 of which were intended for the second largest party or coalition. This so-called "coalition prize" was designed to encourage the parties to coalesce into two blocs. At this stage, Pasquino introduced another novelty: The two blocs would have had to state, openly and in advance of the second ballot, what their legislative priorities would be and whom they had decided to nominate as prime minister. The electorate would thus have a clear choice of personalities and policies. Pasquino further proposed that the prime minister should be given tenure: He would be subject to substitution only in cases of death, resignation or incapacitating illness, whereupon he would be replaced by the deputy prime minister, or fresh elections held.

Pasquino's plan thus attacked most of the acknowledged ills of the Italian electoral system. It reduced the number and political weight of the small parties sharply. It also made the voters, rather than the party leaders, the main protagonists in the political process. Under Pasquino's scheme, the parties would have had to choose their prime ministerial candidates and programs with an eye for the country's real preferences and needs rather than their own internal power struggles. The power of pivot parties like the PSI would also have been diminished. Smaller in numbers relative to either of the big parties, and compelled to choose whose side it was on before the second ballot (rather than after the final results were in), the PSI's power to bargain for a disproportionate number of seats around the cabinet table would have been severely cut back. The concept of tenured prime ministers would have eliminated the ceaseless *crisi di governo* common throughout the 1980s: Political turmoil was usually the result of bickering among the *maggioranza* over the government's leadership and policies. The fixed list technique would have rendered the distortions of the *caccia alla preferenza* obsolete.

Mario Segni

The chief objections to Pasquino's plan were political, not intellectual. The leadership of the PCI were afraid that his plan would lead the PSI into a permanent alliance with the DC. The party was also worried that the PCI would be underrepresented, relative to its electoral strength, after the distribution of the coalition prize. Pasquino did his best to allay such fears, but was unsuccessful. The PSI was naturally opposed to a plan that seemed designed to slash its influence over the political process and was accordingly happy to take advantage of the PCI's hostility to change. Pasquino's scheme also seemed to limit the power of the president to nominate the prime minister and might have required a constitutional amendment: No easy matter in Italy.

There were therefore powerful objections against the improved system of proportional representation Pasquino was advocating. By the mid-1980s, in any case, the conviction was growing among Italians interested in electoral reform that the so-called first-past-the-post (FPTP) system used in the United States and England was more efficacious than any proportional method. Marco Pannella, the leader of the Radical party, never ceased to inveigh against an electoral system that allowed a party as mercurial and oddball as his own to maintain a parliamentary presence. In Pannella's view, the great advantage of the Anglo-

Saxon approach was that it forced *partitini* (little parties) to combine into two main blocs, one representing the right, the other representing the left. In England, the Labour Party and the Conservatives took turns in governing; in the United States, the Democrats and the Republicans alternated in power. As he argued in an article in *Avanti!*, the daily newspaper of the PSI, in January 1986, Pannella preferred the Anglo-American model because "whoever comes first in a fair fight wins and that's that." The electorate, Pannella sustained, would appreciate this system's "literal simplicity."[10]

Pannella's somewhat rosy understanding of the first-past-the-post system ignored the tremendous distortions to which both the British and American systems are susceptible. FPTP penalizes third parties, especially if they have no regional base; it allows for a multiplicity of parties when there are several parties with strong regional support; it enables ideological crusaders to take power with strong parliamentary majorities despite having less than 50 percent of the electorate's consent (Mrs Thatcher's three deeply divisive administrations were all elected by less than 45 percent of those voting). For Italians frustrated with the *partitocrazia*, however, these weaknesses seemed relatively unimportant compared with the fluidity of the Anglo-Saxon model. FPTP allows the voter to hold the parties and individual politicians directly responsible for their performance and to punish them for their mistakes since even a small uniform swing across the nation can lead to a change in government. In October 1986, Pannella united with a number of other politicians, constitutionalists and scholars to form the *Lega per il collegio uninominale* (LCU). Nearly 200 parliamentarians from all the main parties except the PCI and the MSI supported Pannella's initiative.

A fellow founding member of the LCU was Mariotto (Mario) Segni, a Christian Democrat member of the Chamber of Deputies since 1976, and son of Antonio Segni, President of the Italian Republic 1962-1964. Segni had distinguished himself in politics for his unrelenting opposition to the *compromesso storico* with the PCI in the late 1970s and his equally unrelenting efforts to persuade the leadership of the DC to reform the party's internal democracy. His labors had made him the darling of the right-wing daily *Il Giornale*, whose editor, the veteran newspaperman Indro Montanelli, shared Segni's hostility to both communism and corruption, but it had won him few friends within his party. As a result, Segni in 1986 had only just obtained his first ministerial job (as under-secretary at the Ministry of Agriculture), despite his manifest talent, high public profile and family connections. The most influential of these connections, was President Francesco Cossiga, who had attended the same Sardinian *liceo classico* (high school for the study of Latin and Greek language and literature and the humanities) as Segni and his elder brothers.[11]

On the issue of electoral reform, Segni had once placed great hopes in Craxi and had even toyed with the "presidentialist" solution being aired by some members of the socialist intelligentsia in the early 1980s. This solution, which eventually became the official policy of the PSI in 1987, envisaged a strong president directly elected by the people and an alteration of the electoral law to bar small parties obtaining less than 5 percent of the popular suffrage from parliamentary representation. Only the clause proposing the 5 percent limit was ever formally presented as a draft bill to the Italian parliament, however, in part because the party was bitterly split over the kind of presidentialism that should be adopted, with some socialists preferring the French "semi-presidentialist" model (in which executive power is shared by the president and the prime Minister), others the American "full presidentialist" approach. Segni, in common with most Italians, came to regard this policy as tailor-made for Craxi, rather than a serious attempt to meet Italy's institutional needs. These needs could only be met by the adoption of FPTP, he believed, though he thought that a more sophisticated model than the Anglo-Saxon *uninominale secco* ("pure" FPTP) was advisable for Italy.

This model was found on the other side of the Alps. In August 1987, Segni and a group of deputies drawn mostly from the DC, introduced a bill in the Chamber of Deputies that proposed that Italy should adopt the French dual ballot system. Italy would be divided into single member constituencies that did not cross regional boundaries but that were as nearly as possible equal in size (by law, no constituency would be permitted to be more than 5 percent over the average). To win the seat on the first ballot, a candidate would have to secure more than 50 percent of the votes cast, and more than 25 percent of the registered voters in the constituency. In the event that no candidate reached this target, a second round of voting would be held the following week. Slightly absurdly, Segni did not envisage the adoption of a compulsory threshold for accession to the second round. In France, only those parties obtaining more than 12.5 percent are legally entitled to participate in the second ballot: Segni and his fellow legislators allowed for the voluntary retirement of parties that had failed to score well in the first ballot, but did not exclude the *partitini* entirely.[12]

Despite this concession to the smaller parties, Segni's bill was soon bottled up in committee. In order to bring outside pressure to bear, Segni and the socialist intellectual Giuseppe Tamburrano founded the *Movimento per la riforma elettorale* (MRE), on April 22, 1988, at a chic reception at the Rome Hilton. He could boast the support of numerous politicians from all parties, as well as many prominent scholars and industrialists, including Umberto Agnelli of FIAT. Two major national newspapers of widely diverse political coloring, *Il Giornale* and *La Repubblica*, gave Segni's move editorial support.

The rules governing election to the Chamber of Deputies were not the only areas of Italian democratic procedure that Segni's reformers found wanting. The method of electing the Senate and the process of selecting municipal governments for Italy's cities and townships were also the target of reasoned criticism.

The electoral system used for the Senate was criticized largely on grounds of its fake FPTP character and bewildering complexity. Under the system that prevailed from 1946-1993, each of Italy's 20 regions was assigned a number of seats relative to its population: Molise had the smallest number of seats, Lombardy the biggest. Every individual region was then sub-divided into local constituencies, each of which, theoretically, was supposed to elect a single deputy by FPTP rules. The system, in short, seemed designed to warm the heart of Marco Pannella. In fact, only in the autonomous region of Val D'Aosta did straightforward FPTP voting actually take place. Elsewhere, candidates had to reach a threshold of 65 percent of the vote in order to be directly elected: Normally, only in Alto-Adige, where the German-language *Sud Tirol Volkspartei* (SVP) rules all but undisturbed, did any party manage to meet this norm. Ordinarily, therefore, it was necessary to resort to PR. Each region was tranformed into an electoral college and seats were apportioned to the parties, using the D'Hondt formula, according to their share of the vote within the region itself. Seats were assigned to individuals on the basis of how well they had done in their own constituencies relative to other members of the same party in theirs. There were two main weaknesses with this approach. Firstly, it often happened that some constituencies received no representation; secondly, voting this way could lead to the bizarre result of someone who placed fourth or even seventh or eighth in his own individual race being elected (because he was one of the highest scoring members of his or her party), while the candidates who had obtained a higher share of the poll failed to make the cut in their own parties. The example given below illustrates this point well:

Table 6.3: The Senatorial Constituency of Milano II, Election Results: April 1992.

Party	Percentage of the Vote	Elected
1. Lega Nord	16.8	No
2. DC	16.7	No
3. PDS	12.7	No
4. PRI	11.1	Yes
5. PSI	9.5	No
6. PLI	6.7	Yes
7. Rif. Comunista	4.9	No

Source: Massimo Teodori, *Come Voterai*, Rome (Panorama 1000 lire) 1993, p 36

The system for municipal elections was even more complicated than for national polls. Smaller townships with fewer than 5,000 inhabitants chose their municipal governments via a form of FPTP between party lists; the voters, however, could give preference votes to candidates from any party on the ballot form. The final *consiglio comunale* was a compromise between the candidates on the victorious list and citizens from the defeated parties who had picked up a large number of personal preferences. Towns of more than 5,000 inhabitants elected their local authorities by a system that recalled elections to both the Senate and the Chamber of Deputies. The D'Hondt formula was used to ascertain the distribution of councillors among the parties, but voters were given some say in the choice of their representatives by the possibility of allocating five preference votes. All preference votes, however, were limited to the list of the voter's choice. In *comuni* of both kinds, the mayor was selected by the town council.

The MRE's chief complaint about the electoral laws regulating municipalities, especially the larger towns, was precisely that the mayor was chosen by the parties, not by the voting public. The American system of directly electing a visible symbol of the city administration seemed a more appropriate form of local government to Segni's reformers. Accordingly, in October 1989, during discussion of a parliamentary bill to modify the functions of local administrations, Segni proposed a series of amendments to introduce direct mayoral elections. His move was greeted with fury by the CAF, and by their supporters within the DC and the PSI. In January 1990, Andreotti, after arm-twisting by the PSI, imposed a vote of confidence in his government rather than concede to the reformists' proposal.

The Referendum Campaign

The battle lines were thus drawn up. On the one hand, the captains of the *partitocrazia* had unambiguously given notice that they were not prepared to tolerate even the slightest innovation in the field of electoral reform; on the other hand, Segni and his fellow constitutional reformers were determined to make Italian government more accountable to its electors. The squalor of the Goria, De Mita and Andreotti VI governments, with their internecine political fighting, financial profligacy and seemingly acquiescent attitude to the advance of the Mafia, was a vivid demonstration of the ills that could befall a political system if ever democratic accountability was lost. Accordingly, in February 1990, Segni, together with constitutionalists from every band of the political spectrum -- Gianfranco Pasquino, the Catholic historian Pietro Scoppola, Serio Galeotti, the moving spirit of the so-called "Milan Group" of constitutionalists,[13] and the independent Socialist Massimo Severo Giannini -- lodged three referendum proposals with the Court of Cassation (High Court of Appeal). The first, and least important, was to amend the system of preference voting to the *Camera dei deputati*; the second concerned the direct election of mayors in towns with more than 5,000 inhabitants. The third, and most important, abrogated the laws governing election to the Senate in favor of the adoption of a new regime whereby 238 of the Senate's 315 seats would be filled by straightforward FPTP voting, while the remaining 77 would be awarded to the parties in proportion to their share of the national vote.

Refererenda are the wild card in Italy's otherwise party-dominated constitution. The constitution adopted in 1948 gives the legislative branch of government more power than either the courts or the president, and the parties, of course, control parliament. Since 1970, when the enabling legislation activated a dormant constitutional provision permitting referenda, the referendum has offered aggrieved citizens intent on righting a perceived defect in the law or institutions of the state a way to circumvent the Chamber and the Senate, though it is a path littered with obstacles. To begin with, Italian referenda are only abrogative ballots: That is to say, a referendum can annul existing legislation, not introduce legislation on its own account. The form that the new laws that will replace legislation cancelled by a victorious referendum should take is a question for parliament alone, though parliament is legally obliged to heed the views of the referendum's sponsors. Furthermore, calling a referendum is a lengthy process designed to daunt all but the stoutest. The promoters of a referendum must first obtain the valid signatures of 500,000 adults (or else persuade five regional assemblies to press their case). The validity of these signatures must be ascertained by the Court of Cassation; then, the constitutionality of the referendum's proposals must be debated by the Constitutional Court. Since the Constitutional Court is in part nominated by parliament, this last hurdle is a difficult one to jump. Finally, any proposal that succeeds in making this salmon run up the institutional stream must face two further obstructions during the referendum campaign. First, a government that is truly set on blocking a referendum can engineer a *crisi di governo* and elections; by law, a referendum may not coincide with a general election and must therefore be postponed if a national election is called in the interim period between its constitutionality being established and actual polling day (this technique was used to block referenda in 1972, 1976 and 1987). Second, the referendum, to pass, must secure the participation of more than half of the *aventi diritti* (people with the right to vote), as well as, obviously, a majority of those voting. The 1990 referendum promoted by the Greens on hunting and the use of pesticides, for instance, was blocked by its failure to attain the 50 percent threshold. Although a huge majority (92.2 percent) of those voting supported the abolition of hunting, a clever campaign by field sport associations to encourage absenteeism ensured that only 43 percent of the electorate voted.[14]

Segni's referendum set off on this long march through the institutional savannah with no great *élan*. None of the main party leaders evinced any enthusiasm for the reformists' move. The leaders of the smaller political forces, who stood to lose the most from a change in the electoral system, were actively opposed. Even Giorgio La Malfa, the leader of the PRI and a longtime personal friend of Segni's, was vocally critical.[15] The Radicals supported only the motions to reform local elections and the Senate: Pannella came out strongly against merely tinkering with the proportional system of election to the *Camera dei deputati*. As a result, the campaign to collect signatures got off to a slow start in April 1990. Segni's biographer says that "the first month's collection of signatures was an all out disaster," with only 13,000 names being enrolled.[16] Segni's activists, who had expected to meet public enthusiasm, met blank looks and incomprehension when they attempted to explain the purpose of electoral reforms. Worse, the MRE lacked grassroots organization. The Radicals aside, the people agitating for electoral reform were professors and senior statesmen; hardly the people to spend their days collecting signatures in the *piazze* of Italy on wet Wednesdays in April.

This necessary organization was provided in May from two powerful sources. First, prompted by Augusto Barbera, the PCI's former representative on the Bozzi commission, the Communists abandoned their "long march" towards institutional reform and broke into a sprightly trot, mobilizing their militants to help in the mundane work of signature-gathering.[17] Second, Ciriaco De Mita, who alone of the DC's hierarchy had shown any interest in Segni's initiative, mobilized his formidable electoral machine and client network on the MRE's behalf. Rino Formica, a senior figure in the PSI, risked Craxi's excommunication and came out in favor of reform. Against these positive developments, the failure of the referendum on hunting in June 1990 was a major setback: The belief that Italian public opinion was tiring of the referendum strategy briefly caused the MRE's enthusiasm to sag.

The referendum committee, however, could count on one unfailing ally: the party bosses, especially Craxi. As the number of signatures began to mount, so the attacks of the *partitocrazia* multiplied. *Avanti!* and *Il Popolo* (the daily newspaper of the DC) began to assert that the referenda were unconstitutional and to insinuate that Segni was the dupe of a communist plot. The party-controlled television service was evidently whipped into line: Media coverage of the referendum movement's arguments was scarce, to use the kindest possible adjective.[18] Segni hit back, publishing a list of the PSI deputies, including several national figures, who had lent their names to Marco Pannella's LCU in 1986. But Segni had also begun to note something strange: "The more Craxi proclaimed that the referendum was unconstitutional, the more signatures we got."[19] He was noticing the first traces of the popular feeling that would be unleashed in the spring of 1991: The widespread conviction that if Craxi and grey functionaries like Arnaldo Forlani, the leaden secretary of the DC, were against the Segni committee's proposals, then there must be much good in them.

The first overt attempts to block the referendum movement relied on the constitutional argument. In July, a very Italian polemic on the intentions of the original constitutional committee took place: It was oddly suggested that because the "founding fathers" of the 1948 Italian constitution had seriously considered adding the electoral laws to the list of items (finance laws, amnesties and international treaties) not subject to change by referendum, therefore such referenda were invalid, even though the constitution was indisputably silent on the matter.[20] This constitutional challenge prefigured a more serious attempt to block the referendum in December 1990. After 600,000 names had been handed in to the Court of Cassation in August and had had their provenance confirmed in November 1990, Segni's committee was faced with the notoriously high fence of the Constitutional Court, which has 15 members, five of whom are nominated each by parliament, the president and the legal profession. Despite dissent inside the cabinet, the Andreotti administration asked the Court to find the three referenda unconstitutional on the grounds that they exceeded the abrogative function laid down by the constitution. If the three referenda were passed, the government's constitutionalists argued, Italy would be obliged to rewrite its electoral laws completely.[21] The referenda were therefore a de facto imposition of a new law. To the dismay of Segni's reformers, the Court, despite rejecting this argument, still refused to allow two of the three referenda to go ahead, ruling on January 17, 1991, that only the first referendum (the technical change to the number of preferences) was valid. When the Court presented its opinion on February 1, 1991, it argued that the other two referenda, while strictly speaking constitutional, were ill-formulated and disorientating to the electorate. This judgment has been interpreted in different ways. Anna Chimenti in her *Storia dei Referendum* argued that the Court had shown a praiseworthy spirit of judicial independence from the party bosses by allowing one referendum and refusing to be bullied into pronouncing the other two as unconstitutional;[22] Gianfranco Pasquino has said bluntly that "there are many good reasons to believe that the decisive votes within the Court on these two issues were motivated by political rather than constitutional considerations."[23] Whatever the truth of this matter, it is clear that the decision was as much a political compromise as a considered legal judgment. It was also a major blow to the reformists. The blow was compounded by the defection of the Radicals in February 1991: Pannella's all-or-nothing mentality would not permit him to compromise his principles and give his support to a mere palliative, as he considered the reform on preferences to be.

The Court's decision was the second slap in the face Segni had endured in January 1991. Earlier he had been obliged to resign from his chairmanship of the

Secret Services Committee of the Chamber of Deputies under Socialist pressure. In December 1990, it was revealed (see Chapter Seven) that post-war Italian governments had armed and supplied secret undercover networks of "patriots" for the purpose of maintaining resistance to an eventual Soviet invasion. These networks, which were codenamed "Gladio" (after the sword carried by Roman gladiators), were obviously the source of considerable disquiet for the PCI, which wanted to know whether the same groups had been authorized to go into action in the event of a Communist electoral victory. Moreover, in a country that had seen so many instances of unpunished right-wing terrorism, many people also wanted to know whether Gladio's stockpiles of arms had been diverted to illegal uses by deviant factions within the secret services. The PSI, however, were determined to exploit the Gladio story to smear Segni, whose father's presidency had been tainted by the rumor that he was aware of what was arguably a planned coup in 1964 (the so-called Solo Plan) on the part of the then head of the *Carabinieri*, General Giovanni De Lorenzo. Craxi insisted that Segni's family ties rendered him an inappropriate person to head an inquiry into Gladio since the possibility certainly existed that De Lorenzo had intended to make use of the secret networks in his attempt at destabilization. This argument, which seemed to imply that Craxi believed that Antonio Segni was guilty of plotting against the state he presided over, was met with surprising indifference by the leadership of the DC. Although the DC had always strongly denied that Segni had been involved in the Solo plan, both Forlani and Andreotti remained silent in the face of the PSI's attacks. Segni was compelled to give up his committee chairmanship on January 10, 1991, a distressing defeat that caused him to revise his personal opinion of Craxi sharply. He now realized that Craxi was not just a hard opponent of the referendum movement, he was an unfair one too.[24]

Once the referendum campaign was under way in May 1991, Segni was given plenty of opportunities to see Craxi at his most ruthless and domineering. The campaign was dominated by Craxi's contemptuous dismissals of the referendum's objectives, calling them "unconstitutional, anti-democratic, polluting, anti-social and a waste of 700 billion lire in taxpayers' money."[25] In a clear attempt to talk up absenteeism, Craxi made full use of the state television's fawning news programs to proclaim that he would be spending referendum weekend on the beach. The violence of Craxi's attacks on the referendum were such that the cartoonist Altan portrayed him saying "Reducing the number of preferences is dangerous. Let's get rid of the vote altogether" on the June 9 cover of *L'Espresso*. Craxi was joined by De Mita, who made an astonishing about-face in May 1991 and described the idea of reducing preferences as "half-baked."[26] Umberto Bossi, giving rein to a weakness for conspiracy theories that has more than once clouded his judgment, denounced the referendum as a DC plot to avoid genuine electoral reform and announced that he too would be taking his annual vacation on referendum weekend.

There is no question that this unholy alliance of opponents strengthened the referendum committee's cause. First, as Patrick MacCarthy has argued, Craxi's public attacks on the referendum's ideas broke the uncanny silence of the news media and made electoral reform into an issue.[27] People who had not previously given much thought to the electoral system began to do so in large numbers. There is also no question that millions of Italians reasoned that any proposal that could incite the united opposition of Craxi, De Mita and Bossi could not be all bad. The referendum also profited from the hard work of its promoters. The PDS, the PRI and the PLI all backed the idea of reducing preferences, and so did many Catholic organizations. Church newsletters such as *Verona fedele* and *Vita trentina* came out in favor of reducing the number of preferences.[28] PDS militants, energized by the prospect of inflicting a major defeat on Bettino Craxi, worked night and day to spread the referendum's message. Gradually, by the beginning of June, it was clear that almost the only people opposed to the referendum were the party bosses. After two years of struggling against public indifference and outright hostility from the political class, the referendum's promoters suddenly found themselves preaching to the converted.

The main reason people voted for the referendum, however, was well expressed by Achille Occhetto in an article in *L'Unità* on the eve of the poll. Writing in simple heartfelt tones, Occhetto argued that Italy was "a democracy at risk." The parties of government existed to perpetuate themselves in power and were blocking every worthwhile reform, not to mention the fight against the Mafia or the fight for greater social justice. Voting "Sì," Occhetto concluded, might be "the first day of a new spring;" the first act in a much-needed cycle of regeneration in Italian politics.[29] There is no doubt that millions of voters went to the polls with some such thought in mind. As anyone who was in Italy at the time can confirm, the belief that a vote for Segni's proposals was a vote for a better, more genuinely democratic country was absolutely fundamental to the referendum movement's success. Giorgio Bocca was right: Above all, the people were telling the parties that they had to mend their ways.

The parties, however, did not want to hear. Among the senior statesmen of the Republic, President Francesco Cossiga was almost alone in realizing that Italian public opinion was genuinely demanding radical change, not just letting off steam. In April 1991, following the collapse of the Andreotti VI government in a Socialist-engineered government crisis that was dragged on by the PRI's defection from the *pentapartito* after a squabble over control of the ministry of postal services and telecommunications, Cossiga insisted that Andreotti's new mandate was to form a government that would take rapid steps to combat the Mafia, control public spending and undertake institutional reform. The most entertaining feature of Italian politics until May 1992 would be Cossiga's often eccentric ways of reminding Andreotti and the other party barons that he expected this mandate to be fulfilled.

Notes

1. *L'Unità*, June 11, 1991.
2. *La Repubblica*, June 11, 1991.
3. Giovanni Valentini, "Ripulisti," *L'Espresso*, June 23, 1991.
4. Gianfranco Pasquino, *L'Unità*, June 11, 1991.
5. Giorgio Bocca, "E adesso riformiamo i partiti," *L'Espresso*, June 23, 1991.
6. This is a reference to Percy Allum, *Italy: Republic Without Government*, London (Weidenfeld & Nicolson) 1973.
7. A good short survey of the history of electoral reform in Italy, including the "Swindle Law," is Pietro Scoppola, "Dalla Assemblea costituente alla "grande riforma," *Il Mulino* (35), May-June 1986, pp 453-467.
8. Pasquino's draft legislation is reproduced in Sebastiano Messina, *La Grande Riforma*, Bari (Laterza) 1992, pp 180-181. Messina discusses Pasquino's proposals pp 97-107. Pasquino, who is a very prolific author, discusses his plan in *Restituire lo scettro al principe: Proposte di riforma istituzionale*, Bari (Laterza) 1985. Pasquino writes on the theory of sovereignty in his *Alla ricerca dello scettro perduto*, Bologna (Il Mulino) 1990, while his views on the limited power of individual Italian citizens to influence the political system were brilliantly summarized in his essay "Ex voto: gli strumenti della cittadinanza politica," *Il Mulino* (40), March-April 1991, pp 328-337. His short book *La Repubblica dei cittadini ombra*, Milan (Garzanti), 1991, deals with the same theme at greater length.
9. Describing the D'Hondt formula without the help of a diagram is almost impossible. To illustrate the technique, let us look at the following example. A small political association that is divided into three internal factions wants to elect its five-person governing committee. The members vote and the following result is recorded:

Faction A	36	Faction B	20	Faction C	16

How is the composition of the committee decided? Essentially, the number of votes obtained by each faction is divided by a numerical progression, with the highest unrewarded number after each division being awarded a committee placing. After the first division, Faction A is obviously given the first placing. The totals are now divided once more; this time by two. The new quota is 18. Faction B, however, scored higher than 18 in the first division: It gets the second committee place. The process continues until all placings are distributed.

Divider	1	2	3
Faction A	36 [1]	18 [3]	12 [5]
Faction B	20 [2]	10	6.67
Faction C	16 [4]	8	5.33

Note that Faction A, which obtained exactly 50 percent of the votes, is awarded an absolute majority of committee places. The D'Hondt method tends to reward the largest party. The Sainte Laguë method, by contrast, divides by a numerical progression 1-3-5-7, which, by mathematical quirk, gives a more strictly proportional distribution.

10. Marco Pannella, *Avanti!* January 14, 1986, quoted Messina, *La Grande Riforma*, p 153.

11. These biographical details are taken from Primo Di Nicola, *Mario Segni*, Milan (Sperling & Kupfer) 1992.

12. Segni's draft legislation is republished in Messina, *La Grande Riforma*, pp 182-185. Messina discusses the plan pp 117-133. Di Nicola gives somewhat sketchy background detail to this move pp 172-74.

13. The "Milan group" of constitutionalists, which included Gianfranco Miglio as well as Galeotti, was named after its connection with the Catholic University of Milan, one of Italy's most prestigious private colleges. Between 1983-1985, they battled hard for the adoption of a institutional reform that was baptised "the Regime of the Prime Minister." The prime minister would have been directly elected by the people in two rounds of balloting; the first round would have been open to anyone willing to run, the second would have been limited to the two most-voted candidates. At the same time as the second ballot for the prime minister, elections would be held for a 300-seat legislature, elected half by FPTP, half by the German national list system. In addition, the Milan group envisaged the replacement of the Senate with a 100-seat "Chamber of the Regions," elected by the regional assemblies to represent the regions in Rome. A 250-seat "Council of the Economy" would also have played a consultative role. The President of the Republic would have been chosen by parliament from a roster of five candidates approved by the Constitutional Court. The trouble with this proposal, like so many proposals by so-called conservatives, was the radical upheaval to the constitutional order it implied. Italy would have had to tear up her constitution and start over again. For a discussion of the Milan group's proposals, see Sebastiano Messina, *La Grande Riforma*, pp 133-142.

14. This analysis of the referendum process is indebted to Anna Chimenti's excellent *Storia dei Referendum*, Bari (Laterza) 1993, especially Chapters One and Ten.

15. La Malfa said he was against the "abnormal use of the referendum instrument," quoted Di Nicola, *Mario Segni*, p 181.

16. Primo Di Nicola, *Mario Segni*, p 185.

17. This is a reference to Gianfranco Pasquino (ed) *La lenta marcia nelle istituzioni: i passi del Pci*, Bologna (Il Mulino) 1988.

18. The Socialist president of the RAI network justified this scarce coverage on the grounds that the MRE was not an institutional body. How an attempt to revise the electoral laws could be seen as anything other than an institutional question was left unexplained, as was the fact that the RAI saw nothing wrong with giving hours of tedious coverage to the activities of the main party leaders when they were acting in a

purely private or party capacity. See Gianfranco Pasquino, "The Electoral Reform Referendums," in Robert Leonardi and Fausto Anderlini (eds), *Italian Politics: A Review*, (vol. 6), London (Pinter), Bologna (Il Mulino) 1991, p 16.

19. Quoted Di Nicola, *Mario Segni*, p 187.

20. The failure to include the electoral laws in the category of legislation not subject to referendum was originally a clerical error. See Anna Chimenti, *Storia dei referendum*, p 11.

21. A succinct and outspoken summary of the PSI's views on institutional reform is Mario Patrono, "Perchè diciamo no ai referendum elettorali," *Mondoperaio* (43), October 1990, pp 34-40. Patrono argues that Segni's schemes are a "reactionary project" designed to perpetuate the hegemony of the DC and the PCI over the political process. A few days before the Constitutional Court made its decision on the constitutionality of the three referenda, Patrono weighed in with another article "Poche parole in meno, ed ecco nuove leggi" (A few words fewer, and here are new laws), in *Avanti!* January 13-14, 1991. An earlier Socialist critique of the referenda is Giuliano Amato, "Referendum elettorali: la Costituzione violata," in *Avanti!* June 14, 1990.

22. Anna Chimenti, *Storia dei referendum*, p 99-100.

23. Gianfranco Pasquino, "The Electoral Reform Referendums," p 21.

24. Primo Di Nicola discusses the PSI's attack on Segni over *Gladio* in *Mario Segni*, pp 189-194.

25. Quoted in Primo Di Nicola, *Mario Segni*, p 197.

26. Di Mita's actual expression was *una cavolata*.

27. Patrick MacCarthy, "The Referendum of 9 June" in Stephen Hellman and Gianfranco Pasquino (eds), *Italian Politics: A Review*, (vol 7), London (Pinter) and Bologna (Il Mulino) 1992, p 17.

28. MacCarthy emphasizes the importance of these Catholic newsletters in "The Referendum of 9 June," p 21.

29. Achille Occhetto, "L'Italia rassegnata? Non ci credete" *L'Unità*, June 3, 1991.

7

A President Versus the Parties

At this point in the narrative, it is worth pausing for a moment to take a snapshot of Italy in mid-1991. The first point to strike an observer is the complexity and scope of the developments taking place. By June 1991, Italy was in a state of flux. The unity of the Italian state was being called into question by the *Lega Nord*, which could still be regarded a fringe movement, but which was drawing votes away from the traditional parties and challenging their dominance in the richest and most commercially important areas of the country. In the South, the Mafia had taken de facto control of three entire regions, damaging the southern economy and compromising the parties that relied on its electoral clout on polling day, but also provoking fury among ordinary working people in the *Mezzogiorno*. In October 1990, the deposed leader of the "Palermo Spring," Leoluca Orlando, formed a leftist Catholic formation called *La Rete* (Network) to give this anger a political outlet. Two seemingly permanent features of old-style Italian democracy, the electoral system and the PCI, were no longer fixtures. The referendum movement had just humiliated the party bosses on June 9, sending an unmistakeable signal of public unrest at an electoral system that took sovereignty away from the people and consigned it to a handful of unaccountable power-brokers in the higher reaches of the ruling parties. The Communist Party, for so long everybody's favorite bogey, especially at election times, had transformed itself into the far less threatening PDS and was wrestling with an acute crisis of identity as the catastrophic failure of Soviet communism became clear for all to see.

Italy's political compass, in other words, had been decentered and it was anyone's guess which way the country should now turn. Should the traditional parties be entrusted with the role of guide, despite their manifest shortcomings? Or should the country embark upon a risky change of route with unknown quantities like the League and the PDS? Italians did not in fact arrive at a decisive answer to these questions until after the elections in April 1992, when they caught the historical leaders of the national expedition with their hands in the communal funds. The questions, however, were in the air, as anyone who was living in Italy at this time can testify.

The eruption of the *Lega Nord*, the scandal of the Mafia's infiltration into mainstream political life, the transformation of the PCI into the PDS, the huge popular revolt against the electoral system -- any one of these events (not to mention the dire state of Italy's public finances and the massive adhesion of people from all walks of life to the movement protesting national involvement in the Gulf War) would have dominated the front pages in any normal country for months. The extraordinary fact about Italy is that these major political squalls were often drowned out by the clamor of the still more tempestuous institutional storm that was blowing concurrently. The King Lear of this storm, defying the lightning, and (in the judgment of some, losing his wits) was the President of Italy, Francesco Cossiga.

Gladio

Italy's youngest ever President (he was a few weeks short of his fifty-seventh birthday when he was elected in June 1985), Cossiga had been an unpolemical figure for most of the early part of his mandate. His election had been characterized by exceptional goodwill between the parties -- Cossiga was made President on the first ballot, thanks to strong support from the PSI and the PCI -- and until 1990, Cossiga fulfilled his duties with courteous but somewhat grey dignity. This was despite the fact that controversy had dogged Cossiga throughout his career. A brilliant student (he was awarded his *laurea*, or master's degree, when he was just twenty years old), he was involved in politics in his native Sardinia from his early teens. In 1958, with the backing of a powerful *padrone*, Antonio Segni, Cossiga was elected to the Chamber of Deputies. In 1964, Cossiga became embroiled in the Solo plan scandal, acting as President Segni's go-between in meetings with General De Lorenzo. Most of Cossiga's ministerial work in the 1970s and 1980s would be connected to the murky worlds of the secret services and the police. His first government job was as under-secretary for defense in 1966; in 1974 he was made minister without portfolio with the specific task of reforming the secret services, which were widely accused of harboring sympathizers of fascist terrorism. In 1976, at the height of a bribery scandal in which a number of top Italian ministers, including a former prime minister, were accused of taking money from Lockheed, the American aerospace and defense company, he became minister of the interior, in charge of the Italian state's struggle against the *Brigate rosse*. His efforts in this job won him the nickname of "Kossiga" from the radical left, but he was generally successful until the kidnapping in March 1978 and brutal murder in

May 1978 of Aldo Moro. The lamentable failure of the police to track down Moro's makeshift prison cell rebounded on Cossiga, who behaved honorably and resigned as soon as the former prime minister's corpse was found. Conspiracy theorists have since revelled in speculating that the police's failure to find Moro was due to political interference from Cossiga and Andreotti, who are alleged to have come under CIA pressure to leave Moro, the architect of the *compromesso storico* with the PCI, to his fate. Neither this accusation, which has obviously never been substantiated, nor the tragic end of the Moro kidnapping, prevented President Sandro Pertini from choosing Cossiga to form the two governments that bridged the gap, 1979-1980, between the collapse of the government of national solidarity and the formation of the *pentapartito*. Cossiga's spell as prime minister, however, was also cut short by scandal. In May 1980, shortly after the formation of his second government, the PCI accused Cossiga of complicity in the flight from justice of Marco Donat Cattin, the terrorist son of a prominent DC faction leader, Carlo Donat Cattin. Cossiga was eventually tried and absolved by parliament. The affair, which was complicated by a family clash (Enrico Berlinguer, the leader of the PCI, was Cossiga's cousin), brought down Cossiga's administration and almost drove him to leave politics.[1]

After a career as tumultuous as this, it is hardly surprising that Cossiga should have chosen to "put on his slippers," to use the expressive Italian idiom, in the job of president. He handled the acrimonious 1987 *crisi di governo* with great skill, and managed thereafter to stay off the front pages. In October 1990, however, he was catapulted to public attention once more with the discovery by the *Carabinieri* of letters written by Aldo Moro during his time as a prisoner. When communicated to parliament, it was found that these letters were severely critical of Cossiga, Andreotti and the then secretary of the DC, Benigno Zaccanigni, for their inaction in tracing the group holding him hostage. Shortly afterwards came the eruption of the Gladio affair, in which he was cast as the villain of the piece.

Gladio first came to public attention in August 1990 when the PCI asked Andreotti whether or not he could confirm that there existed in Italy "an occult parallel structure that allegedly operated within the secret service with the aim of influencing the political life of our country." Andreotti replied that there had been secret networks of patriots prepared to resist an eventual Soviet invasion, but that these networks had been disbanded in 1972. Later, in October 1990, Andreotti was obliged to retract this statement and confirm that the networks were still in being. In all, there had been some forty "stay-behinds," or commando units, plus five "rapid action forces" that would have conducted underground sabotage operations against an occupying power in the event of an invasion by the USSR. These "stay-behind" networks had been supplied by 139 hidden caches of guns, plastic explosives and other military equipment. In the 1970s, 127 of these caches had been recovered; some of the other twelve had been rifled by unknown hands. This information, which was elicited by the investigation of a Venice assistant DA, Felice Casson, put a menacing cat among the political pigeons. Casson had discovered the arms caches in the course of an inquiry into the murder in a car bomb attack of three police officers in 1972; the obvious suspicion raised by the news of the missing weapons and explosives was that the caches had been used by right-wing terrorists to carry out massacres such as the Piazza Fontana bombing in Milan in December 1969 and the Bologna railway station bombing of August 1980, in which 80 people lost their lives. This suspicion deepened in January 1991 when the names of the "gladiators" were revealed and it became clear that disproportionate numbers of them held neo-fascist political views. The failure of the Italian state to fight "black" terror with the same efficiency as it displayed in the struggle against the "red terrorism" of the *Brigate rosse* is an issue that arouses passionate feelings in Italy's more leftward-leaning regions and in the fall of 1990, these feelings were running particularly high. In July 1990, the Court of Appeal had found a group of neo-fascist activists not guilty of the Bologna bombing, prompting Cossiga and Andreotti insensitively to suggest that the memorial to the victims of the attack should be amended to exclude the words "fascist massacre." A huge tenth anniversary rally on August 2, 1990, underlined that "Red Bologna" had no doubts that right-wing terrorists had been to blame.

Quite apart from possible terrorist links, the real question raised by the Gladio networks was "What was their purpose and who controlled them?" From the onset, Cossiga and Andreotti claimed that the networks had been an exclusively NATO operation with no connection to internal political developments. The PCI was convinced that the contrary was true: From their perspective, the networks were a plot cooked up by the CIA and right-wing members of the DC to subvert any legitimately elected Communist government. There were certainly good reasons to believe this latter hypothesis. The closeness of the CIA's connections with Italy's alphabet soup of different secret services has never been denied; references to the CIA's involvement in the 1964 Solo plan were cut out of the documents Andreotti presented to parliament. NATO's press office originally denied having anything to do with Gladio, only to retract the denial the following day after an official request by the Italian government. Moreover, only politicians judged thoroughly reliable by American intelligence seem to have been informed of the networks' existence. Amintore Fanfani, a six-time prime minister between the late 1950s and 1987, seems not to have been told anything at all: Fanfani is well-known for his personal integrity and (to quote Franco Ferraresi) "sense of the state." The diminutive former prime minister was presumably not trusted to keep such sensitive information to himself. Craxi and Spadolini, the first "lay" prime ministers, seem to have been informed in only the most general terms of Gladio's existence, though it is also possible that they preferred to give the impression of ingenuousness rather than collusion. Cossiga and Andreotti, by contrast, were clearly fully aware of the networks and their activities.[2]

Externator

Whatever the truth about the purpose of Gladio, the polemics surrounding its discovery unleashed a new Francesco Cossiga. The grey statesman of the previous five years was substituted by a garrulous, sometimes wild-eyed figure with a tendency to shoot from the lip. Cossiga's *esternazioni* (outbursts) were to become a prominent feature of Italian political life from December 1990 onwards, winning the president the nicknames of *il picconatore* (the striker of pick-axe blows) and, after the release of Arnold Schwarzenegger's Terminator movie, Externator. The *Economist*, less charitable, described him as the "Mad March Hare," in the Spring of 1991, a remark that was extremely hurtful to the Italian President, who is a keen Anglophile.[3]

The initial target of Cossiga's outbursts was critics of Gladio. Cossiga refused to cooperate with Casson's inquiry in November, and threatened to resign on December 7, 1990, (inviting Andreotti to do the same) after the Socialist and Republican ministers in the cabinet had advocated his answering the questions of a parliamentary commission of inquiry instead. This threat of a major constitutional crisis did the trick: The cabinet did an abrupt about-turn and described Gladio as a legitimate organization on December 8, 1990. After waiting a couple of weeks, Andreotti dropped the idea of a commission on Christmas Eve. Cossiga still had to face an attempt by the extremist Democratic Proletarian Party to indict him for high treason, but from mid-December onward the parties of government (the increasingly frustrated PRI aside) maintained a solid defense of Gladio's legality that rendered him impervious to such moves.

Cossiga then began a long-running saga of clashes with the *Consiglio superiore della magistratura* (CSM), the governing body of the Italian judiciary, of which he was by constitutional right the titular head (though every president, including Cossiga, had delegated his authority to the CSM's elected vice president). On November 22, 1990, Cossiga effectively rescinded this delegation of powers by vetoing discussion in the CSM of the climate of political intimidation surrounding Felice Casson, a matter in which he obviously had a stake. In February 1991, interfering again, he urged the vice president of the CSM, Giovanni Galloni, to discipline more than 100 judges who had signed a letter of opposition to the Gulf War. In May, he "externated" on the subject of what he called *giudici ragazzi* (kid judges), ridiculing the fact that fresh young scholars were sent to the South to combat the Mafia straight after passing their legal examinations. This subject was a sore one since the justice minister, Claudio Martelli (PSI) had been trying in vain from the moment of his taking office to obtain greater political control over judicial appointments in order to ensure that older, more experienced state prosecutors did not use their seniority to escape service in Italy's three "frontline" regions of Campania, Calabria and Sicily. From the CSM's point of view, Cossiga and Martelli were engaged in an unwarranted invasion of its constitutional privileges. The affair ended with Cossiga officially revoking his delegation of powers to Galloni, and Galloni hitting back, in June, with an ambiguous speech that hinted that "those at the pinnacle of power" were leading an attempt to revolutionize Italy's constitutional order. Cossiga, with by now standard hyperbole, described Galloni's remarks as "subversive demagoguery" and threatened to resign.[4]

Galloni later claimed that he had been referring to Martelli, but Cossiga's other actions gave the lie to this remark. By June 1991, it had become clear that Cossiga's trial of strength with the judiciary was just part of a wider vision of an enhanced presidency. During the March 1991 government crisis, Cossiga, who by now was followed everywhere he went by a troupe of top journalists, hectored the DC (which he referred to as his ex-party), laying down specific policy objectives in the field of institutional reform that he expected the new administration to meet. Rather than consent to a reshuffle of the same old faces, Cossiga menaced, he would call fresh elections. Cossiga's behavior led Achille Occhetto to comment ironically that the sight of those "principally responsible for the political and institutional disarray" of Italy presenting themselves as "denouncers" of that disarray was "the height of absurdity."[5] *L'Unità* fulminated against Cossiga's supposed *qualunquismo* (a word that literally means "everymanism," and which owes its origin to a populist post-war mass movement called *L'Uomo Qualunque*) and the PDS pressed for a parliamentary debate to clarify the government's attitude to the constitutional novelty of a President who, to quote Gianfranco Pasquino, was not content "to exercise his formal powers, but instead, against every norm, practice and usual procedure wants to have substantive powers at his command too."[6]

Pasquino's comment went to the heart of Cossiga's strategy. In two speeches in May, first at St John's University in New York, then during an official visit to Iceland (foreign countries would have to get used to Cossiga's *esternazioni*; his outbursts did not follow the normal rules of protocol), Cossiga explained in elliptical language that he believed that a president elected by a plebiscite of the whole people should be the "dynamic guarantor" of the "entire politico-institutional system." Since the Italian constitution of 1948 fuses most power into the legislative branch, Cossiga was effectively saying that Italy should rip up its constitution and start again. He was taken to task for this radicalism on June 2 by Ettore Gallo, the president of the Constitutional Court, who used emotive language himself by pointing out that Adolf Hitler had been a plebiscitary leader. Cossiga interpreted these remarks as an attack on Bettino Craxi. After denouncing Gallo, Cossiga sent a letter of solidarity to Craxi condemning the "ignorance, bad faith and demagoguery" of Gallo's insinuations. The PSI, in the person of Justice Minister Claudio Martelli, also joined in the criticism of Gallo's words.[7]

It is just possible that the connection between Craxi and Hitler is not immediately obvious. Quite apart from the fact that Craxi was more usually lampooned by Italy's brilliant and irreverent newspaper cartoonists as a reincarnation of Mussolini, Cossiga's assumption that Gallo was referring to the leader of the PSI may well appear a back-handed libel. In fact, everyone knew that Cossiga's pro-presidentialism was a coded signal of support for Craxi and the PSI. The PSI (see Chapter Six) was the most vocal champion of presidential government in Italian politics. The most cogent explanation of Cossiga's behavior in the first half of 1991, especially during the March *crisi di governo*, is that he was hoping Craxi would break with the DC and ride the rising tide of protest by campaigning for a presidentialist republic. On June 26, on the eve of the PSI's Congress in Bari, Cossiga sent a message to the two chambers of the Italian parliament that pointedly argued that there was an "authentic and stupefying contradiction" between Italy's remarkable economic and social development in the post-war years, and the "stark malfunctioning" of its institutions.[8]

Craxi, however, as *L'Unità* pointed out, was "the prisoner of the White whale."[9] -- the DC. For the first time since 1983, the leadership of the DC was in the driver's seat in its relationship with Craxi. Compared to the PSI, the DC had escaped much of the blame for the referendum debacle as regional elections in Sicily on June 17 confirmed: The DC took more than 40 percent of the vote, while the PSI lost ground. Speaking on June 27, at Bari, Craxi took an uncharacteristically cautious and almost fearful line, all but pleading with the DC to continue its alliance with the PSI. Craxi knew, even if Cossiga did not, that the presidentialist option was not a real one. Apart from the hostility it would meet from the other two major parties, any attempt by the PSI to seize the banner of reform and to ride like a white knight to the defense of democracy was certain to be greeted with derision by public opinion. By opposing the referendum campaign with such violence, Craxi had indelibly stamped himself with the mark of the *partitocrazia*: The PSI could no longer seriously pretend that it was in the government but not of it. In July, when Cossiga threatened once more to dissolve parliament and call elections, the PSI, after a short period of hesitation, did not give the president the support he had expected. For better or worse, the PSI had become part of what *L'Espresso* columnist Giampaolo Pansa called, in his best-selling book of the same name, "the Regime."[10]

By appealing to Craxi, Cossiga was missing his public. His increasingly scornful critiques of the entire institutional structure of Italian democracy were meat and drink to the many disaffected citizens who bought Pansa's books and who watched and participated in television programs such as RAI 3's

Samarcanda. This program, which was conducted by the half-showman, half-intellectual Michele Santoro, created a public forum for angry citizens to hurl insults at harrowed-looking representatives of the government coalition. More alarming still for the politicians, the same audiences sometimes subjected them to well-informed criticism. In the previously sycophantic world of Italian television, these developments were an unprecedented innovation. People seemed to like it, however. *Samarcanda*'s viewing share, which was almost zero in 1987 when the series started, zoomed to almost 40 percent of the viewing population during the 1992 election campaign. Its success led to similar shows being put on the air, most notably *Profondo Nord*, which was conducted by the formidably intellectual journalist Gad Lerner, and later evolved into the still more stimulating *Milano Italia*. Lerner, despite being scheduled after the mid-evening news at 11pm, attracted several million viewers every night to his blend of audience interrogation of leading political figures and high-level discussion between politicians, writers and academics. Umberto Bossi of the *Lega Nord* was one of the first politicians to realize the possibilities of Lerner's program, giving several bravura displays of the political and theoretical case for federalism that won the League greater intellectual credibility.

It is only a slight exaggeration to say that these hugely popular discussion programs became a kind of nightly town meeting for millions of Italians. They were not, moreover, an amended form of what Joseph LaPalombara called "politics as spectacle" in *Democracy, Italian Style*. The complaints one heard before, during and after the referendum campaign were not the stylised protests of self-conscious participants aware of their role in the show, but outbursts of genuine fury and disgust. One had only to listen, on *Samarcanda*, to the irate voices of over-taxed small businessmen from Lombardy, or the desperate pleas of unemployed artisans from the grim outskirts of Naples, Bari and Palermo, or the disdainful protests of talented young professionals denied fitting jobs by the stifling control of the parties over the plum jobs within society and the state to realize that there was an edge to this particular wave of public dissent that the parties would do well to take seriously. The critics were divided among themselves -- the ideological gulf between the *leghisti* of the North and the liberal Catholic supporters of Leoluca Orlando in Sicily was enormous -- but their message was essentially the same -- *Il sistema fa schifo, dobbiamo cambiarlo* (the system is rotten to the core, we've got to change it).

By the fall of 1991, Cossiga was to all intents and purposes saying the same thing in much the same colloquial language.[11] Although his *esternazioni* had originally been greeted with public skepticism and amusement -- many believed that he was trying to put up a smokescreen to cause people to forget the Gladio revelations -- Cossiga gradually found himself becoming almost popular. In September 1991, for instance, he launched an all-out attack on the role of the political parties in the RAI television networks, defining the propagandistic tone of news broadcasts "intolerable in a free state."[12] License payers across Italy cheered. This new popularity survived even his quixotic plea for a pardon of a convicted Red Brigades' terrorist, Renato Curcio, and a renewal of his war with the CSM. In November 1991, Cossiga threatened to use the police to prevent the CSM meeting to discuss an agenda of issues he had not approved. This decision provoked a national strike by the judiciary on December 3, 1991, and provoked the Senate to debate and finally on January 15, 1992, pass a law clarifying the right of the CSM to decide its own subjects for discussion. In the meantime, the PDS, rightly alarmed by strong statements of support for the president and of condemnation for other institutions by the *Carabinieri*, started impeachment proceedings against Cossiga (a move that led him to wonder whether a hundred years on, the trial of "Francesco Cossiga, Sardinian" might not have the same status in the history books as the trial of Charles Stuart and Louis the Sixteenth). When the DC defended him only tepidly from what he regarded as an act of aggression, Cossiga broke with his old party in a lengthy letter to the January 24, 1992, edition of *Il Popolo*. Earlier, on New Year's Eve, he had limited his midnight address to the nation to just three minutes, to the frustration of watching millions who had been expecting him to use this forum to spectacular effect.

The Run-Up to Judgment Day

Elections were due in the Spring of 1992, and this fact, along with Cossiga's fulminations, shaped the course of the political debate in the Fall of 1991. Intent on doing nothing unpopular before the poll, the Andreotti cabinet approved a budget that was viewed as plainly inadequate by the IMF; the EC, which was pressing Italy to get its public finances in order as part of the Maastricht process; and the governor of the Bank of Italy, Carlo Azeglio Ciampi. All these authorities were adamant that the Italian government was risking bankruptcy by its failure to get the budget deficit under control.

Italy's rapidly worsening public finances would not prove to be a major theme in the campaign proper, however. Other questions -- notably the Mafia and the murky, pro-soviet history of the old PCI -- would dominate. The campaign began at the end of January 1992, when the government majority voted to end the legislature early. On February 2, Cossiga formally announced that parliament, being "no longer able to fufil any kind of institutional reform" had been dissolved. Italy was being given a chance to forge a new "national pact" by electing a parliament that would renew the institutions of the nation and found a second republic on April 5. The fine rhetoric of this appeal would soon be swamped by the sordid realities of the electoral battle. Few, if any, modern election campaigns in the developed world can have been fought with quite the same bitterness, hysteria, lack of intellectual scruples, smear tactics, and brazen manipulation of the media, as Italy's in 1992.

The party guiltiest for this descent into the gutter was the PSI. The actions of the PSI and the PSI-controlled press from February 1992 onward seem to have been dictated by a strategy of unrelenting aggression towards the other "lay" parties. The obvious intention of this strategy was to offset any damage done to the PSI's reputation by its now unambiguous identification with the DC by slinging mud at the parties capable of eating into the PSI's vote, namely the League and the PRI. It also seems clear that there was a genuine expectation among the leadership of the PSI that the PDS's vote would disintegrate if the voters were reminded often enough that Italian communism had been associated with the beaten and discredited Soviet experiment. The PDS was thus made the victim of a coordinated press campaign in the first two weeks of February 1992 that was designed to highlight its Stalinist past and to tarnish the new party's program and ideas with its former leaders' misdeeds.

This campaign began following a discovery in the newly opened archives of the Comintern in Moscow. The discovery consisted of a wartime letter signed by Palmiro Togliatti in which he gelidly refused to plead with the Soviet authorities for the lives of captured Italian *Alpini* (the *Alpini* are a division of the Italian army specialized in mountain combat). This news not unnaturally aroused much genuine indignation and led -- inevitably -- to an outburst from Cossiga. Taking advantage of the live television coverage provided by all seven national networks of his dissolution of parliament, Cossiga publicly expressed his hope that Togliatti had not written the letter. He added, however, that if the letter should prove to be genuine, he felt obliged as "representative of the nation" to "beg the forgiveness of the dead soldiers and their families."[13] A couple of days later, Cossiga announced the formation of a team of historians who would be entrusted with the task of assessing the letter's authenticity.

The letter was actually published by Silvio Berlusconi's news magazine *Panorama* on February 3. Strangely, the magazine seemed reluctant to make the most of its scoop. A short, two-column account, the article was consigned to the nether regions of the paper (page 72) and was accompanied by an editorial that called the document a "disquieting piece of evidence" but reminded the paper's readers of the unusual circumstances ("the harsh winter of 1943") in which it had been written. Other newspapers were less reticent. The publication of *Panorama*'s story was followed by what can only be described as an orchestrated explosion of news stories, op-ed pieces and hostile radio and television coverage. This propaganda barrage lasted almost two weeks and must have been damaging to the PDS's electoral prospects. No stone was left unturned. Two newspapers and Italian state radio interviewed an anti-communist who had shot Togliatti in the head on the steps of parliament in 1948. The man's claims that he had acted for patriotic motives were left unquestioned and uncondemned. The PDS Speaker of the Italian Chamber of Deputies, Nilde Iotti, who had lived with Togliatti for many years, came in for savage accusations of complicity in Togliatti's crimes. Achille Occhetto's claims that he too had found the letter "heart-rending" were brusquely written off as too half-hearted, while every refusal by any of the leaders of the PDS to denounce not just Togliatti's sentiments in the letter but his whole legacy were ballyhooed as evidence that "beneath the oak tree communism remains."[14] PSI scholars and intellectuals were naturally at the forefront of this onslaught on the PDS: With shining hypocrisy, *Avanti!* explained on February 5 that its concentration upon the Togliatti affair was "not a question of cynicism." The paper asserted that it was merely trying to highlight the "fanaticism" and "dogmatism" of the former leadership of the PCI and illustrate to the PDS that its renunciation of Marxist doctrines would "have to be unqualified."[15]

Although the Socialist press's real motives were clear for all to see, there was much truth in the charge that the PDS was refusing to give all the Stalinist skeletons in its closet a thorough airing. Had the anti-Togliatti campaign not been halted by a fortuitous accident, it seems certain that the pro-government press would have exploited other unfortunate episodes in the PCI's history to berate the party's fellow-travelling past right up to election day. The PDS, however, was saved by an unlikely rescuer, the Agnelli family's Turin newspaper, *La Stampa*. On February 14, *La Stampa*'s Moscow correspondent, Giulietto Chiesa, documented no fewer than twelve "inconsistencies" between Togliatti's original letter and the version that had prompted *Panorama*'s article. The historian who had originally presented *Panorama* with the scoop, Franco Andreucci of the University of Pisa, had transcribed certain words wrongly, invented others when the original was unclear, missed other words out. Much had been made of the fact that, according to Andreucci, Togliatti regarded the authoritarian German philosopher Hegel as *il divino Hegel* (divine Hegel): Now, it transpired, Togliatti had really written *il vecchio Hegel* (old Hegel). *Panorama* defended itself by arguing that the inconsistencies were minor and did not really change the substance of Togliatti's opinions. *Il Tempo*, another pro-government paper that had been especially sanctimonious in pursuing the PDS, had no such excuse. *La Stampa* also revealed that *Tempo* had received a photocopy of Togliatti's original document, had realized that the *Panorama* version contained errors, and had forged Togliatti's handwriting to match the words *Panorama* had reported.[16]

The effect of Chiesa's revelations on the propaganda carnival was dramatic, however. The campaign stopped overnight. Once the essential artificiality of the polemic was exposed, the journalists of the pro-government newspapers no longer knew how to carry on the battle. The whole affair had been less a way of discussing the genuine question of the PCI's pro-Soviet past than, to quote Sandro Curzi, the editor of the evening news on RAI 3, a "serious attempt at brain-washing; a method of cancelling from [our] minds the issues we face today."[17]

One such issue was the Mafia. Shortly before Cossiga dissolved parliament, Italy's Court of Appeal, reversing a long series of favorable judgments to the Sicilian Mafia (see Chapter Three), had rejected the appeals of Michele Greco and other mafia *capi* against a sentence of life imprisonment. Then, on March 12, the election campaign was rocked by the news that Salvo Lima, now a Euro-deputy and the head of Andreotti's faction in Palermo, had been brutally killed by a squad of expert killers as he was driven away from his home by a friend, a professor at the university in Palermo. Lima was a controversial figure, who had long been suspected of mafia ties, although no concrete proof had ever been adduced. Press speculation immediately began to suggest that the Court's decision and Lima's death were linked: The Mafia was warning Rome that it expected its friends in politics and the judiciary to keep their pact with the devil. For the DC, Lima's death was an even worse embarrassment than Lodovico Ligato's murder in August 1989. A number of influential politicians, including Giorgio La Malfa, the leader of the PRI, openly cast doubt on Lima's bona fides, others silently distanced themselves. Of the highest representatives of the State, only Andreotti, Lima's close friend since the late 1960s, dared to attend the funeral. Cossiga, Spadolini (president of the Senate), Nilde Iotti, Enzo Scotti (minister for the interior), and the leaders of all the major parties except the DC failed to attend Lima's memorial service. In Italy, where politicians seem to spend much of their time at the funerals of political figures far less important than Lima, these absences were a major snub. The DC soon pulled itself together, however. Andreotti announced that "denigrators are worse than killers. Or at any rate equal. My friend Salvo Lima was denigrated for years." Arnaldo Forlani, striking the note that would characterize the DC's attitude to Lima's killing until election day, declared that the Sicilian politician had been murdered as part of a "general plan to subvert the institutions of the State."[18] Over the next ten days, the DC diffused the idea that Lima's death was part of a plot by sinister unnamed forces to throw the country into chaos. On March 19, the interior ministry even officially circulated a message stating that the secret services had learned of a plot to kidnap a possible successor to Cossiga and which connected Lima's murder to the killing of a PDS town councillor in the South of Italy and a Socialist found dead in Brussels. Not one shred of proof was offered for this fantastic assertion.[19] While most newspapers treated this blatant attempt to manipulate the elections with relative caution, the pro-government press did its best to whip up a climate of fear in the few days remaining before the poll. The PSI-controlled media, as always, was in the van of this effort. RAI 2's coverage of the election reached Bulgarian levels of sycophancy toward the party line in the last few days before what *La Repubblica* called the "Day of

Judgment."[20] Giampaolo Pansa has described RAI 2's handling of the election campaign with splendid scorn:

> How farcical the evening debates on the second channel were. There would be a supporter of Craxi with a party card, another supporter without official membership, an ex-communist who had since become a supporter of Craxi, as well as an "oak tree huckster" with an office in the headquarters of the PDS but his head in Via del Corso, the Craxi-ite motherland. The whole program would be conducted by a carnation-wearing guy or a gal who had even played a bit part in one of Bettino's campaign adverts.[21]

The hysteria of the campaign betrayed the importance of the moment. It was commonplace to say that the elections rivalled 1948 and 1976 (when there was the threat of a Communist *sorpasso*) as the most important post-war tests of public opinion. Actually, in many ways, the 1992 poll was more similar to the election in 1953. Just as in 1953, when the electorate punished the DC for its arrogance in attempting to impose the *legge truffa*, so, in 1992, Italians cast their ballots against politicians who were veering dangerously near to the shoals of undemocratic sentiment and techniques. Craxi's opposition to the referendum, the recklessness of the Andreotti cabinet's use of public funds to buy votes, the Togliatti sham-scandal, the attempt to whip up public fear, the obsequiousness of the party-run media, the domination of organized crime over the electoral process in the *Mezzogiorno*, fused into a public perception that the ruling parties were overstepping the limits on the use of public power permissable in a democracy. As in 1953, the electorate gave the ruling coalition a sharp rap across the knuckles, though it is arguable that the punishment meted out to the parties at the poll was milder than they deserved. A flood of votes switched from the DC to the *Lega*; the old PCI, even adding the votes of the PDS and *Rifondazione* together, suffered a major defeat; the PSI's *onda lunga* failed to reach its high-tide mark and the "lay" parties of the center enjoyed a minor victory, albeit one that was eclipsed by the size of the League's win.

The results of the April 5 poll also underlined the extent to which Italy had become divided into North and South. In northern Italy, the League established itself as second party behind the DC, with 17.3 percent of the vote. In northern Lombardy (Como, Varese, Sondrio), the League scored 28.5 percent and became the largest party. Bossi himself obtained nearly a quarter of a million personal preferences, easily the largest total of any candidate. The League, by a whisker, also emerged as the largest party in Milan. 650,000 citizens of Italy's second city voted for the *Carroccio*; 3,000 more than voted for the DC and 200,000 more than voted for the PSI. The League also reached 20 percent in northeast Italy. Cities like Belluno, Pordenone, Udine and the border town of Gorizia proved fertile new ground for the League's ideas. The League's appeal, however, was only widespread north of the river Po. Less than 2 percent of the electorate in the center of the country voted for the League, while in the South, the League's support was all but non-existent. These regions were dominated by the traditional parties, though *La Rete* scored well in Sicily. In the Center, the DC inched out the PDS, though if *Rifondazione comunista*'s vote is added to the PDS's, the left retained its traditional advantage in the middle parts of the country, albeit by a reduced margin. In the South, illustrating the power of client voting, the PSI arrived at almost 18 percent, while the DC hovered at just under 40 percent. There was thus an unprecedented geographic polarization of the vote. In the North, only 40 percent of the electorate voted for the four parties of the governing coalition; in the South, approximately 65 percent did. [22] Nevertheless, despite the crumbs of comfort brought to the parties of the coalition by their performance in southern Italy, the size of their defeat could not be obscured, as a direct comparison with the previous national elections convincingly demonstrates:

Table 7.1. A Comparison of Elections to the Chamber of Deputies, 1987 and 1992

Party	Percentage Share		Seats		+/-
	1987	1992	1987	1992	
DC	34.3	29.7	234	206	-28
PCI-PDS	26.6	16.1	177	107	-70
PSI	14.3	13.6	94	92	-2
MSI	5.9	5.4	35	34	-1
PRI	3.7	4.1	21	27	+6
PLI	2.1	2.8	11	17	+6
PSDI	2.9	2.7	17	16	-1
LEGA	0.7	8.7	1	55	+54
RETE	-	1.9	-	12	+12
RIF. COM	-	5.6	-	-35	+35
OTHERS	8.7	5.2	37	29	-8

Source: *La Repubblica*, April 4 and April 8, 1992.
Others (1987) *Verdi, Democrazia proletaria, Partito radicali*, Regionalist parties.
Others (1992) *Verdi, Lista Pannella*, Regionalist parties.

In the light of these figures, nobody in Italy was under any illusions that a major upset had occured. Even though the four-party coalition had managed to preserve a wafer-thin majority in the Chamber (331 out of 630) and had also squeaked through by a handful of seats in the Senate (the DC scored only 27.3 percent in the Senate poll, which is limited to voters over 25 years old), the size of the North-South divide, and the extent of the DC's decline, led jubilant critics of the *partitocrazia* to proclaim that the "Christian Democrat wall has tumbled down."[23] Longtime critics of the party system had a field day in the two or three days of anguished debates that followed the poll. Giampaolo Pansa, to give just one instance, appeared on television on the night of April 7 with a Cheshire cat grin that broadened visibly as he listened to discomfited and disconsolate representatives of the beaten parties trying to come to terms with their defeat. The parties' slim majorities, everyone knew, were a sham. They were a testimony to the power of client voting and the hold of organized crime over the southern electoral process and as such they were morally illegitimate. The North of the country (and to a lesser extent the Center) had lost confidence in the regime.

The Election of a President

The election over, Cossiga stepped back into the limelight. His seven-year mandate elapsed in June, which gave him time, if he wished, to preside over the formation of the new government. Speculation was rife that Cossiga would give the *incarico* (burden) of forming the new administration to Craxi, whose PSI had emerged from the April earthquake with fewer broken bones than the DC. The election campaign, in which institutional propriety had compelled him to take a more passive role (Cossiga announced a moratorium on his *esternazioni* on February 9, though at various times during the campaign he polemicized with both Andreotti and Nilde Iotti and called the Chamber of Deputies "zombies" for deciding to debate a measure he disapproved of), seems to have provided Cossiga with time for reflection, however. He plainly did not like what he had seen. On April 25 he resigned, in tears, in the course of a lengthy television broadcast that won him the praise of even his bitterest critics. Defining himself "a lonely figure," he attacked the "political oligarchs" for not having understood that the country was in need of genuine reform and for trying to impose their own "party liturgies" on the people's will for change. *La Repubblica*, the following day, entitled its editorial comment "At the very end he has understood," and gave Cossiga warm, though double-edged, praise for having had the courage to acknowledge that his critics of the past year -- the PDS, Leoluca Orlando, the philosopher Norberto Bobbio, *La Repubblica* itself -- had been right about the party system.[24] Cossiga's quixotic year-long attempt to persuade the parties to reform had ended in rueful recognition that his erstwhile colleagues had neither the intention nor the will to put the country's interests ahead of their own.

The new parliament thus had the task of electing Cossiga's successor. The president of Italy is chosen by a secret vote of both branches of parliament, together with representatives of the regions. Just over a thousand people are entitled to cast a vote. To be elected, a candidate must obtain two-thirds of the vote in the first three rounds of balloting. Thereafter, a simple majority is needed.[25] This process is usually a hard fought one. Cossiga, who was elected on the first ballot during a cease-fire in the DC-PSI guerilla war in parliament, was an exception to the rule in this respect. In 1992, the election followed more traditional lines. Balloting started on May 13 and did not conclude until May 25. By the time balloting was over, Craxi, Andreotti and Forlani had had the limitations of their power in the new parliament cruelly exposed; an instance of suspected ballot-rigging had been overcome; the parties had put on a virtuoso display of confusion, wheeler-dealing and factionalism; Giovanni Falcone had been murdered, along with his wife and bodyguards, in a bomb explosion near Palermo; and Italy, quite perceptibly, was a different place.

The election was characterized by the dramatic failure of the DC to vote as a bloc. As the balloting went on, the DC sank, in full view of the Italian people, into a morass of factional infighting. The biggest casualty of this internal conflict was Arnaldo Forlani, whose candidature was defeated amid controversy on May 16, a defeat that was only a prelude to his losing the party secretaryship later in the balloting. Forlani entered the lists in the fifth ballot, with the strong support of Antonio Gava and Craxi, who ignored an appeal from the PDS to find a joint candidate of the left. Theoretically, Forlani was a shoo-in. The parties backing him controlled 539 votes: The required majority was 508. Everyone knew, however, that Segni's reformists and the left of the PSI were opposed to Forlani's nomination. In the fifth ballot, in spite of all the efforts of the party whips, Forlani obtained just 469 votes; in the sixth, only 479. This failure was greeted with raucous jubilation by the League (which voted en bloc in every ballot for Gianfranco Miglio), the MSI (whose candidate was Cossiga) and the PDS, though the festive mood turned sour when it became clear, in the evening, that five electors had voted twice -- 999 votes had been cast, but only 994 electors were present. On February 17, Forlani decided not to risk further humiliation. The baton was thus passed to the PSI. After acrimonious discussions with the PDS, Craxi proposed a candidate unacceptable to the left, Giuliano Vassalli, the former minister of justice. At first, the DC was unwilling to go along with this suggestion, but after two days of confusion agreed to back Vassalli's nomination. The word of the party bosses, however, was no longer law on the backbenches. On May 22, Vassalli scored more than a hundred votes less than Forlani as DC *franchi tiratori* shot down Craxi's candidate. Mortified by this result, Forlani resigned as party secretary, though he continued to fulfil his duties pending the selection of a new leader by the National Council of the DC.

By this time, parliament seemed to be "thrashing about in a swamp."[26] There was a lot of febrile activity, but the party bosses were getting nowhere. Had external events not given an impulse to the balloting process, the indecision, politicking and chaos may well have dragged on for several more weeks. On May 23, however, *Cosa Nostra* exploded a ton of explosive under the car carrying Giovanni Falcone from Palermo airport to the *Palazzo di Giustizia* downtown. The blast left a crater twenty meters across and killed, apart from Falcone and his wife, three members of the prosecutor's escort.

It is hard for an academic account to capture the wave of revulsion that swept through Italy as news of *la strage di Capaci* (the Capaci massacre) was diffused. The prosecutor, whose patience, dedication, intellect, spirit of self-sacrifice and extraordinary courage had inspired young lawyers, officials and police officers throughout the country, had been a symbol that all was *not* wrong with the Italian state. Now he was dead. As *La Repubblica* argued in an emotional leading article on May 24, Falcone's death proved that there was "no more time." Italy was simultaneously facing a financial crisis (the need to cut the deficit was becoming acute, but there was no government to do the cutting), an institutional one posed by the parties' failure to elect a president, and a direct criminal challenge to the authority of the state.[27] But even this immediate demand for political action does not encompass the whole change of mood inspired by Falcone's murder. The tragedy of Falcone's death was such that the maneuvers and squabbles of the parties -- so important just a day or two before -- seemed simply grotesque. From Syracuse to Bolzano, millions of Italians were brutally reminded that they had been governed by parties that had knowingly nourished Falcone's killers with the warm broth of public money. At the funeral, on May 25, public emotion -- half outrage at the parties, half self-disgust -- spilled over into disorder. Former prime minister Giovanni Spadolini, the acting head of state, and Enzo Scotti, the minister for the interior, were jostled by huge crowds accusing them of being murderers. Giovanni Galloni, representing the judiciary, was assaulted by a furious policeman. Inside the church, however, the distraught young widow of Vito Schifani, one of Falcone's bodyguards, made a heart-rending appeal to the killers of her husband that reverberated around the world: *Mafiosi io vi perdono. Ma dovete mettervi in ginocchio* (Mafiosi I forgive you. But you should get on your knees). As Simona Dalla Chiesa said in *L'Unità*, Rosaria Schifani's anguish, pain and dignity were "burning slaps to the civil conscience of our nation."[28] For far too long, the Italians had let themselves be ruled by men who had been morally unfit to govern. It was time to make a change.

Aware that the public mood would tolerate no further delay, parliament made the first significant change by electing Oscar Luigi Scalfaro, the newly elected Speaker of the Chamber of Deputies, as President of the Republic on the day of Falcone's funeral. Scalfaro, a dignified Piedmontese, had been one of the original

123

members of the Constitutional Assembly elected in 1946. Despite his strongly Catholic views and his collocation on the right of the DC, he was also reasonably popular with the PDS. *L'Unità* called him a "moderate we can trust" on May 26. Moreover, nobody could question Scalfaro's fitness to govern. Famously honest and frugal in his personal life, Scalfaro had been one of the few senior members of the DC to try to prise open the lid on the Pandora's box of scandal surrounding Irpinia and the death of Lodovico Ligato.

Honesty was going to be at a premium in the coming months. Since February 1992, Antonio Di Pietro, a pugnacious, heavy-set prosecuting magistrate in the Milan District Attorney's office, had been digging hard to uncover the extent to which the DC and the PSI in particular had extorted *tangenti* (pay-offs) in exchange for the award of public works contracts in Milan and the Milanese hinterland. Shortly after Scalfaro's election, Di Pietro and his fellow investigators, Gherardo Colombo, a jeans-wearing intellectual with a bemused air, and Piercamillo Davigo, the financial brains of the trio, asked the Chamber of Deputies to authorize the first of what would eventually become hundreds of *avvisi di garanzia* (subpoenas) against parliamentarians. Among those named were two Socialist former mayors of Milan, Carlo Tognoli and Paolo Pillitteri, who is also Craxi's brother-in-law. At this point, *Operazione mani pulite* (Operation clean hands), as Di Pietro's investigation was known, became a major political issue. The scene was set for a square-off between the party bosses, especially Craxi, and the judiciary. In May 1992, however, few if any of Italy's leading politicians foresaw that this brush with the law would lead to a knock-out blow for the political system.

Notes

1. Biographical information is taken from Enzo Biagi, Paolo Guzzanti, Pasquale Chessa et al, *Externator: Discorsi per una repubblica che non c'è,* Rome (Panorama) 1992, pp 12-24.
2. For my discussion of Gladio, I have relied heavily upon Giovanni Maria Bellu and Giuseppe D'Avanzo, *I giorni di Gladio: Come morì la prima repubblica,* Milan (Sperling & Kupfer) 1991, and Franco Ferraresi, "A Secret Structure Codenamed Gladio," in Stephen Hellman and Gianfranco Pasquino (eds), *Italian Politics: A Review,* vol 7, London (Pinter), Bologna (Il Mulino) 1992.
3. The European edition of the *Economist* portrayed Cossiga as the "Mad March Hare" on March 30, 1991. The more demure American edition relegated Cossiga to an inside page (p 45) under the heading "March Hare." Cossiga was described as "increasingly tormented" in the American story.
4. For my discussion of Cossiga's battle with the magistrates I have made use of Enzo Balboni's excellent essay, "The President of the Republic, Judges, and the

Superior Council of the Judiciary: Chronicle of a Bitter Constitutional Struggle," in Hellman and Pasquino (eds) *Italian Politics: A Review*, vol 7.

5. Achille Occhetto, quoted *L'Unità*, March 25, 1991.

6. Gianfranco Pasquino, "Così il presidente apre la crisi della prima repubblica," *L'Unità*, ibid.

7. This paragraph owes a great debt to Balboni, "The President of the Republic." The quotation is from Balboni, p 55. The text of Cossiga's Iceland speech is reprinted in *Externator*, pp 41-44.

8. Francesco Cossiga, message to the Chamber of Deputies, June 26, 1991, partly reprinted in *Externator*, pp 45-50. The quotation is from p 47.

9. "Il prigioniero della balena bianca," *L'Unità*, June 28, 1991.

10. Giampaolo Pansa, as well as being the chief columnist of *L'Espresso*, has written a series of books that chronicle events in Italy since the mid-1980s. In order (the publisher in every case is Sperling & Kupfer of Milan), the books are: *Lo Sfascio* (1987), *Il Malloppo* (1988), *L'Intrigo* (1990), *Il Regime* (1991), *I Bugiardi* (1992), *L'Anno dei barbari* (1993). The books are often side-splittingly funny and are also a useful source of unofficial history.

11. At various times Cossiga described Occhetto as a "zombie;" called Paolo Cirino Pomincino, the budget minister, "the illiterate minister" and "a failed psychiatrist;" and wondered aloud why the Mafia was so strong in Sicily, seeing that the DC got over 40 percent of the vote there and was so passionately committed in the struggle against organized crime. In July 1991 he said that while he was alone in the midst of the parties, he had the backing of the armed forces. He added that it was lucky that the Italian army's tanks were inferior even to the Iraqis'. A full list of Cossiga's *esternazioni* would cover pages.

12. For the text of Cossiga's outburst against the RAI, see *Externator*, pp 55-58.

13. Quoted in Pansa, *I Bugiardi*, p 77.

14. Giulio Scarrone, "Sotto la quercia il comunismo rimane," *Avanti!* February 5, 1992.

15. The quoted comments are translations of the titles of articles by Vittorio Strada and Antonio Landolfi in *Avanti!* February 5, 1992.

16. Key documents for the whole Togliatti scandal are the original February 3, 1992, article in *Panorama* (see also *Panorama*'s much more exuberant presentation of the story on February 10 and its reluctant retraction on February 17). *La Stampa*'s February 14 article is obviously important. *La Repubblica* published a comment on the whole affair on February 15 by Norberto Bobbio -- the philosopher dourly remarked that history had been pressed into the service of politics. Pansa's *Bugiardi* gives a whole chapter (Chapter 6: pp 76-92) to the episode.

17. Quoted Pansa, *I Bugiardi*, p 91.

18. Quoted in Giovanni Mari Bellu and Sandra Bonsanti, *Il Crollo*, Bari (Laterza) 1993, p 125; *La Repubblica*, March 14, 1992.

19. Gianni Rocca asked rhetorically in *La Repubblica* of March 19, "in che paese viviamo?" -- what kind of country are we living in? -- when the ministry of the interior could lend itself to an electoral scare of this nature.

20. Eugenio Scalfaro, "E infine arriva il giorno di giudizio," *La Repubblica*, April 6, 1992.

21. Pansa, *I Bugiardi*, p 129. The quotation is an example of Pansa's style at its best. "Oak tree huckster" is my not entirely satisfactory attempt to translate the sarcasm of Pansa's original *querciaiolo*: His reference, of course, is to the PDS's oak tree symbol (La quercia means oak in Italian). "Carnation-wearing" is the best I could do to translate *garofanista* -- the *garofano*, or carnation, was the symbol of the PSI. The whole passage runs thus: "Che sballo certi dibattiti notturni del Tg-2. C'era il craxiano tesserato, poi il craxiano senza tessere, poi l'ex-comunista diventato craxiano, poi il querciaiolo con la stanzà alle Botteghe Oscure ma con la testa già in via del Corso, casa madre del craxismo. Il tutto moderato da un tizio o da una tizia così garofanisti dall'aver persino lavorato come comparsa negli spot elettorali di Bettino."

22. For a full -- indeed, exhaustive -- analysis of the 1992 election results, see Jean Besson and Genevieve Bibes, "The General Elections of 1992" in Stephen Hellman and Gianfranco Pasquino (eds), *Italian Politics: A Review*, (vol 8), London (Pinter) and Bologna (Il Mulino), 1993, pp 13-33.

23. "È crollato il muro DC," headline in *La Repubblica*, April 7, 1992.

24. Eugenio Scalfari, "E alla fine ha capito..." *La Repubblica*, April 27, 1992.

25. The rules regulating the election of the president of Italy are laid out in article 83 of the Italian constitution. A recent translation is to be found in David Hine, *Governing Italy*, Oxford, (The University Press) 1993, Appendix 5.

26. Bellu and Bonsanti, *Il Crollo*, p 156. The Italian is "agitarsi in un pantano." An academic account of Scalfaro's election is Vincent Della Sala, "The Cossiga Legacy and Scalfaro's Election: In the Shadow of Presidentialism?," in Hellman and Pasquino (vol 8), pp 34-49.

27. Eugenio Scalfari, "Non c'è più tempo," *La Repubblica*, May 24, 1992.

28. Simona Dalla Chiesa, "Le parole di Rosaria," *L'Unità*, May 26, 1992.

8

Operation Clean Hands

Operation *Mani pulite* began in mid-February 1992, when detectives under the command of assistant DA Antonio Di Pietro arrested Mario Chiesa, the Socialist manager of a Milanese charitable institution, the Pio Albergo Trivulzio (PAT), in the act of taking a 7m lire ($4000) bribe from the owner of a cleaning company. As the police searched Chiesa's office, the manager asked to go to the bathroom and there flushed a further 37 million lire down the lavatory.

Chiesa was almost a caricature of the class of youngish professionals who had flocked to the PSI in the 1980s. A snappy dresser and a high liver, he had wedded politics with business throughout his career. He had made a meteoric rise through the ranks of the party in Milan in the 1980s and had achieved a reputation as someone who commanded a large personal "packet" of votes. These votes were mostly provided by the employees of the companies with whom he did business at the PAT. As director of the PAT -- a position that he naturally owed to his political connections rather than any particular expertise -- he commanded a substantial business empire. The PAT owned more than a thousand flats in the centre of Milan, as well as shops and offices, so Chiesa had plenty of contracts -- for maintenance, cleaning, and funerals (the beneficiaries of the PAT's charity are mostly impecunious old people) -- to hand out. He soon won a reputation as "Mr 10 Percent." As Chiesa would himself later admit, he took a slice of every contract he awarded (including a fixed tariff of 100,000 lire per corpse levied on the undertakers) and used it to finance his political ambitions. The chief of these ambitions was to become mayor of Milan. To that end, Chiesa took care to ingratiate himself with the Craxi family, since Milan was Craxi's home power-base and fief. Much of the money Chiesa extorted from the businessmen with whom he had dealings was spent on dinners, conferences, costly gifts and electoral publicity. At substantial personal expense, Chiesa supported the election campaign of Vittorio "Bobo" Craxi, the Socialist leader's son, in the May 1990 local elections. Not all the money was spent on politics, however. When the police finished their inventory of his assets, Chiesa, whose job had paid less than $50,000 a year, was discovered to have $9 million in real estate and bank deposits. This suspicious private wealth would prove to be typical. As the *Mani pulite* investigation broadened its scope in the spring of 1992, it would emerge clearly that much of the money that greased the wheels of politics in Milan and other leading Italian cities finished in the private bank accounts of individuals at all levels of the political process.[1]

High-Living Comrades

The Craxi connection made Chiesa's arrest a political hot potato. His arrest made the front page of every national daily in Italy, except *Avanti!* The Socialist Party newspaper -- so scrupulous about the necessity for full and frank disclosure of every detail in the case of the Togliatti letter -- relegated Chiesa's arrest to the inner pages and mentioned his party affiliation merely in passing.[2] *Avanti!* could not stop tongues from wagging, however. Gossip -- and something more than gossip -- had swirled around the Milanese PSI, and Craxi personally, since the early 1980s. During the investigations of the Milanese *procura* (DA's office) into the crash of the Banco Ambrosiano in 1981 and into the activities of the notorious Propaganda-2 (P2) masonic lodge, a document naming Craxi as the beneficiary of slush fund money from Roberto Calvi, (a financier who was later found hanging under Blackfriars' bridge in London,) was found in the home of Licio Gelli, the occult leader of Italian freemasonry and a man with reputed links to right-wing terrorist groups and the Mafia. In the clearest possible terms, the documents recorded a payment in October 1980 of $3.5m into bank account 633369 of the Lugano branch of the Union Bank of Switzerland. The payment, the first of two for the same amount, was explicitly stated to be "for Claudio Martelli on behalf of Bettino Craxi." Martelli protested that the bank account in question was not his and appealed to the UBS for confirmation. The UBS did confirm this fact, but was reticent over who the account-holder actually was. By the time the UBS was ready to reveal details in September 1981, the investigation had been taken away from the Milanese authorities and transferred to Rome, on orders of the Court of Cassation. The Rome *procura*, historically far friendlier to the government than the one in Milan, consigned the case to the archives. In the meantime, however, the PSI-controlled press had conducted a propaganda war against the Milanese inquiry, defending Calvi (who was arrested in July 1981) and accusing the judiciary of launching a politically motivated attack.[3]

The suspicion was that the leaders of the PSI were impeding an investigation into their own misappropriation of public funds. Calvi's $7m was alleged to be a payoff to the leaders of the PSI for having arranged for a $50m hand-out from ENI, the then cash-rich state oil refining company, to the Banco Ambrosiano, which at that moment was on the edge of bankruptcy. This $50m was one of several transfers by executives close to Craxi and the PSI for a total of more than $150m and 100m Swiss francs in the period 1978-1980. The PSI, in other words, was suspected of using public funds to bail out a troubled private bank and taking a middleman's cut for doing so. For more than a decade, the *omertà* of the executives involved, plus the reticence of the Swiss authorities and the collusion of the Rome *procura*, allowed Craxi to keep a lid on the scandal.

The Milanese prosecutor who had the Banco Ambrosiano investigation whipped away from under his nose was Gherardo Colombo. Other Milanese prosecutors, including Piercamillo Davigo and Antonio Di Pietro, were also frustrated in their efforts between 1983-1991 to expose the extraordinary corruption existing in the Milanese construction industry. As Elio Veltri has written, in the 1980s, numerous cases of alleged corruption of officials and politicians were dismissed for lack of proof (even when the proof was overwhelming) or were never brought to court, yet it was an open secret that permission to build anything larger than a garden shed in Milan required payments in cash to the political parties, especially the PSI.[4] Parliament was no help. At a time when the Italian state was indulging recklessly in every imaginable form of public spending, budget constraints ensured that the *procure* of Italy were short of the technology and qualified personnel they needed to do their job. When prosecutors in Milan did manage to piece together a convincing case against a leading politician, parliament simply refused to lift the offending deputy or senator's parliamentary immunity. The most blatant example of this behavior came in November 1990, when the Senate refused to allow the Milan prosecutors to complete an investigation into the affairs of Antonio Natali, the Socialist president of the Milanese metropolitan railway 1972-1987, despite the precise, well-documented nature of the allegations against him. This was quite simply an abuse of power: Parliament's constitutional right to vet judicial complaints against its members extended only to ensuring that the parliamentarian was not a victim of a campaign of persecution -- which Natali certainly was not. Nor was Natali's case unique. In the 1987-1992 legislature, the Chamber of Deputies approved only 34 of 224 judicial requests for authorization to proceed with their inquiries. The Senate was even less forthcoming. It approved just 9 out of 113 cases.[5]

The high living of the PSI's leadership was both notorious and perfectly open. Throughout the 1980s, sycophantic newspapers and glossy weeklies published glowing articles about the new breed of Socialists Craxi had brought into government. Craxi, Martelli and the flamboyant Gianni De Michelis, who became foreign minister in Andreotti's last two administrations, were social lions in Rome, maintaining suites at the capital's best hotels, eating in the best restaurants and living in the *haute monde*. De Michelis, in particular, was a popular figure with the scandal magazine *Novella 2000*, which regularly photographed him dancing the night away in Rome's trendiest discoteques in the company of mini-skirted models half his age. De Michelis actually published a guide book to European night clubs. The tone for the party as a whole was set by the leadership. Craxi kept a luxurious flat in Milan, a country retreat on Lake Como and a private villa in Hammamet, Tunisia. His Rome residence was a large two-room suite at the luxury hotel Raphael, which was always available for his use. His attitude toward the perks of government life was cavalier, to use the kindest possible adjective. To cite one notorious example: In November 1986, he and Andreotti, the then foreign minister, made an official visit to China. Andreotti was accompanied only by his wife. Craxi was accompanied by 65 friends and family, including his wife, his son and daughter, his son's girlfriend, his chauffeur, the Socialist mayor of Venice, secretaries from his private office and a personal photographer -- all at the expense of the Italian state. Abuse of public funds on this scale made headlines even in Italy. One sardonic parliamentarian censured Craxi in the Chamber of Deputies for having only taken 65 guests when there were plenty of empty seats on the plane; the comic Beppe Grillo cast caution to the winds on national television by wondering out loud who the Chinese stole from if they were all socialists. It is indicative of the power of the political parties over the television service that Grillo, despite being the most popular comedian in the country, thereafter became a marked man on state TV and was eventually driven off the network.[6]

At the end of March 1992, Chiesa began to confess.[7] Worn down by Di Pietro's well-informed questioning and the grim conditions of Milan's forbidding San Vittore prison, and offended by Craxi's dismissal of him as a *mariuolo* (a Neapolitan word meaning "little rascal"), the would-be mayor of Milan started naming names and quoting figures. In the run-up to the election, and during the post-electoral period, there was an ominous lull, as the magistrates held their fire in order to avoid charges of interfering with the political process. In May, however, the arrests began. Within weeks, the cream of Milan's business and political class had seen the inside of "Hotel San Vittore." Most told all they knew after just a few hours. At the beginning of June, the first *avvisi di garanzia* against national political figures were sent to Rome for confirmation by parliament. The two most recent mayors of Milan, Tognoli and Pillitteri, but also three second-rank deputies from the DC, the PSDI and the PCI, were accused of twenty-six specific cases of corruption. In particular, they were accused by the testimony of Chiesa and other prominent figures within the Milan PSI of having knowingly accepted bribes when awarding contracts for the Milanese metropolitan railway, for the tramway system, for the construction of car-parking facilities during the 1990 World Cup and for the modernization of an indoor sports stadium in Milan. The sums involved were huge, though they would be dwarfed by the amounts uncovered later in the investigation. Counts five and six of the document sent by the Milanese procura to Rome accused Pillitteri and Tognoli of receiving nearly $5,000,000 for the Metropolitan railway contract alone. Though the PSI had been the party with its hands deepest in the marmalade, none of the traditional parties could claim to be clean. The share-out of resources generated from public works contracts was explicit and governed by clear rules. The PSI took the lion's share and distributed a few crumbs to the PSDI. The DC took a lesser cut and looked after the PRI; both the DC and the PSI reserved a large part (as much as 25 percent) of any single *tangente* for the nominal opposition, the PCI. Reading the indictments prepared by Di Pietro, Colombo and their two seniors within the Milan *procura*, Gerardo D'Ambrosio and Francesco Saverio Borrelli, one is left with a strong sense of conspiracy against the public weal. The parties, which should have been the political expression of civil society, were in fact colluding to rob it. Milan, which is a proud city that is very conscious of its status as Italy's most "international" metropolis, now found itself being called *tangentopoli* (bribesville) by influential publications in Italy and abroad.[8]

Milan, moreover, was only the (substantial) tip of an iceberg of corruption. By the time the *avvisi di garanzia* were sent to Tognoli, Pillitteri *et al.*, investigations had begun to flower all over Italy. In Venice, Felice Casson, who after his experiences of the previous year undoubtedly relished the opportunity, had begun an inquiry that would shortly lead to *avvisi di garanzia* being sent to Gianni De Michelis; the *procure* of Turin, Bergamo, Naples, Foggia, Verona, Pavia, Varese and more than twenty other cities were also hard at work unmasking corruption in the areas under their jurisdiction.

The sheer scale of the corruption being uncovered is hard to comprehend. One of the first books to be rushed into print on *tangentopoli*, Giuseppe Turani's *I Saccheggiatori* (The Looters), estimated that in the decade 1980-1990, corruption had cost the Italian economy $1 trillion.[9] Not all of this money went in direct bribes to politicians, though tens of billions of dollars did. The real waste, in economic terms, was on the thousands of public works undertaken in the 1980s with no other purpose than the generation of bribes. Turani, who is probably Italy's leading financial journalist and a prolific author, offers no source for his figure, and arguably exaggerates the extent to which contractors were able to "buy" government contracts. Nevertheless, that public works for tens of billions of dollars were contracted every year in the 1980s, by provincial and regional governments as well as the national government, and that the political parties creamed off 5-15 percent of many or most such contracts, is an undoubted fact. The parties were paying for their glamorous congresses, subsidized newspapers and intellectual magazines, lavish receptions and extravagant electoral campaigns with what amounted to a disguised tax.

A Long Hot Summer

The rising tide of scandal surrounding the party system as a whole and the PSI in particular had one immediate political consequence. President Oscar Luigi Scalfaro felt unable to nominate Craxi to the premiership. Instead, Craxi had to be content with the appointment in June of the most gifted of his satellites, the diminutive, English-speaking former treasury minister Giuliano Amato. "Dr Subtle," as Amato is ambiguously known, formed a rickety government based on the *quadripartito*, after frantic consultations had failed to persuade the PRI to add its weight to the majority. As a sop to public opinion, Amato's administration contained an interesting novelty. The DC decided that membership of the government should henceforth be incompatible with being a member of the legislature. The DC's ministerial nominees were therefore obliged to choose between the lures of office and the dubious honor of being a member of what would soon become the most publicly reviled parliament since 1945. This decision had one historic consequence. Andreotti, who had been a near-permanent fixture in government since the end of the 1940s, opted to renounce any ministerial ambitions. Subsequent events would prove that this was a wise decision. By privileging his life membership of the Senate over his desire to be at the heart of government, Andreotti retained his parliamentary immunity from arrest.

Amato's government got off to a shaky start. The day before Scalfaro gave Amato the "burden" of forming an administration, the provincial secretary of the PSI in the town of Lodi killed himself after becoming embroiled in the corruption scandal; on June 27, at the end of Amato's consultations with the other parties, the Lombardy regional secretary of the PSI admitted that he had sent bribes to the national party headquarters in Rome. Disaster followed disaster in July. Amato's first act as prime minister was to impose an emergency tax raise on July 5: This act was a bleak reminder of the financial costs of a corrupt political system. On July 16, another major arrest took place. Salvatore Ligresti, a construction magnate personally friendly with Craxi, and one of the wealthiest men in the world, took up residence in San Vittore. Ligresti, a dour Sicilian, would resist Di Pietro's interrogation techniques and the joys of prison life longer than most, enduring more than 100 days of confinement before cracking in November. Finally, and most dramatically, on July 19, Italy was shocked by the bomb-blast murder of Paolo Borsellino, Falcone's colleague and fellow mafia fighter. Once more, there were angry scenes: Scalfaro and Amato were called murderers by mourners outside the cathedral in Palermo. Within days, another calamity hit the government. The foreign minister, Enzo Scotti, decided to resign his post rather than give up his parliamentary position.

The outrage displayed at Borsellino's funeral and the almost daily arrests of second-tier political figures seem to have belatedly stirred the chiefs of the *partitocrazia* to a realization of their position. Italy's leaders had not previously seemed unduly bothered by the winds of public indignation howling around them. Born survivors, they were used to Italian public opinion's occasional squalls. In mid-Summer 1992, however, it seems to have dawned upon them that this particular storm could sink the ship and rob every crew member of his accumulated share of the cargo. When respected commentators such as Giorgio Bocca could write, as he did at the beginning of August 1992, that "This democracy is a corpse, a revolution would be better," even the dullest party leaders knew that urgent measures were needed.[10] Craxi resolved to act. In August, the Socialist leader wrote a series of *corsivi* (italicized editorials) on the front pages of *Avanti!* that insinuated that the Milanese prosecutors were politically motivated and that Antonio Di Pietro was tainted by his prior friendships with some of the people who had been arrested in the course of the *Mani pulite* investigation.[11] For a few days at the end of August 1992, the political environment pullulated with rumors that Craxi had a "poker" ("Royal flush") that he was about to play at the expense of the Milan inquiry. When he put his cards on the table, however, it was clear to all that Craxi had been bluffing. Di Pietro was reputed to have links with a couple of prominent *mariuoli* within the party hierarchies in Milan, but no proof was offered that these friendships were anything other than normal social contacts of somebody who, after all, occupied a position of some official importance. Even Craxi did not pretend that Di Pietro had given the two men favorable treatment. In the days following his failed attempt at a "poker," Craxi had to put up with a form of press coverage he was simply not used to: Being the butt of ribald humor. He was also asked to explain, and signally failed to do so, who had been responsible for collecting the information in his dossier on Di Pietro.

The extraordinary sight of a former prime minister doing his best to derail a judicial investigation by publicly peddling gossip brought home to the electorate how weak Craxi's position was becoming. The arrest of Ligresti, as Craxi well knew, was a ticking bomb for his own position. For the first time since 1980, moreover, Craxi was anxious for his position within the PSI. Claudio Martelli openly described the attacks on Di Pietro as a mistake and argued that the PSI needed to detach itself from its alliance with the DC. On September 12, ten days after a PSI parliamentary deputy, Roberto Moroni, had killed himself upon receipt of a subpoena, Martelli announced his "divorce" from the Socialist leader.[12] The PSI, Martelli argued, had lost its dynamism, had become too closely associated in the mind of public opinion with the DC and needed to become the rallying point of a new progressive coalition that would include the PDS, the PSDI, the PRI and the Radicals. At the end of September, in local elections in Mantua, this idea received its official baptism when the local branch of the PSI, which was *martelliano* in sympathy, campaigned in the company of the PDS. Martelli, Occhetto and Carlo Vizzini, the secretary of the PSDI, shared a platform at a successful mass meeting shortly before the vote. Mantua, however, had been designated as the capital of the Republic of the North, and the *leghisti* were on the march. The long hot summer drew to an end with another spectacular triumph for the League. 34 percent of the *Mantovani* voted for Bossi's slate, up from 22 percent in April. The PSI fell from 13 percent to 7 percent; the DC dropped to just 14 percent. The PDS did comparatively well, losing just two percentage points and staying second party in the city. The *Lega Alpina*, a party formed by Bossi's dissident sister Angela, took almost 7 percent of the vote. Its greatest attraction, so far as anyone could see, was that it had the word *Lega* in its name.

Checkmating the Red King

At the beginning of September, the lira collapsed, nullifying all the Amato government's efforts to shore up the currency. Within a few weeks, the lira plummeted from 750 to the Deutschmark to 940 in October, though once the worst of the storm on the currency markets was over it eventually crept back toward 900. Italy's beleagured exporters cheered, but for everyone else, the crisis was a symbolic affirmation of the country's weakness. True, other countries, especially Britain, had been dragged into the maelstrom of speculation that had surrounded the run-up to the French referendum on the Maastricht agreement, but Italy's humiliation had been the worst. Italy was the sick man of Europe; its national debt was a third of the debt of the EC as a whole, its politics was the most corrupt and ineffective. On September 30, adding insult to injury, the entire regional government of Abruzzo was arrested for defrauding the EC's regional aid fund. In its cover article of September 17, *L'Espresso* printed mug-shots of Andreotti, Craxi, Forlani, Gava, Vizzini, the Liberal minister for health Francesco De Lorenzo, the PLI's leader, Renato Altissimo, and a lugubrious Gianni De Michelis, with the word "Wanted," superimposed (in English) across the page. A sub-heading asked: "Can the men who destroyed the lira ever resuscitate Italy?"

The answer to this question was no. The DC, which was less in the thrall of a single figure, realized this fact sooner than the PSI. Forlani, who had resigned in May, but then hung on as caretaker secretary of the party, re-resigned after the Mantua defeat. The DC, desperately anxious to find someone respectable in the eyes of public opinion, chose as his replacement the dour lawyer, Mino Martinazzoli, on October 12. Martinazzoli, who was a long-time ally of Ciriaco De Mita and had been defense minister in the Andreotti VI administration, was the best option open to the DC, but time would prove that the job was too big for him -- as it would have been for anyone. Martinazzoli's credentials, however, were undisputed. An intelligent, reflective man, Martinazzoli was also known for his personal honesty, a commodity in short supply in the top ranks of the DC. He was also a northerner, from Brescia, and thus seemed likely to restore the DC's credibility with the slice of the electorate that had defected to the *Lega Nord*. On the downside, Martinazzoli was hardly given a free hand to reform the party. Important powerbrokers within the *balena bianca*, notably Antonio Gava, were hostile to Martinazzoli's reforming instincts, though they realized that his election was necessary for the party's public image. Martinazzoli was also arguably too clever for the role he had to play. The DC needed someone who could fire up the party's membership and lift morale. It got someone who looks permanently morose and whose intellect told him -- as he said to the assembled DC parliamentarians after his election -- that the party was "at death's door."[13] Though the corruption scandals had hit the PSI worse, the DC had not emerged unscathed. The treasurer of the party, Senator Severino Citaristi, had begun to pick up the first of what would become dozens of *avvisi di garanzia* as businessmen and political small fry in Milan and elsewhere revealed how the proceeds of their illicit activity had been transferred to Rome to fill the coffers of the national party. A businessman close to Arnaldo Forlani had been arrested and accused of defrauding the state of $100m by failing to build a road he had been contracted to construct in the seaside town of Ancona. Dozens of regional and provincial councillors belonging to the DC had by now spent nights in prison cells all over Italy.

The DC's final ignominy, however, would not occur until the Spring of 1993. Until March 1993, the tribulations of Craxi, the Red King of the 1980s, would dominate the front pages. Craxi's strategy during the autumn of 1992 was to defend the political system with arrogant, startling vigor. On October 9, Craxi, responding to growing unrest in parliament, accused the *procura* of Milan of using techniques more appropriate for a dictatorship to extract confessions. Much ado was made of alleged abuse of the *procura*'s power of "preventive detention," especially in the case of Ligresti, who had lost 30 pounds in weight during his lengthy stay in prison. This power, which gives the Italian judiciary the right to hold suspects who might, upon release, destroy or taint evidence valuable to the state's case against them, is certainly a sweeping one. On the other hand, it is difficult to see how the *Mani pulite* inquiry could ever have got off the ground without some such power. The businessmen and the second-tier politicians arrested at the beginning of the investigation would have had every incentive to sit tight had they known that there was a fixed limit on the time Di Pietro and his colleagues could keep them. Fear of political retribution alone would have caused most of them to keep their mouths stitched -- to translate an Italian idiom. One can also provide a similar "the ends justify the means" justification for the way the Milan *procura* handled the press. To the disgust of the leaders of the PSI, who, of course, had never stooped to manipulating the press, the *Mani pulite* investigation leaked like a sieve. As soon as someone was arrested, details of his confession were reported all but verbatim in *L'Espresso*, *La Repubblica* and other sympathetic newspapers and magazines. While there is no suggestion that any of the prosecutors most closely involved in the investigation deliberately fed the press titbits of information, the leaks did serve a useful purpose. The constant stream of revelations kept public interest high and the party leaderships on the defensive. Craxi, especially, was not accustomed to being in the humiliating position of having constantly to reply to charges, and to having the political agenda set by others.[14]

The Socialist leader did his best to take the offensive on two fronts. Within the party, he cracked down on the growing dissent. The editor of *Avanti!*, Roberto Villetti, was sacked in the middle of November. As Villetti's parting article made clear, he was tired of directing a newspaper that the party leadership regularly hijacked for propaganda purposes: His comments about the party's loss of dynamism and sense of purpose were almost identical to Martelli's views.[15] At the end of the same month, the National Assembly of the PSI met to discuss Craxi's leadership. Craxi was faced with a challenge from Martelli and from a representative of the party's left, Valdo Spini. Craxi won, taking the votes of 63 percent of the delegates, but the party's disunity was visible for all to see. Martelli's faction took 33 percent of the votes, including one cast by Giuliana Nenni, the grand-daughter of Pietro Nenni, the historic leader of Italian socialism, and the man who had launched Craxi on his career.

Craxi also spoke out more and more aggressively in public against the *Mani pulite* prosecutors. He blamed the death at the beginning of November of Vincenzo Balzamo, the national treasurer of the PSI, on the stress he had had to bear since he received his first *avviso di garanzia*. More generally, Craxi bawled on a daily basis that he and his party were victims of a conspiracy -- who the conspirators were, he generally didn't say. Like Hitler in his Berlin bunker, or Lear on the heath, he bellowed threats and warnings that he no longer had the power to execute. Had his manner been less overbearing, one would almost have regarded him as a pathetic figure. In its December 6 edition, *L'Espresso*, which had somehow obtained the official transcripts of Ligresti's confession, revealed that the Sicilian contractor had been paying substantial sums to the PSI, often at the PSI's explicit request, for most of the 1980s, though Ligresti insisted that he had neither handled the transactions directly, nor been aware of the exact amounts paid out. His chief financial advisor, Luciano Betti, filled in the details. According to Betti, the Ligresti group had laid out approximately 800-900 million lire per year ($500,000-600,000) since 1985 for the privilege of belonging to "an exclusive club of entrepreneurs who had shown themselves to be friends of the PSI." Betti insisted that these payments had been essential to ensure that the group had a fair chance of winning public works contracts. One such contract had been for repairs to the *Palazzo di Giustizia* in Milan. Payments had been made to Vincenzo Balzamo directly. Though neither Ligresti nor Betti said that Craxi had received money from them, these revelations naturally worsened the Socialist leader's position. For how could Craxi not have known of a cash inflow of this order being made to the PSI?[16]

Municipal elections were held in many major cities at the beginning of December. The results were a new calamity for the DC and the PSI: The League got almost 40 percent of the vote in the northern towns of Monza and Varese; the MSI did well in the South. Once the elections were out of the way, the prosecutors moved against Craxi. The former prime minister received his first *avviso di garanzia* on December 15, an 18-page document that listed all the information received by the *Mani pulite* team from Luciano Betti as well as from the confession of another entrepreneur, Mario Lodigiani. Craxi was accused of corruption, extortion and breaking the law concerning the financing of political parties. Craxi, who had said in parliament in July that all the political parties had taken "black" contributions from business to finance their activities, but had always maintained that these donations had not been the price of obtaining public contracts, claimed in tortuous prose that the prosecutors' move was a "wholly unfounded initiative that is being transformed into an all-out act of aggression against my person for ends that may be political but certainly have nothing to do with justice."[17] He refused to resign as leader of the PSI. The following day, *Avanti!* denounced the "Campaign of Falsehoods" that was being launched against the PSI; an editorial lamented that "Socialist hunting" had become the national sport.[18] Craxi himself contributed a *corsivo* in which he declared that he was not personally corrupt, nor had he ever corrupted anyone else. More subtly, he argued that he was being "called to account" for matters that rightly pertained to the administrative branch of the party, rather than the political leadership.[19] For someone whose control of the party apparatus had been notoriously tight (Eugenio Scalfari of *La Repubblica* had long been pointing out that "not a thing has moved in Milan these last 17 years without Craxi's knowing and wanting it"[20]), this defense was both implausible and unseemly. Craxi had shed tears at Balzamo's funeral, and had suggested that an innocent man had been hounded to his death by the prosecutors and a scandal-seeking press. Now, he appeared to be implying that any wrong-doing had been Balzamo's responsibility.

Craxi's defense looked even more implausible when the precise nature of the prosecutor's charges became publicly known. In the second week of January 1993, another *avviso di garanzia* was served on Craxi, and on January 13, full documentation of the charges arrived in Rome. Craxi, it transpired, was not merely being accused of having turned Italy's oldest political party into a glorified shake-down operation, he was also alleged to have been the ultimate beneficiary of tens of billions of lire in *tangenti* from several companies and entrepreneurs. According to Di Pietro, Davigo and Colombo, a large part of the cash that the PSI raised in Milan had allegedly been paid over not to Balzamo, but to a close friend of the Socialist leader, Silvano Larini, who had been wanted for questioning since the previous summer, but was by then one of several important figures in the Milanese political world on the run from justice. Larini, who was officially an architect (it would later emerge that he did not have the correct credentials to claim this title), had long worked just six months of the year in Milan: He spent the rest of the year idling in Polynesia on board his ocean-going yacht. At a press conference on January 16, 1993, Craxi affirmed that Larini was a "trusted person who collaborated with the party administration." This party role was news to most people: Larini had always been linked to Craxi personally, rather than to the party itself. Just a few days after the press conference, *L'Espresso* revealed that Larini and another Socialist architect, Filippo Panseca, were the proprietors of the company from which Craxi leased his two opulent villas in Como and Hammamet. At the end of January, it became known that Larini was also the titular owner of the notorious *Conto protezione* in the UBS in Lugano. Almost simultaneously, Vittorio D'Urso, Balzamo's former assistant who was arrested on January 29, contradicted Craxi's claim that the party treasurer alone had been responsible for the party's financial well-being. D'Urso stated that the PSI had required a minimum of 30 billion lire ($20m) a year in illegal contributions and that Craxi had given Balzamo the task of raising the wind. Confirming Luciano Betti's thesis that there had been a "club" of entrepreneurs willing to put up large sums of money annually in order to be on the inside track in the awarding of public works contracts, D'Urso named a number of enterprises that had been regular suppliers of funds to the PSI.[21]

Silvano Larini gave himself up to the police on February 7, 1993, and admitted both that the PSI had used his account with the UBS as a conduit for illicit cash and that he had acted as an intermediary between Craxi's headquarters in Milan and the business community of Milan for the payment of bribes. Larini's confession, which was backed up by the testimony of Licio Gelli, was the knockout blow. Craxi had already been served with two more *avvisi di garanzia* at the end of January. His credibility could not withstand this latest disaster. On February 10, it was announced that Craxi and Martelli were being investigated for their role in the crash of the Banco Ambrosiano, though the prosecutors fought shy of accusing Craxi and Martelli of having ordered ENI to risk public funds in the troubled bank (the Milanese attorneys argued instead that Calvi had hoped to strengthen his position with ENI and the PSI by using the bank's own money to reduce the PSI's substantial debt to the Banco Ambrosiano).[22] Claiming he was innocent, Martelli resigned from his post as minister for justice and from the PSI. Craxi resigned as leader of the PSI the following day, though he still had enough influence to impose his own choice of successor, the former trade unionist Giorgio Benvenuto, as party secretary. The reign of the Red King was over, though Benvenuto himself would resign within a hundred days, claiming that Craxi and his supporters were sabotaging his attempts to renew the PSI.

Craxi also exerted influence over the government. Giuliano Amato owed his prime ministership to Craxi; now, as Dr Subtle soared in popularity relative to any other major political figure in the country, Craxi called in his loans. On March 2, he gave an odd speech to the Chamber of Deputies, in which he announced that he was a victim of a plot cooked up by the *Mani pulite* prosecutors and the Milanese civic action group *Società civile*. Three days later, the Amato government jeopardized its credibility by attempting to pass a piece of decree legislation (one, in other words, that was not subject to debate in parliament) that retrospectively decriminalized the law concerning illegal financing of the political parties and imposed the threefold restitution of any illegal contributions. A concurrent parliamentary bill was introduced allowing plea bargaining for cases of extortion and corruption. Amato's newly appointed minister for justice, Giovanni Conso, a former president of the Constitutional Court, presented this measure as a necessary lifeline for the administration of justice. By the beginning of March, the Milan *procura* was buckling under the strain. One day in February, Di Pietro had to deal with fifteen businessmen who spontaneously presented themselves in his office to confess to having paid bribes.[23] Hundreds of politicians were being investigated all over Italy, and would eventually have to be brought to trial. Justice is a time-consuming affair in Italy, and the hearings and subsequent appeals of the men (practically no women have been accused) involved in *tangentopoli* threatened to clog up the nation's higher courts for years. Moreover, the politicians in Amato's cabinet were aware that things could only get worse. New inquiries were starting almost daily, the most dramatic being at ENI, which the political parties had seemingly used as a private bank, and at ANAS, the state highway authority that had been the fief of the notoriously corrupt Giovanni Prandini in the late 1980s. Everybody knew that the scandals likely to emerge from these branches of the *Mani pulite* inquiry were quite simply staggering: Just for starters, one arrested former executive, Florio Fiorini, revealed on February 16, 1993, that ENI alone had paid out 1,500 billion lire ($1 billion) to the political parties between 1970-1980 -- i.e., in the decade before serious corruption really began.

Conso's proposed decree, however, effectively gave credence to a fiction that the party leaderships had been earnestly bleating for months. This fiction was that Italian politicians had "only stolen for the party." However, as Gianfranco Pasquino pointed out in *L'Unità*, "nobody steals just for the party."[24] If Italy's leading statesmen had been looking out for the welfare of their parties, those parties would not have been all but bankrupt. The PSI, in particular, as an increasingly strained-looking Giorgio Benvenuto was finding out, was disappearing into a vortex of debt -- approximately $200m of interest on loans, unpaid salaries, printer's and telephone bills, and rent on buildings. The truth of the matter, as Pasquino underlined, was that most of the cash raised by illegal means had been used to finance factions within the various parties and to fund individual campaigns. Italian politics was similar to Japanese "money politics" in which every political boss kept his own slush fund to use as he saw fit. Political funds and private affairs were thus inextricably linked. But Conso's legislation gave no hint of how such funds were to be reclaimed. The money was hidden in Luxembourg, Switzerland and the Cayman Islands. It was obvious that unless the guilty politicians themselves volunteered the numbers of all their bank accounts and the names of all their shell companies, none of the cash was going to come back.

The Conso decree, in short, as the *Indipendente* fulminated on March 6, was a "self-administered amnesty."[25] It was, to use the phrase current at the time, *un colpo di spugna* (literally, "a wipe of the sponge.") The Amato government was saying -- in the face of mountains of evidence -- that the principal partitocrats had used *tangenti* as a means of financing the party system, not as a means of personal gain; that this had been wrong, but not so wrong that it deserved imprisonment; and that those whose activities had benefitted -- the parties -- should repay three times the sum they had extorted: a manifest impossibility. The proposed legislation did not even ban self-confessed crooks from running for office in the future. The legislation, in other words, was made to Craxi's measure, and though Amato said in an interview that Craxi's case had not been on his mind when he and Conso drafted the legislation, it is hard to believe that he was not being economical with the truth.[26]

The way in which the legislation was presented to public opinion confirms this hypothesis. A sheepish-looking Conso appeared on the evening discussion program of the notoriously pro-Craxi journalist Giuliano Ferrara and extolled the merits of his proposed decree while Ferrara, obediently following the line laid down by Craxi in parliament, brandished mysteriously obtained photographs of Antonio Di Pietro laughing and joking in the company of Nando Dalla Chiesa, a founding member of *Società civile*.[27] If the moment had not been so serious, the program would have won only amusement for its surreal partisanship; as it was, the nervous viewer was left worrying that this counter-offensive might have some effect on public opinion.

The prosecutors in Milan were certainly afraid that the parties were trying to rob them of the results of their investigation. On March 7, a visibly nervous Francesco Saverio Borrelli gave a press conference at which he read out a statement signed by all the members of the *Mani pulite* team. Politely but clearly, Borrelli expressed his subordinates' view that the "forseeable result" of the proposed legislation was the "total paralysis of all inquiries."[28] Public opinion responded immediately to Borrelli's words. The presidential palace and all the national newspapers were inundated with faxes, letters and telephone calls imploring Scalfaro not to sign the legislation into law. An ex-friend of Craxi, the former European commissioner Carlo Ripa di Meana, resigned from his post as minister of the environment in disgust. Schools all over Italy went on strike-- for once with good reason -- and street demonstrations of students waving sponges and chanting "Bring out the loot, put away Bettino" (it rhymes in Italian) took place. Scalfaro bowed to the public mood and refused to add his name to Conso's proposal. By so doing, he dealt what seemed to be a heavy blow to the credibility of Amato's government. By comparison with the blows that would rain down on the four--party coalition in the rest of March, however, Scalfaro's dignified refusal to let Craxi off the hook would soon appear as hardly more than a caress.

The Unmasking of the DC

Until March 1993, the chief powerbrokers of the DC had managed to escape Craxi's fate. Andreotti, De Mita, Gava and Forlani had still not received a single *avviso di garanzia*, though Forlani's position was looking perilous. On March 4, Forlani's private secretary was brought handcuffed into court to face serious corruption charges -- a sight which sent a collective shiver of apprehension through Italy's political class, and led to vocal protests from nervous parliamentarians. The party was as deeply implicated as the PSI in the corruption inquiry at a local level, but nationally, the party had the useful lightening rod of the party treasurer, Severino Citaristi. Subpoena after subpoena landed on the uncomplaining Citaristi's desk, while the political leaders that had guided the party in the previous decade remained free of judicial woes.

The kingpins of the DC's hierarchy were about to be skittled, however, by growing evidence of their longstanding links with the Sicilian Mafia, the *'Ndrangheta* and the Camorra. Ever since the deaths of Falcone and Borsellino, the judiciary and police of southern Italy, together with the anti-mafia task force, the DIA, that was Falcone's legacy, had been working round the clock to get even. This burst of activity had soon produced results. The number-two man of *Cosa Nostra*, Giuseppe Madonia, was arrested near Vicenza, in northern Italy, on September 6, 1992. A few days later, an important *camorrista*, Carmine Alfieri, was also captured. The state was also being helped by increasing numbers of *pentiti* (collaborators with justice). In the summer of 1992, two of them, Leonardo Messina and Gaspare Mutolo, named Salvo Lima as the Mafia's man in Rome. A third *pentito*, Giuseppe Marchese, who had been closer to the top ranks of the Mafia than either of the other two, confirmed this allegation on September 7. On November 16, Tommaso Buscetta, who had always refused to name politicians, returned to Italy from his hiding place in the United States. Citing the murders of Falcone and Borsellino as his motive for speaking out, Buscetta revealed that Lima had met him in Rome in 1980, while Buscetta was on the run from justice, to apologize for being unable to do anything to assist his case. All the *pentiti* agreed that the murder of Lima was no mystery. *Cosa Nostra* had ordered his killing as punishment for his failure to keep his Faustian bargain with organized crime -- votes for political and judicial protection. Enzo Scotti and Claudio Martelli's genuine efforts to strike back at the Mafia, and the condemnation of Michele Greco by the Court of Cassation in January 1992, had signed Lima's death warrant, not to mention Falcone's.[29] But if this theory was true, it raised disquieting questions about Giulio Andreotti. For how could Andreotti not have known that his right-hand man in Sicily was a mobster? And to whom but Andreotti could Lima turn to block ministers and fix ongoing trials? When the *New York Times* published this allegation, however, Andreotti angrily protested at the words of ex-mafia gumbas being given credibility by such a prestigious source.[30]

The Mafia by now was on the defensive. On January 15, 1993, the police arrested Toto Riina in an obscure suburb of Palermo. *Cosa Nostra*, seemingly invincible five months previously, was suddenly bereft of its leadership. In the 1980s, it had been fashionable to say that the state would never eliminate the Mafia, because it was too deeply rooted in the Sicilian way of life. In the days after Riina's arrest, experts like Pino Arlacchi and Claudio Martelli dared to say the unthinkable -- Yes, the Italian state could win. The state was now co-ordinating its activities against organized crime efficiently; financial necessity had led to the flood of public money to the South being reduced to a trickle; the murders of Falcone and Borsellino had weakened the hold of the clans on the sympathies of the Sicilian people and the political class.[31]

The *pentiti*'s revelations about Lima were an appetizer for the series of confessions and allegations that would destroy the DC at the end of March. On March 19, a member of parliament, Alfredo Vito, a close ally of Antonio Gava, decided to co-operate with prosecutors in Naples. Vito, who was already under investigation for having bought votes with the promise of jobs, seemingly experienced a genuine attack of conscience. Disillusioned with the political system, he revealed his own role as a collector of *tangenti* for the DC in Naples. A few days later, an arrested PSI city councillor talked of a *cupola* of politicians who determined the allocation of public works projects and decided the amount of bribes. As in Milan, all the parties, including the PLI and the PRI, had got their cut. On March 24 and 26, *avvisi di garanzia* were served on Enzo Scotti and Paolo Cirino Pomicino of the DC, on Francesco De Lorenzo of the PLI, on Giulio Di Donato of the PSI, Giuseppe Galasso of the PRI and a PDS deputy, Alberto Pastore. These were big names. De Lorenzo was minister of health; Scotti's success as minister of the interior had led to his being talked of as a potential prime minister, Pomicino was the head of the *Andreottiani* in Campania and had been minister of the budget during the Andreotti VI and VII administrations. Di Donato had been vice-secretary of the PSI, and was one of the leading powerbrokers on the Italian political scene.

The use of the word *cupola* (literally, dome) recalled the Mafia. Buscetta had revealed in the 1980s that *Cosa Nostra*'s operations in Sicily were arbitrated by a commission of bosses who met in a domed room in a villa in Palermo. On March 27 and 28, 1993, the glass ceiling that had prevented the judiciary from alleging political ties to the Mafia and the Camorra was shattered. On March 27, Gian Carlo Casselli of the *procura* of Palermo sent an *avviso di garanzia* to Giulio Andreotti, who was accused by Gaspare Mutolo of having been the "person to whom the honorable Salvo Lima constantly turned for the decisions to be taken in Rome, concerning the interests of Cosa Nostra."[32] As always when a long-rumored event actually takes place, the shock was traumatic. *La Repubblica*'s headline the following day was "Now it is Beelzebub's Turn." The title was accompanied by a spine-chilling cartoon by Forattini showing a hunched figure in a black overcoat and cap holding a mask of Andreotti's face by the ears. The figure's new face was a skull, with socketless eyes and huge teeth; carrion crows hovered in the background.[33] *L'Unità*'s cartoonist, "Ellekappa" was slightly kinder. He portrayed two men discussing the accusations against Andreotti. One says: "Why is Andreotti being investigated for his mafia links?" The reply is: "You know how it is, you always start with the minor offences."[34] The following day, Antonio Gava, along with Paolo Cirino Pomicino, Alfredo Vito and a sprinkling of other parliamentarians from the Naples area, was also sent an *avviso di garanzia*. He, too, was accused of consorting with known gangsters and protecting the interests of organized crime. On March 29, Judge Claudio "Sentence-killer" Carnevale was also warned that prosecutors were investigating allegations that he had been the Mafia's protector on the Court of Cassation. Mutolo accused him of being easily "maneuvered" and of having "a special personal relationship" with Andreotti that rendered him favorable to the Mafia's interests.[35]

Being investigated, of course, is not the same thing as being guilty-- a distinction that some Italian newspapers indisputably blurred. Andreotti pointed out -- with some justice -- that his government had been responsible for the creation of the DIA and for the laws permitting plea bargaining for mafiosi: These laws had led directly to the phenomenon of the *pentiti*. Andreotti argued that the revelations of Mutolo and Messina were *Cosa Nostra*'s way of revenging itself on him for taking the fight against organized crime seriously. The accusations themselves, moreover, were technically hearsay. Mutolo's confession was based partly on conversations he had had in Sicily with boastful gangsters, partly on what he had picked up in prison in conversation with other captured mafiosi. On the other hand, Salvo Lima's association with the leading crime families was by now doubted by nobody. On April 9, with the support even of the DC, the president of the anti-mafia commission of the Italian parliament, Senator Luciano Violante (PDS) presented the report of his lengthy investigation into links between politics and the chief Sicilian clans. Over 70 numbered paragraphs long, the report was a meticulously written and scrupulous reconstruction of the history of the growth of the Mafia's political and economic importance since the 1960s. The key paragraph, however, was number 64. Violante wrote:

> Salvo Lima's links to men in *Cosa Nostra* are regarded as certain by the commission. Lima was the point of reference in Sicily for the DC faction headed by Giulio Andreotti.
> Parliament will have to decide the extent to which Senator Andreotti should be held politically accountable for his links to Salvo Lima. [36]

The accusations against Andreotti were fleshed out by additional confessions from Tommaso Buscetta and Francesco Marino Mannoia at the beginning of April. Mannoia, who had been a prominent "man of honor" in the Bontade family in Palermo, had been regarded as a believable witness by Giovanni Falcone. This was fortunate, because his story was so extraordinary that nobody would have believed it in the absence of some guarantee of his credibility. Mannoia's revelations began with the 1980 murder of Piersanti Mattarella. According to the *pentito*, Mattarella had long used his political clout in favor of the Bontade family, but at the end of the 1970s, he had determined on breaking with the clans and renewing the Sicilian DC as a popular political force. A well-known local politician supposedly passed this information along to Salvo Lima, who himself gave the word to Andreotti. Mannoia then alleged that Andreotti was so disturbed by this unwelcome development in the Sicilian DC that he came to Palermo, where he held a secret meeting "sometime between the Spring and Summer of 1979" with Lima and a gaggle of prominent local gangsters. Mannoia himself did not attend, but was told by Stefano Bontade, the chief of the Bontade clan, that "everybody present" had complained to Andreotti about Mattarella's unacceptable behavior. Shortly after the meeting, the "provincial commission" of *Cosa Nostra*, including Toto Riina, decided to murder Mattarella. Andreotti, however, by Mannoia's account, was angered by the Mafia's action. "A few months" after the killing -- the absence of precision in the dates is a common thread running through all Mannoia's evidence -- Mannoia was summoned to a gathering of all the main Palermo crime bosses at an obscure villa in a suburb of Palermo. He testified that about an hour after his arrival, Andreotti arrived in a dark-colored Alfa Romeo together with Antonino and Ignazio Salvo, two wealthy businessmen with mob ties. A heated meeting ensued, at which Mannoia did not participate, since he was on guard duty outside the house. He claimed, however, that after the meeting Stefano Bontade gave him a summary of what had been said. Andreotti had come to Sicily to "clear up" the motives behind the murder of Mattarella. He had been told in no uncertain terms that the Mafia commanded in Sicily, not the DC. Bontade allegedly warned Andreotti that the clans would use their electoral influence against the DC all over southern Italy if the DC did not jettison Mattarella's reformist approach, and hinted that there would be other "serious occurences" if the national government implemented emergency anti-mafia measures.

Stefano Bontade was himself murdered by Toto Riina shortly afterward. According to Mannoia, the victorious Corleonesi wanted to maintain the Andreotti connection, but Andreotti was less forthcoming with the bloodier new Mafia. Mannoia's testimony, in this context, seems more plausible than the evidence of another *pentito*, Baldassare di Maggio, who accused Andreotti on April 20, 1993, of meeting Toto Riina in Palermo in September 1988. According to Di Maggio, the two men had exchanged a kiss of greeting. Mannoia finished his testimony with a couple of observations relatively favorable to Andreotti. In his opinion, Andreotti had actually tried to fight organized crime since 1987. Mannoia also did not believe that Andreotti had had anything to do with fixing the trials of Judge Carnevale. He explained, plausibly, that Carnevale was a native of the same part of Sicily as several prominent mafiosi, and had thus been open to persuasion throughout his career. Mannoia also put a different spin on the murder of Lima. In his view, the killing had been less a warning to Andreotti than the removal of a potential hazard. Unlike a real "man of honor," Lima was inclined to talk too much, and Mannoia believed that this character flaw had been the cause of his death.[37]

Mannoia's testimony was backed up by further revelations from Tommaso Buscetta, who had always previously refused to mention the top political contacts of the Palermo clans. Now, Buscetta alleged that Antonino and Ignazio Salvo had referred to Andreotti as *lo zio* (uncle) and that they themselves had frequently met with Andreotti in Rome, without availing themselves of Lima as a go-between. Stefano Bontade and the head of another major Sicilian crime family, Gaetano Badalamenti, also met with Andreotti in his private studio in Rome. According to Buscetta, Andreotti's willingness to favor the Mafia was tied up with the murder of General Carlo Alberto Dalla Chiesa and the killing in 1979 of a writer and magazine owner called Mino Pecorelli, who was a member of the P2 masonic lodge and a specialist in muckraking journalism. Buscetta's theory was that both men knew secrets, especially about the Moro affair, that Andreotti preferred not to have disclosed publicly. Basing his testimony on information he had received from Bontade and Badalamenti, Buscetta implied that Andreotti had ordered the murder of Dalla Chiesa and explicitly stated that Pecorelli's murder had been a "political crime" committed by the Salvo cousins at the express wish of Andreotti.[38] This latter accusation led to Andreotti receiving a further *avviso di garanzia* at the end of May, this time from prosecutors in Rome. Andreotti, it was alleged, had had Pecorelli murdered because the journalist had obtained, probably from Carlo Alberto Dalla Chiesa (the two men were friends), a copy of secret passages from Aldo Moro's prison memorial, which Dalla Chiesa had almost certainly retained and privately passed to Andreotti with the purpose of avoiding scandal. On the basis of articles written by Pecorelli in the weeks before his death, and comments in the parts of Moro's memorial that had come to light, it was suggested that these passages had contained information about Gladio, and had also painted a savage portrait of Andreotti, accusing him of using the central controlling agency of Italy's rural banks network as a political slush fund. A mock cover of Pecorelli's magazine OP (*Osservatore politico*) showed that the Roman journalist was certainly on the point of publishing a scoop on the subject of Andreotti's financial affairs. Strengthening the prosecutors' case for further investigation was testimony from Franco Evangelisti, Andreotti's longtime private secretary, and Ezio Radaelli, a financier, both of whom had apparently cashed mysterious checks for large sums on Andreotti's instructions.

Andreotti, after trying and failing to persuade the Senate that he was a victim of a plot, renounced his parliamentary immunity and asked for a quick trial on all the charges that were being levelled against him. He did not get his way. In May 1994, the prosecutors said that they would be pressing for an indictment of the former premier, but at the time of writing (November 1994), Andreotti has still not had the chance to reply in court to any of the serious offenses imputed to him.

The same can be said for Antonio Gava, Paolo Cirino Pomicino and the other *onorevoli inquisiti* (parliamentarians under investigation) of Naples. Without entering into the merits of their cases, however, it must be said that the accusations levelled against them seem at first sight still more substantial than those directed at Andreotti. As Pino Arlacchi emphasized in his preface to *La Repubblica*'s reprint of the superb dossier sent by prosecutors in Naples to parliament, Gava and Pomicino were being openly denounced for "willing and knowing participation" in "quintessential mob activity."[39] They were not, in other words, being accused of collusion and corruption -- of turning a blind eye, in exchange for cash or votes, to mafia-run companies winning contracts. The thesis of the Naples *procura*, in fact, was nothing less than that Gava and Pomicino, especially Gava, were the godfathers of criminal activity in Naples.

The prosecutors based their claim on the confessions of a senior member of the Alfieri crime family, Pasquale Galasso, who had given several detailed accounts of the underworld in Naples since he first began to talk in August 1992. Galasso was far from the stereotype of a gangland hoodlum. A former university student and an able businessman, his revelations were clear, concise and persuasive. He explained that the fusion of political and criminal power in Naples had begun in earnest at the beginning of the 1980s after the kidnapping of a DC politician called Ciro Cirillo by the Red Brigades. Antonio Gava and his

146

brother Silvio, as well as Enzo Scotti, allegedly used the Camorra as a go-between with the terrorists and eventually secured Cirillo's release.[40] Galasso insisted that both the Alfieri family and its principal rivals, the Cutolo family, had been contacted by Gava through a trusted intermediary. Carmine Alfieri had preferred to stay out of the affair, Raffaele Cutolo, the leader of the *Cutoliani*, had been bolder. Cutolo, however, had subsequently overplayed his hand. He waged a war of aggression against the Alfieri and tried to blackmail Gava into surrendering more of the DC leader's power than he was prepared to give. Gava therefore supposedly sided with Carmine Alfieri. One of Raffaele Cutolo's most prominent henchmen was murdered in Rome and from then on, according to Galasso, Naples was run as a fiefdom by Gava and Alfieri with Pomicino playing an important secondary role, especially during the distribution of the Irpinia earthquake cash. To give substance to his revelations, Galasso listed a number of important local political figures who were, he said, both Gava's men and Alfieri's.[41] Telephone taps ordered by the *procura* to verify these allegations turned up strong evidence to suppose that Galasso's evidence concerning these men's links to organized crime was accurate. Galasso's most shocking revelation, however, concerned Pomicino. According to Galasso, Pomicino "did not bat an eyelash" when he was presented to Carmine Alfieri in 1980, even though he must have known of Alfieri's reputation as a gangland figure. Instead, he allegedly made use of Alfieri's muscle to build himself an illicit construction empire that enriched itself on Italian government aid to the South.[42]

Perhaps Galasso's detailed and partially proven testimony will be found insufficient to convict Gava and Pomicino; perhaps Andreotti has been the victim of a plot. Riccardo Misasi, who was accused by the *procura* of Reggio Calabria of having colluded with the *'Ndrangheta* on April 8, 1993, has since been found innocent. Italian public opinion's overwhelming reaction to the testimony of the *pentiti*, however, was to suppose that there was too much smoke for there to be no fire. Eugenio Scalfari best summed up the public mood in a brilliant leading article entitled "The Lord of the flies has taken your soul." Whether or not the specific allegations against the leading DC politicians were accurate, Scalfari argued, it was obvious that a "malignant spirit" -- the spirit of Beelzebub, the lord of the flies -- had taken over the political parties. Scalfari instructed his readers to take a long look at the kind of men who had prospered in the DC:

> Look at them, these lords of the flies, these Pomicinos, these Gavas, these Vitos ... look at their greasy faces, their eyes flashing with craftiness, smarminess, and an appeal to complicity ... look at their search to find the lowest possible common denominator, where every vice can be included and every divisive virtue ignored ... these are the lords of the flies... that have transformed a party of Catholic democrats into a confederation of feudal

fiefs that are run in more or less the same way all over Italy, though they get more degraded the further south you go. [43]

The Two-Week Roller-Coaster Ride

By mid-April 1993, the Italian electorate was ready to cry *basta!* The voters got their opportunity on April 18 when they went to the polls to cast a ballot on a large number of referendum initiatives proposed by various political movements. A number of the referendums on the ballot were absurdly technical -- there was a referendum on whether the ministry of tourism should be abolished, another on abolishing the ministry of agriculture, yet another on deciding whether the USL should have their environmental functions assumed by local government authorities. The referendum that attracted everybody's attention, however, was the one advocated by Segni's MRE, on the abrogation of the rules for elections to the Senate. As soon as the June 1991 referendum result was in, the MRE had begun campaigning for the two referendums *bocciati* (found wanting) by the Constitutional court in January 1991. The scheme for the direct election of mayors had actually been adopted by parliament -- it passed into law earlier in 1993. In the days before April 18, Segni, who resigned from the DC at the end of March after the first *avviso di garanzia* was sent to Andreotti, used the campaign as a platform for extolling the virtues of a first-past-the-post system. Pointing to the abuses being revealed by the *Mani pulite* investigations, he contended that had Italy had an electoral system that allowed the electorate to "vote the rascals out," the worst excesses of *tangentopoli* would have been avoided. Italian politics had degenerated into moral squalor because the electoral system had guaranteed permanent majorities for the DC and its allies. Feeling themselves to be politically immune, the bosses of the DC and the PSI, and their hundreds of imitators at local level, had behaved as if they were above the law.

Segni's argument was plausible and the electorate was in no mood to quibble. Despite the opposition of some smaller parties, notably Leoluca Orlando's *Rete* party, the MSI and *Rifondazione comunista*, the voting public turned out en masse on polling day and voted by huge majorities for Segni's proposal and for any referendum that struck at the party system. Segni's plan obtained the consent of over 80 percent of those who cast a ballot; a referendum advocating the abolition of state financing of the parties unsurprisingly passed by a 90 percent majority; referenda to end party control over nominations for director-level appointments to savings banks, and to abolish the ministry for state participation in industry, passed by equally dramatic margins.

From under the rubble, Amato's voice was heard, pleading to be allowed to resign. One of the few statesmen whose political stature had actually been enhanced since the April 1992 elections, Amato was now anxious to give the burden of government to someone else. Amato resigned on April 21, and though the notion of an "Amato bis" government was hypothesized by some, it was never a real possibility. As Scalfaro's *giro di consultazione* proceeded, it became clear that the new prime minister would have to be an "institutional" one: Someone above the political fray who was not in any way tainted by links to one of the old government parties and who could pilot the country through the turbulent waters ahead. For it was clear to all that the current parliament could not last. Thoroughly delegitimized, with dozens of its members under investigation, parliament needed renewal. There was widespread agreement among Italian opinion-makers that the main task facing the new prime minister was to pass a new electoral law, which would open the way for fresh elections. President Scalfaro's eventual choice, Carlo Azeglio Ciampi, the governor of the Bank of Italy, was widely hailed as an inspired decision. It was also a novelty. Ciampi was the first non-parliamentarian to be appointed prime minister since the unification of Italy in 1861. He was also the first prime minister in the post-war period to be exempted from the duty of cutting deals with the party leaderships before assembling his administration. As a consequence, Ciampi moved swiftly to assemble a cabinet of experts which was a distinct step up, intellectually, from any recent Italian administration. Several leading university professors were called in, including the ascetic figure of Luigi Spaventa, one of Europe's leading economists, who was made minister for the budget. Another expert, the well-known journalist and writer, Alberto Ronchey, continued as minister for *Beni culturali* (arts and museums): Since his appointment by Giuliano Amato, Ronchey had given this ministry, which was a byword for sloth and incompetence, a rapid and public shakeup. The biggest novelty, however, was the inclusion in the government of three members of the PDS and a leftist green, the youthful Francesco Rutelli. The three PDS ministers -- Augusto Barbera, Vincenzo Visco and Luigi Berlinguer -- were all university professors of outstanding gifts: Their presence was a symbol of the non-factional character of Ciampi's government, though influential figures in the PDS, including D'Alema and Ingrao, were worried that the PDS would seem to be giving the new administration its blessing.

Ciampi's government, in short, was a brave attempt at creating a government that prized competence and integrity over party connections. The traditional parties of government nonetheless maintained a strong foothold in the cabinet. The DC and the PSI provided 12 of the 24 ministers, and though most of these figures, such as the foreign minister, Beniamino Andreatta (DC), and the minister for work, Gino Giugni (PSI), had nothing in common with the crooks that had populated Andreotti's last two governments, the naming of such a large bloc of ministers with links to the DC and the PSI caused enthusiasm for the new administration to be muted. *La Repubblica* called Ciampi's team a "So-so government;" *L'Indipendente*, a new newspaper that had grown increasingly close to the League in its first year of publication, greeted Ciampi's nominations with the headline "Like before, only worse."[44]

Ciampi's problem, of course, was that he had to win an initial vote of confidence from the two chambers of parliament. To do that, he needed the support of the parties that had won a majority in 1992, however discredited they had become. His decision to include so many DC and PSI ministers was presumably dictated by this consideration. He was certainly wise to take this precaution. Government deputies and senators had begun to suggest -- extraordinarily -- that they were victims of *tangentopoli*. DC and PSI members of parliament felt threatened and unloved. On April 1, the MSI had organized a demonstration against parliament. The usual handful of leather-jacketed thugs had gathered outside the entrance to the Chamber of Deputies and had jostled one or two parliamentarians as they tried to enter the building. Earlier, in March, one of the *Lega Nord*'s less sophisticated followers had caused a punch-up in parliament by dangling a noose in the course of a debate. Many deputies also felt, with almost childish stubbornness, that it was unfair for them to be punished for misdemeanours that everybody had taken for granted in the past, even if they had been forbidden by the statute books. Public derision must also have been hard to bear. Long treated with obsequious respect, parliamentarians now found themselves regarded as pariahs in their everyday lives and as the butt of sometimes cruel humour. To give just one (relatively mild) example that made the entire nation laugh, RAI 3's satirical show, *Avanzi*, celebrated the annual popular song festival held in the Mediterranean town of San Remo by performing the song that Ugo Intini, Craxi's personal spokesman, would have sung had he been taking part. The melody, which was sung as a splendid parody of a typical San Remo winner by one of Italy's funniest young comics, Rocco Guzzanti, was entitled "The system just can't collapse (for the sake of a few irregularities)." There is no question that had Guzzanti really entered his song in the festival itself, he would have won by a mile. Its satirical strength lay precisely in the fact that its title was hardly a parody of what most parliamentarians were saying.

Before Ciampi's administration had even had time to take the oath of office, the "victims" took a golden opportunity to assert themselves against public opinion. On April 29, despite a room full of documentary evidence and the signed confessions of literally dozens of businessmen, PSI functionaries, and personal friends, parliament refused to allow the *Mani pulite* pool to proceed with its investigation into Bettino Craxi's role in the corruption scandals and refused to remove his parliamentary immunity from criminal prosecution on four of the six serious charges he faced. By so doing, it gave its solemn judgment that the "clean hands" investigation was a judicial conspiracy to discredit Craxi politically. Who had voted for such a farcical verdict? Craxi had managed to rake together a bloc of around 300 deputies to vote in his favor on every one of the Milanese prosecutors' accusations of corruption and extortion. 316 deputies had voted against the prosecutors' being allowed to search Craxi's home or personal effects.The DC and PSI had seemingly voted solidly for him, but by themselves these parties did not have enough deputies in the chamber on that day to provide the former socialist leader with support of these dimensions. The leadership of the PDS, furious, accused the League and the MSI of voting tactically to cause a public uproar. The League's spokesmen responded by pointing to the long-standing links between Craxi and the *miglioristi. La Rete*'s deputies and the deputies of *Rifondazione comunista* were also suspected of having voted in favor of Craxi in the hope of provoking an election under the old electoral rules. Whatever the truth of the matter, the real culprits were clearly the DC and the PSI. By voting so compactly for Craxi's absolution in the light of such abundant evidence, they were deliberately challenging the rule of law.

Had public opinion accepted this decision passively, it would have been a black day for Italian democracy. Without wishing to suggest for one moment that the parliamentary representatives of the DC and the PSI dabbled with the idea of authoritarian solutions to their predicament, Craxi's absolution arguably did reflect a subconscious desire on the part of the poor bloody infantry of the *partitocrazia* to free themselves from the attacks of the furies of the press, the opposition parties, public opinion and the judiciary with a single undemocratic gesture. Even more vehemently than at the beginning of March, however, the Italians greeted this latest act of political arrogance with street demonstrations and public displays of disgust and disdain. They were incited to rebel by the most authorititive voices in the Italian press. Indro Montanelli wrote a scornful *corsivo* for *Il Giornale* that asked how members of parliament could continue to use their formal title of "honorable" and appealed for a public trial of Craxi and "all the fixers who surround him."[45] *La Repubblica*, whose cover stories are normally a model of restraint, printed the words "Infamy Craxi Absolved" in huge type on its front page.[46] Thousands of people, young and old, turned this front page story into an impromptu placard in the spontaneous protests that erupted all over Italy. One such protest took a violent turn. A chanting crowd of people who had gathered outside Craxi's residence in Rome became a mob when Craxi left the building to attend a television interview. Hundreds of coins and stones were thrown and had he not been protected by a massive police escort, Craxi would certainly have been manhandled. The consequences of the Chamber of Deputies' decision for Ciampi's one-day-old government were equally dramatic. Creating a record even for Italy, Ciampi's administration immediately collapsed as the PDS's ministers and Rutelli resigned en bloc. They were replaced on May 4 by non-party experts.

Within a year, in other words, a combination of dogged detective work by prosecutors all over Italy and public repugnance at the corruption, venality, hypocrisy and arrogance of the political class, had succeeded in sweeping away the whole stultifying apparatus of the old party system. Its most emblematic figures -- Craxi, Gava, Andreotti, De Michelis, Cirino Pomicino, Forlani -- had been humiliated in the eyes of public opinion. Although there had been one or two unwelcome casualties -- the talented leader of the Republican party, Giorgio La Malfa, honorably resigned in March 1993 after admitting that he had accepted illegal contributions for his 1992 election campaign -- most people regarded the *Mani pulite* investigations as a long overdue clear-out of unwanted and malodorous junk. It was for this reason that the whole two-week roller-coaster ride from the April referendum to the public protests against Craxi's escape from justice seemed more exhilarating than perilous. Despite the fact that parliament had been thoroughly discredited by events, few thought that there was any danger of the institutional switchback car coming off the rails. There were visible and impressive safeguards against accidents. The judiciary had shown itself to be a model of probity. There was a strong president, who had amply demonstrated his sympathy for the corruption inquiry in March. The new prime minister and his chief cabinet colleagues also promised well. A world away from the tawdry boss-politicians the Italians had long been used to, Ciampi's new administration seemed to be an ideal government of transition: one which would last long enough to pass a new electoral law based upon FPTP principles. By October at the latest, Ciampi's emergency government would give way to a new administration and a new parliament genuinely representative of the people's will. The Rome Spring, in short, was a time of hope. At the time, few guessed that Ciampi would hang on until January 1994 and that his heir would be not Mario Segni, or Umberto Bossi, or Achille Occhetto, but a newly created political movement called *Forza Italia!* led by the notoriously pro-Craxi entrepreneur Silvio Berlusconi.

Notes

1. A brief summary of Chiesa's career is given in Giuseppe Turani and Cinzia Sasso, *I Saccheggiatori*, Milan (Sperling & Kupfer) 1992, pp 18-27.
2. *Avanti!* buried news of Chiesa's arrest on page 6 of its February 19, 1992, edition. It underlined that Antonio Di Pietro and his superior, Borrelli, were part of the judicial pool that had roused a *polverone* (storm in a teacup) over corruption in the Milan metropolitan area and stressed that the PSI was absolutely extraneous from the entire affair.
3. For a succinct account of the Banco Ambrosiano scandal see Elio Veltri, *Da Craxi a Craxi*, Bari (Laterza) 1993, pp 176-184 and 223-226.
4. For a full account of all the scandals in Milan in the 1980s, see Elio Veltri and G. Barbacetto, *Milano degli scandali*, Bari (Laterza) 1992.

152

5. The statistics are from Sebastiano Messina, *La Nomenklatura*, Milan (Mondadori) 1992, p 148.

6. Veltri, *Da Craxi a Craxi*, pp 124-126 is my main source for this account of Craxi's free-spending ways.

7. *L'Espresso* published a version of Chiesa's confessions to Di Pietro on June 28, 1992. It would be the first of a long line of strategic leaks to the paper.

8. The dossier sent by the procura of Milan and signed by Antonio Di Pietro, Gherardo Colombo, Gerardo D'Ambrosio and Francesco Saverio Borrelli is included as an appendix to Turani and Sasso, *I Saccheggiatori*, pp 145-177.

9. Turani and Sasso, *I Saccheggiatori*, p 11.

10. Giorgio Bocca, "Questa nostra democrazia è un cadavere. Meglio la rivoluzione," *L'Espresso*, August 2, 1992.

11. Craxi's *corsivi* appeared in *Avanti!* on August 22, 24 and 26.

12. Claudio Martelli, interview in *La Stampa*, September 12, 1992.

13. Quoted Giovanni Maria Bellu and Sandra Bonsanti, *Il Crollo*, Bari (Laterza) 1993, p 215.

14. Francesco Saverio Borrelli discussed both the use of preventive detention and the numerous leaks from the *Palazzo di giustizia* in an interview with *L'Espresso*, December 20, 1992.

15. Roberto Villetti, "La nave, il nocchiero e la rotta" *Avanti!* November 14, 1992.

16. "E a via del Corso sette miliardi," *L'Espresso*, December 6, 1992.

17. Bettino Craxi, "Finalità non certo di giustizia" *Avanti!* December 16, 1992.

18. Francesco Gozzano, "La caccia ai socialisti è lo sport nazionale," *Avanti!* December 17, 1992.

19. Bettino Craxi, "Superata la frontiera di verità e giustizia," ibid.

20. Eugenio Scalfari, "Che baldracca questa moglie di Cesare," *La Repubblica*, June 8, 1992.

21. Vincenzo D'Urso's revelations were printed in *L'Espresso*, February 14, 1993, under the heading "Craxi e Balzamo? Due cuori, un conto."

22. Text of the documentation sent to the Chamber of Deputies by the district attorney of Milan, Francesco Saverio Borrelli, and his subordinates, on March 6, 1993, to request the lifting of parliamentary immunity from Bettino Craxi and Claudio Martelli. Reprinted in *Avvenimenti* (11), March 1993, under the title *Conto protezione: il documento dei giudici di Milano per l'autorizzazione a procedere contro Craxi e Martelli*. See especially p 19 and pp 28-29 of this edition.

23. Di Pietro complained in a speech to the carabinieri of Bergamo, reprinted in *Il Di Pietro Pensiero*, Rome (Panorama) 1993, pp 51-57, with a preface by Francesco Cossiga.

24. Gianfranco Pasquino, "Nessuno ruba solo per il partito," *L'Unità*, March 4, 1993.

25. "Si son dati l'amnistia," *L'Indipendente*, March 5, 1993.

26. Giuliano Amato, interview in *La Repubblica*, March 14, 1993.

27. *L'istruttoria*, presented by Giuliano Ferrara, *Canale 5*, March 5, 1993. Ferrara has been appointed minister for relations with parliament in the new Berlusconi administration.

28. Borrelli, quoted *La Stampa*, March 8, 1993.

29. For a good account of Messina's, Buscetta's and Mutolo's initial revelations, see Bellu and Bonsanti, *Il Crollo*, pp 193-200.

30. John Tagliebue, "Informers in Italy Accusing Ex-Premier of Ties to the Mafia," *New York Times*, December 31, 1992.

31. See the interviews with Arlacchi and Martelli in "Mafia L'ultimo atto?" special report in *Panorama*, January 24, 1993.

32. Text of the documentation sent to the Italian Senate by the district attorney of Palermo, Gian Carlo Caselli, and his subordinates, on March 27, 1993, to request the lifting of the parliamentary immunity of Giulio Andreotti. Reprinted in *Avvenimenti* (13), April 1993, under the title *Indagate su Andreotti*. For Mutolo's remarks concerning Andreotti, see especially pp 41-42.

33. Forattini, *La Repubblica*, March 28, 1993.

34. "Ellekappa," *L'Unità*, March 28, 1993.

35. *Indagate su Andreotti*, especially pp 42-43.

36. Luciano Violante, text of a report presented to the parliamentary commission on the Mafia April 8, 1993, reprinted in *La Repubblica* on April 10, 1993, as *Mafia & Politica*, with a foreword by Pino Arlacchi. See especially p 18.

37. Text of the documentation sent to the Italian Senate by Gian Carlo Caselli on April 14, 1993, as an adjunct to the earlier request for the lifting of the parliamentary immunity of Giulio Andreotti. Reprinted as a special insert in *L'Espresso*, April 25, 1993. The substance of Mannoia's testimony is to be found in pages 5-9 of the *Espresso* version.

38. Testimony of Tommaso Buscetta, ibid. pp 9-12.

39. Text of documentation sent to the Senate and the Chamber of Deputies by the district attorney of Naples, Paolo Mancuso, and his subordinates, on April 6, 1993, to request the lifting of the parliamentary immunity of Paolo Cirino Pomicino, Vincenzo Meo, Antonio Gava, Alfredo Vito and Raffaele Mastrantuono. Reprinted by *La Repubblica* as *Camorra & Politica*, April 15, 1993, with a foreword by Pino Arlacchi pp 1-3. Quotes are from p 1.

40. The best account of the Cirillo case is to be found in Isaia Sales' contribution to Nicola Tranfaglia (ed), *Cirillo, Ligato e Lima: Tre storie di mafia e politica*, Bari (Laterza) 1994, pp 33-97.

41. *Camorra & Politica*, p 11.

42. Ibid., p 19.

43. Eugenio Scalfari, "Il signore delle mosche vi ha preso l'anima," *La Repubblica*, April 7, 1993.

44. *La Repubblica*, "Un governo così così," *L'Indipendente*, "Come prima, solo peggio," both April 29, 1993.

45. Indro Montanelli, "E continuano a chiamarli onorevoli," *Il Giornale*, April 30, 1993.

46. *La Repubblica*, banner headline "Vergogna Craxi assolto," April 30, 1993.

9

Three Elections and a Trial

The disgrace of the *partitocrazia* in the Spring of 1993 left Italy without a clear political identity. In the short term, public opinion was content to allow Ciampi and Scalfaro to guide the country, but in the long run, the country had a difficult choice to make between all the vendors of ideas setting up stall in the political market place. In the early summer of 1993, the voice bawling loudest was the *Lega Nord*'s, but even Umberto Bossi's formidable lungs could not wholly drown out competing cries from the PDS, and from the *Alleanza democratica*, a forum for the concerned middle-class intelligentsia whose leaders hoped to build a broad progressive coalition encompassing the PDS, the PRI, the Greens, a sanitized PSI and -- crucially -- progressive Catholics like Mario Segni. Segni, whose electoral reform activists were a nebulous political party, was a prize wanted by reformers inside the DC too. Farther left, *La Rete* and *Rifondazione comunista* were exhibiting their wares. At the other extreme, the only traditional force that had escaped *Mani pulite* unscathed, the MSI, was beginning to sense that good times were round the corner. For so long an outsider, the MSI had spent much of the 1980s immersed in an internal debate over its ideological identity. After a turbulent interlude in 1990, when the party secretaryship had briefly passed into the hands of a leader, Pino Rauti, who had proclaimed the revolutionary rather than conservative character of fascism and who had articulated an anti-American, anti-capitalist ideology full of scorn for the shallow and tawdry values of modern consumerism, the MSI had returned to voicing the views of its traditional middle-class conservative voters. At the same time, the Rauti parenthesis had left its mark. Post-Rauti, the party was less virulently racist, and more attuned to modern issues such as the environment. In short, it was more electable.[1] While many members of the *ceto medio* continued to turn up their noses at the quality of the goods on offer from the MSI, others were starting to take an interest. Before long, the number of voters clustering around the MSI's stall would be matched only by the PDS and by a latecomer whose merchandise was marketed with consummate professional skill.

The year would be signposted by three elections and a trial. In June 1993, and then again in November-December, municipal councils were selected all over Italy: The new rules proposed by the MRE, including direct mayoral elections, were employed for the first time in these polls. In March 1994, national elections, under a mixed FPTP/PR system agreed at the beginning of August 1993, also took place. In the meantime, Antonio Di Pietro had used the trial of a financial consultant with close links to the upper reaches of the PSI, Sergio Cusani, to subject some of the most prominent barons of the old political class to ruthless questioning, and to call into question the bona fides of the League.

The Stalingrad of the League

The first of the elections, those of June 1993, were fought in an atmosphere of extreme tension and polemic. In May, bombs began to explode in the centers of Italy's principal cities. Rome was the first town to be hit: On May 14, a car bomb seemingly aimed at one of Italy's leading television personalities, the chat-show host Maurizio Costanzo, badly damaged a block of flats and injured 15 people. On May 27, another explosion, this time in Florence, killed five people and caused substantial damage to the collection of the Uffizi museum. On June 2, a potential massacre was avoided by good luck when an alert passerby spotted an elderly FIAT 500 full of explosives just 100 meters from Palazzo Chigi, the prime minister's residence. The minister for the interior, Nicola Mancino (DC), was inclined to blame the Mafia for this onslaught. There was some evidence for this theory: Costanzo had presented a number of televised anti-mafia initiatives in the previous year; on May 18, moreover, the *Carabinieri* arrested perhaps the most important member of *Cosa Nostra* still at liberty, the crime-boss Nitto Santapaola. Most people, however, were inclined to regard the bombs as part of a *strategia di tensione* perpetrated by right-wing terrorists, or "deviant" members of the secret services, in the hope of derailing the on-going political transformation. The Florence attack, which took place the day after Andreotti had received an *avviso di garanzia* for the murder of Mino Pecorelli, added particular grist to this mill.

Even without the bombings, the political atmosphere would have been electric. All the parties were aware that the municipal elections would provide a genuine sign of the role they would play in Italy's political future. At the beginning of the campaign, after the April referendum, the DC, the PDS and the League had been the front-runners. An opinion poll published in *La Repubblica* on April 23 showed the DC as the largest party in the country with 20 percent support; the PDS second, with 17.5 percent; the League third, with 16 percent;

the Radicals, the MSI, *Rifondazione* and *La Rete* were the other forces scoring more than 5 percent. The PSI had declined to just 4.5 percent. These broad figures, however, disguised important regional variations. In the North, the League was by far the biggest party. Twenty-nine percent of northern voters favored the *Carroccio*, nearly as many as the combined total of the DC and the PDS, the two next largest parties. In the Center, the PDS, with 24 percent, was the strongest political formation, though its position was less commanding than the League's. The DC was just 8 percent behind the PDS; *Rifondazione*, the Radicals and the MSI were all in double figures. In the South, the DC retained nearly 30 percent of the vote, well down from the plebiscite-like margins of the past, but still way ahead of its nearest challenger, the PDS, which could count on just 16 percent of the votes. The MSI (9.5 percent) and *La Rete* (7.5 percent) were the next most popular forces south of Rome.[2] The three "big" parties were not so far ahead, however, as to be invulnerable to coalitions of their opponents. The new electoral law for municipalities provided for a dual ballot. In the first round of voting, the electors voted for a party list and for a mayoral candidate. If no candidate scored more than 50 percent on the first ballot, the two strongest candidates would run off in the second round, with the winner receiving a guaranteed majority of town council seats to ensure that he had a stable majority with which to govern. This procedure obviously gave small parties an incentive to cluster around a single attractive candidate for mayor, as a way of maximizing their influence.

The left realized this fact earlier and better than the right. All over Italy, the leftist parties struck local bargains on mayoral candidates and lists. The PDS took the lead: In some places, the PDS combined with *Rifondazione comunista* and *La Rete*; in others, they allied with the Greens, the PSI, the PRI and *Alleanza democratica*. The League and the DC, by contrast, fought the elections in splendid isolation: The DC, in particular, paid a heavy price for this choice.

The left's clever decision to sink its differences and fight the elections in relative unison opened the prospect of inflicting the first defeat to the League since its arrival on the scene as a major political force in the late 1980s. In all, 122 municipalities were electing their communal administration, including 15 provincial capitals. Eight of these (Milan, Turin, Vercelli, Novara, Pavia, Pordenone, Belluno, and Lecco) were in the North. With the exception of Turin, a bastion of the former PCI, the League found itself opposed in all these cities by slates of united left candidates, all explicitly intent on braking the *Carroccio*'s progress. The most intense struggle came in Milan. The PDS, *La Rete*, *Rifondazione*, the Greens and a civic action group called "List for Milan" rallied around the candidacy of Nando Dalla Chiesa. The League, after havering for a while over a last-minute candidacy by Bossi, stuck to its original decision to run Bossi's number-two, Marco Formentini. It proved to be a wise choice. Angered by press jubilation over opinion polls showing Dalla Chiesa in the lead, throughout the campaign Bossi gave nightly displays of the worst aspects of his personality and rhetoric. Among other excesses, he called Dalla Chiesa a "cuckold," and "Nando Dalla Cosa Nostra," and insinuated, with demented logic, that the Florence bomb had been planted by occult forces in order to raise the specter of organized crime and consequently help the campaign of Dalla Chiesa, one of the best-known anti-mafia activists in the country.[3] To the rest of the political world, Bossi's abusive performances seemed like a sign of desperation. Mino Martinazzoli, ignoring the fact that the DC theoretically had a candidate in the race, gloated a few days before the poll that Milan would be the League's Stalingrad, and all but urged former DC voters to back Dalla Chiesa, *Rifondazione comunista*'s preferred choice.[4] Formentini, however, was proving to be an inspired choice as candidate. The personification of the typical Milanese white collar worker, Formentini's quiet, rational, thoughtful style contrasted sharply both with Bossi and with Dalla Chiesa, who also gave way to some ill-considered rhetoric during the campaign. The two candidates met in televised debates on several occasions during the run-up to the election, and Formentini impressed for his ability to dampen down the hysteria surrounding the campaign and to stick to local issues. Promising to slim down the city's bureaucracy and workforce and to introduce greater transparency in the award of public works contracts; but also to beautify the city through new public works paid for by the issue of municipal bonds, Formentini above all else sounded unideological and competent.

In the event, the Milanese electorate concluded that Formentini's low-key approach was what it wanted. Giving lie to the opinion polls, the League took 41 percent of the vote in the first ballot on June 6, more than double its showing in the April 1992 general election. The left coalition took only 28 percent. The mayoral race was slightly closer: Formentini was supported by 39 percent of the voters: Dalla Chiesa, proving to be fractionally more popular than his party backers, obtained 30.5 percent. Nothing could detract from the immensity of the League's victory, however. No party since the war had ever obtained 40 percent of the vote in Milan: The next largest party in the city was *Rifondazione comunista* with 11 percent. The DC and the PDS both slipped to below 10 percent; the PSI got just 1.6 percent of the vote.

In other cities of the North, it was the same story: The *leghisti* triumphant, the other parties scrambling for second place. The only exceptions were Turin, where the candidate sponsored by *La Rete* and *Rifondazione*, the ex-mayor Diego Novelli, beat the candidate backed by the PDS, the Greens and an alliance of local progressives, with the *Lega Nord* coming a disappointing third, and Novara, where the League's candidate was forced into second place (though he emerged victorious in the run-off). In the Center and in Emilia-Romagna, the PDS did even better than expected. Towns such as Ancona, Ravenna and Siena gave the PDS's candidates resounding votes of confidence.

On June 20, the run-off elections took place. The PDS's skilful coalition strategy was confirmed: So was the power, in the North, of the League. The PDS, either alone, or in alliance with other leftist parties, was part of the winning coalition in 74 of the 122 municipalities. It provided more mayors than any other single party, and pulled a surprise by winning the run-off in Turin. The League obtained just 16 mayoralties, but its wins were prestigious. In addition to Milan (where Formentini scored 57 percent in the run-off), the League won every northern provincial capital being contested except Turin and Belluno (where it remained easily the largest single party). In Pavia, the League's candidate obtained 64 percent in the run-off and 43 percent in the first ballot -- more than double its nearest challenger. The DC, meanwhile, experienced *its* Stalingrad: Or perhaps it would be more apt to say its *Caporetto*. The once-proud hegemon in the Italian political system proved capable of winning a mere 9 mayoralties: Its share of the vote plummeted to less than 19 percent. Within weeks of this disaster, the party's National Council, pressed by impatient reformers from northern cities such as Padua, Venice and Brescia, authorized Martinazzoli to begin the process of changing the DC's name to the *Partito popolare italiano* (PPI), a name that recalled an anti-fascist Christian party formed by a philosopher-priest, Don Luigi Sturzo, after World War One. The DC, however, did remarkably well compared with the PSI, which scored just 3.7 percent of the vote. In the same municipalities in April 1992, the PSI had obtained over 14 percent.

The June 1993 elections were a "historic shove" that finally pushed the old party system over the edge of the cliff.[5] At the time, they appeared to have given a broadbrush outline of the shape of the political system to come. On the left, the PDS had proved that it could act as a rallying point for Italy's heterogeneous progressive forces. On the right, Bossi and the League ruled seemingly undisturbed. A new center also seemed to be emerging. Mario Segni's *Popolari per il riforma*, the pressure group he had founded to work for the April referendum, worked successfully with *Alleanza democratica* and the "lay" parties to obtain substantial percentages in several large towns. Segni and *Alleanza democratica* also cooperated with the reformist wing of the DC in Belluno to rob the *Lega Nord* of the mayoralty in the second ballot, and with the PDS in Turin and the large Sicilian city of Catania. If the DC could renew itself, becoming a progressive Catholic party of the kind wanted by the DC's grassroots membership in the northeast corner of Italy, the outlines of a centrist force with real electoral weight would begin to emerge. Segni's success worried Bossi enough to prompt the League's leader to turn down the rhetorical volume as soon as the first round ballots were counted. Bossi said that the results proved that "there is a new center in Italy, namely the League."[6]

Few were convinced. Bossi's language and actions during the campaign caused *La Repubblica* to talk of the "new barbarians" at the gate of Italian democracy. The first lesson of the election seemed to be that the country was on the brink of a crucial choice between the new right -- the *Lega* -- and the new left -- the progressive parties headed by the PDS. The swing vote was Segni, *Alleanza democratica* and the would-be *Partito Popolare*. Who would the civilized center of Italian democracy support, once it had solidified into a coherent whole? *La Repubblica*, for one, was in no doubt that it should back the left.

In retrospect, this immediate analysis of the June 1993 results was flawed. The League was not "national" enough in its electoral appeal and ideology to provide a real alternative to the PDS. In the aftermath of the poll, Bossi envisaged the abolition of all alternatives to the League within two years; of the general acceptance of federalist doctrines throughout Italy. At that point, Bossi predicted, the League would split into "left federalists" and "right federalists," though both groups would favor the free-market policies that had proved so popular a part of the League's program in Milan.[7] This mood of hubris would not survive the year. The PDS was capable of building a firewall on the south bank of the River Po that could stop the *Lega* conflagration from spreading into the Center and South. The League's success, moreover, had been principally dependent upon its association in the public mind with free-market ideas and outspoken hostility to statism and clientelism. In June 1993, the League had a near-monopoly of such themes: a state of affairs that would not outlast the year. Milan, in short, was less the League's Stalingrad than its Moscow. For a few brief weeks in the summer of 1993 Bossi commanded the citadel of Italian politics -- but the movement did not have the resources to occupy it indefinitely.

The second lesson to be learned from the municipal elections was that Italy was a country suffering from political schizophrenia. The vote against the old political parties could not have been clearer: Italy wanted new leaders whether of the left or the right. Parliament and the Ciampi government, however, were packed with representatives of the parties that had been so humiliatingly defeated. This same parliament now had the legal obligation to pass an electoral law embodying the FPTP principles endorsed by the April referendum. Since the passage of a new electoral law would clear the way for fresh national elections, the shocked troops of the old *partitocrazia* found themselves in the macabre position of having to vote themselves out of existence. Naturally, they used every means at their disposal to avoid this fate. Consequently, while the new electoral law approved at the beginning of August 1993 did introduce FPTP for elections to both chambers of parliament, it also retained a substantial element of proportional representation. The main virtue of this dodge for the party grandees was that it offered a backdoor way to stay in power.

The new law also pulled off the difficult feat of surpassing the old system for fiendish complexity. Briefly, the legislation adopted by parliament in July assigns 75 percent of the seats in both houses of parliament through FPTP and 25 percent by PR, though in elections to the Chamber of Deputies, small parties must reach a German-style threshold of 4 percent of the national vote in order to receive seats through PR. For the Senate this means that 232 seats are elected directly and 83 are allocated by PR. For the Chamber of Deputies, the country is divided into 475 individual constituencies, distributed in 27 electoral colleges, thus leaving 155 seats to be shared out proportionally. In the case of the Senate, voters are given a single ballot form. They vote for the candidate of their choice in the constituency where they live. All votes that do not directly contribute to the election of a winning constituency candidate are thrown into a regional pool where the the D'Hondt method is used to allocate the region's quota of indirectly elected senators. For the Chamber, the elector is given two ballot papers. The first ballot, for the direct election of the constituency's representative, shows a list of candidates and the symbols of the parties supporting him or her. The second ballot, for PR purposes, shows the full list of party symbols. In the case of the Chamber of Deputies, PR preferences are transferred into a single national constituency after a complex formula designed to reduce the number of preferences awarded to the parties that won direct representation has been applied.[8] The purpose of subtracting winners' votes in both the Senate and Chamber elections is clear. Just as effectively as under the old system, it ensures that medium-small parties get their fair share of indirectly distributed seats. By so doing, it gives such parties an incentive to maintain their individual identities and dilutes the prospect of single-party government to almost zero. Insofar as Italian proponents of electoral reform had made a reduction in the number of small parties and the achievement of greater governability their holy grail throughout the previous decade, the new law must be regarded as a failure. It is only a half-hearted shuffle away from the pure proportionality of the past.[9]

The Mother of All Bribes

While parliament had been deliberating over the new electoral law, the *Mani pulite* inquiries in Milan, Naples and Rome had uncovered evidence of political wrongdoing that dwarfed anything previously revealed. In July, Francesco De Lorenzo, the former health minister, managed the extraordinary feat of becoming more publicly reviled than Bettino Craxi when his private secretary alleged that he had organized rake-offs for the political parties and individual politicians from the money being disbursed to pay for the fight against AIDS. De Lorenzo was also accused of allowing pharmaceutical products to be sold on the Italian market in exchange for cash. Many of these products were regarded as useless by other European countries; others were subsequently sold with inflated claims for their curative properties at equally inflated prices.[10] Public hostility to De Lorenzo was such that there was public uproar of almost Craxian proportions in September 1993, when the Chamber of Deputies, while authorizing the continuance of the investigation into De Lorenzo's tenure of the health ministry, refused to sanction his arrest. This decision so angered President Scalfaro that he came within an ace of dissolving the parliament and calling fresh elections under the old rules (the electoral commission was still elaborating the new constituency boundaries and parliament still had to pass a constitutional amendment to legalize one of the articles of the new law). Meanwhile, when the government official in charge of issuing licenses for new pharmaceuticals was arrested in his home, police discovered that he possessed thousands of Kruggerrands, gold sovereigns, and diamonds; kilograms of gold in ingot form, and Swiss bank accounts stuffed with tens of millions of francs. His total net worth would later be estimated at more than 300 billion lire (approximately $200 million).[11]

Sanitopoli, as the investigation into the murky world of Italian health spending was quickly dubbed (*Sanità* means "health" in Italian), was sensational stuff by any standards. Antonio Di Pietro and his colleagues in Milan, however, were tenaciously piecing together an understanding of an even bigger scandal: The political parties' defalcations from Italy's public and private chemical industries. Back in February and March, the Milan prosecutors had decapitated the upper reaches of ENI, arresting, among others, the Socialist president, Gabriele Cagliari, and forcing the resignation of the Amato government's finance minister, Franco Reviglio, who had preceded Cagliari as the head of the petrochemical giant. For the several months, Cagliari resisted Di Pietro's interrogating techniques, admitting finally that ENI had paid approximately 27 billion lire ($18 million) to the parties during his four years at the helm of the company. On July 20, 1993, Cagliari suffocated himself in prison. Before killing himself, he wrote a long suicide note to his wife in which he explained that he could not endure the brutality and neglect of prison life and the ruthlessness of the prosecutors any longer. Writing with evident disdain of "them," Cagliari accused Di Pietro and his colleagues of treating people involved in the *Mani pulite* investigation "like unpersons, like dogs to be whipped back into their kennel." The aim of the prosecutors, Cagliari alleged, was nothing less than the creation of an "authoritarian state." Like many politicians, Cagliari also seemed to think that he was being treated unjustly. Corruption had been the way the system worked; the former president of ENI could not see why he should have to expiate the sins of society in general by rotting in a prison cell. The Italian revolution, he wrote, had been a "national tragedy."[12]

Cagliari's condemnation came at a delicate moment for the *Mani pulite* team. A few days previously, President Scalfaro had also voiced worries about the use of preventive detention. After Cagliari's suicide, the minister of justice, Giovanni Conso, without waiting to inform himself of the circumstances, took Cagliari's complaints of neglect and judicial terrorism at their face value, and spoke out in strong condemnation of the Milan pool. All over Italy, nervous members of the judiciary, fearful that the *Mani pulite* investigations would now be blocked, released politicians from custody. Two events kept the investigation's momentum from faltering. First, President Scalfaro clarified his attitude with an explicit statement of support for the prosecutors in Milan. Second, three days after Cagliari's death, another leading figure in Italian business, Raul Gardini, the flamboyant former chief executive of the Ferruzzi group, a fertilizers, chemicals and refining company long regarded as Italy's second largest business after FIAT, shot himself in his luxury office cum apartment in Milan. Gardini -- like Cagliari -- had learned that the prosecutors were about to bring to light all the circumstances surrounding the collapse of the Ferruzzi group's finances (the group had just announced that it was sinking under the burden of $20 billion in debt and had made losses of more than $200 million dollars in 1992: A figure that was later revised to nearer $500 million as evidence of systematic fraud and illegal accounting was added into the balance). In particular, he knew that Di Pietro was in a position to explain the murky 1990 affair of the Italian state's buy-out of the Ferruzzi group's 40 percent stake in Enimont, a joint venture between ENI and Montedison, the group's chemical subsidiary. This affair, according to information provided to the prosecutors by the Giuseppe Garofano, the former president of Montedison and Carlo Sama, Gardini's successor at the Ferruzzi group, had resulted in the pay-out of the "mother of all bribes" to Craxi, Forlani, Pomicino and other political figures. The amount disbursed by Gardini was startling even by the standards of *Mani pulite*: at least 150 billion lire (at the time, over $100 million).

All Italian billionaires have nicknames. Giovanni Agnelli of FIAT is almost invariably called *L'Avvocato* (the lawyer). Carlo De Benedetti, the proprietor of the computer manufacturer Olivetti and the *Espresso-Repubblica* media group, is known as "the Engineer." The TV, advertising and publishing magnate Silvio Berlusconi is called both *Sua Emittenza*, (an untranslateable pun on the Italian for eminence and for broadcasting) and *Il biscione* (the big snake), as well as *Il cavaliere* (the knight). Gardini's *soprannome* was "The Peasant." Despite this name, there was nothing of the country bumpkin about Gardini. A glamorous figure (he was the owner and sponsor of the *Moro di Venezia*, the yacht which came within a hairsbreadth of winning the Americas' Cup in 1992), Gardini was Italy's real-life equivalent of the financier Gordon Gekko in the movie "Wall Street." After taking over the Ferruzzi group's finances in 1980, Gardini swiftly expanded the family's holdings, purchasing the agri-chemical group Montedison in 1986. In the process, he severely over-extended the company. In 1988, Gardini joined with ENI to create a new chemical giant, Enimont, and incidentally unload some of the Ferruzzi group's debt mountain on the new company. By the terms of his agreement with the state gas company, Montedison could not own more than 40 percent of the shares. In 1990, however, Gardini broke his word and mounted a *scalata* (hostile takeover) of

Enimont. His motive appears to have been a combination of vanity and pride. By the end of the 1980s, Gardini had lost the provincial simplicity that had won him his affectionate nickname, and was driven by an overweening desire to become the "King of Chemicals," and be recognized, internationally, as Italy's premier corporate boss.

Gardini's ambitions, however, aroused political resistance. According to testimony given on oath in December 1993 by Giorgio La Malfa, the ex-leader of the PRI, the secretaries of the *pentapartito*, plus Andreotti, had met in Rome in September 1990 to discuss Gardini's move. According to La Malfa, Craxi and Andreotti agreed that Gardini had "excessive pretensions."[13] The politicians, however, were not content to block Enimont's passage to the Ferruzzi group. They also smelled money. In November 1990, at Enimont's request, a Milanese judge, Diego Curtò, suspended all dealings in Enimont's shares and appointed (for the astronomic compensation of more than $100,000 per day) a well-known banker, Vincenzo Palladino, as custodian of Enimont's stock. Palladino was also known for his links with Craxi. The message was clear, and Gardini hastened to back out of the deal, agreeing to sell Montedison's full quota of shares in Enimont to the government for the sum of 2805 billion lire (approx $2 billion). This price enormously overstated the value of Montedison's stake, but there was a catch: The politicians, in return for their profligacy with public funds, wanted 5 percent of the gross sum. Gardini, with the help and advice of Sergio Cusani, a Milanese financial consultant close to Craxi and Claudio Martelli, raked the cash together and paid the parties off. Craxi, Forlani, Cirino Pomicino, Martelli and other leading political figures all certainly received huge sums, though tens of millions of dollars remain unaccounted for even today. Cusani kept a few billion lire in his safe until the run-up to the 1992 election, when it was passed out to the PRI (campaign slogan: "The Party of The Honest People"), among others. It would later emerge that Curtò (whose wife, by one of those quirks of fate that no novelist would dare to invent, is called Antonia Di Pietro) had received substantial sums from Palladino as a reward for his intervention. A number of journalists, ENI executives and industrialists are also alleged to have dipped their fingers in the gravy in return for their cooperation.[14]

Cusani was arrested on July 23. His lawyer, a prominent specialist in high-profile cases who had also represented Toni Negri, immediately began to make vocal demands for an early trial. To his horror, Di Pietro went along with his demands. Cusani was remanded for trial in September 1993 and was arraigned at the end of October. He eventually came before the court at the end of November 1993.

Cusani's trial would become *La Norimburga dei partiti* (The Nuremburg of the parties). Craxi, Forlani, Pomicino, La Malfa, Martelli, and Citaristi would all be called as witnesses and subjected to Di Pietro's forensic questioning. So, too, would Umberto Bossi, who, in a sensational development, was called to respond to an allegation in December 1993 by Carlo Sama that he had given the *Lega Nord*'s treasurer a 200 million lire donation during the 1992 election campaign. The League had not subsequently registered this gift. Compared with the sordid immensities of the Enimont affair, the League's lapse was trivial. No corruption was involved; no public money had been wasted. The *Lega*'s precious reputation for purity was violated, however. If the warriors of Pontida would take money illegally before they came to power, what might they do once they were in government?

This question would prove to be a vital one. When the Cusani trial started, the League was riding high in the polls, though the Italian public had mixed feelings about both Bossi's leadership style and the movement's character. While people admired Bossi's "concreteness" and "tough-mindedness," they also regarded him as "intolerant." By 70-30 percent margins, public opinion regarded the League as "reactionary" rather than "progressive," "right-wing" rather than "left-wing," and "destructive" rather than "creative."[15] The League, in short, had no national groundswell of support to propel it to replace the DC as the center party in the Italian political system. It was not *un partito pigliatutto* (a catch-all party), so much as a movement that was perceived to be both divisive and challenging. It excited respect even among its opponents, but also unleashed strong negative emotions of disgust and fear. The arrest of its treasurer and the revelation that the League, like the traditional parties, would go cap in hand to business in search of illegal contributions, would tell electorally against the League in the new year, when the *Lega* suddenly found itself with ideological competition on the center-right.

The Short-Lived Victory of the Left

Even before January 1994, however, proof of the League's inability to establish nationwide appeal had come in the second batch of municipal elections in November-December 1993. Conditions could hardly have been more favorable for another stride in the League's hitherto relentless advance. At the beginning of November, the last institutions left untainted by scandal, the presidency and the judiciary, were both dragged into the mire. Five judges were placed under investigation in Sicily for their alleged mob ties. Coming after the Curtò case, this seemed to indicate that there was a need for *toghe pulite* (clean robes) as well as clean hands. President Scalfaro, meanwhile, was accused, along with every other minister of the interior since 1980 except Amintore Fanfani, of having been the beneficiary of slush fund payouts of more than 100 million lire a month during his tenure of the Viminale (as the palace housing the interior ministry is called). His accusers, five important ex-officials of the secret services being investigated on corruption charges, were hardly a font of irreproachable limpidity, but the shock to the political system was palpable. Scalfaro's reputation for honesty, along with Ciampi's manifest competence, were the glue keeping the fractured vase of the Italian state intact. If the glue were to dissolve, the Republic might dissolve too. Aware of this, Scalfaro made a televised statement condemning his accusers in the strongest of terms. Explicitly linking this attack on his credibility with the bombings in Rome, Florence and Milan (where five people had been killed in August), the president said "first they used bombs, now they are trying the most ignoble and shameful of scandals" for the motive of damaging or reversing the process of change under way in the country. Angrily, he asserted that he would not "stand for" this smear campaign against him.[16] Unfortunately, he had no choice. Scalfaro would not be cleared of wrong-doing until the beginning of March 1994, and the allegations would hang like a shadow over his conduct for the next five months.

To add to the institutional chaos, parliament was busy discrediting itself even further in the eyes of public opinion. Article 8 of the new electoral law had provided for the representation of Italians living abroad. Thirty "world" deputies would be elected by Italians living abroad: Mega-constituencies (including one for Asia-Africa-Australia) were envisaged. Simply judged as a law, this piece of legislation was a grotesque work of Fellini-esque proportions (the much-revered film director died in November 1993). As Sebastiano Messina pointed out, it reversed the great motto of the Declaration of Independence by providing representation without taxation.[17] Inevitably, the 30 world deputies would become nothing more than lobbyists for the Italian community abroad; using their parliamentary clout to win concessions and privileges that their constituents would never have to pay for. Worse even than the law's inherent defects, however, was the maneuvering that accompanied its passage through parliament. A constitutional amendment was necessary to allow article 8 to pass; this meant that the Senate had to give its assent by a two-thirds majority. Italian constitutional law, however, offered another possibility. If 50 percent plus one of the Senate approved the law, Scalfaro would only be able to sign the bill into law after a three-month waiting period, in which time 500,000 citizens or one fifth of the members of the two chambers of parliament could call a referendum on the issue. With characteristic Machiavellianism, the DC and the PSI planned to coordinate their forces to ensure that this latter option prevailed. Their motive was obvious: By so doing, they could drag out the legislature a few months longer (for until the constitutionality of article 8 was established, Scalfaro could not call a national poll under the new electoral rules). They had left Bossi and Occhetto out of their calculations, however. As soon as the chief opposition parties got wind of the trick being played, they put aside their differences, reversed their previously positive attitude toward the bill and either abstained or voted against article 8. The DC and PSI were stranded with too few senators in the chamber to reach the quorum to pass the bill, and article 8 was thus struck from the electoral law amid heated -- and plainly absurd -- claims from the DC that the vote had invalidated the new electoral law as a whole. At long last, six months after the referendum, Scalfaro had *via libera* to call the new national elections the country so desperately needed.

The municipal elections thus represented a gigantic opinion poll on the country's future. In addition, the mayoralities of some of Italy's most important cities were to be decided, including Rome, Naples, Genoa, Venice, Palermo, and Trieste. Three main questions hovered over the poll. Would the League obtain an "outlet to the sea" by breaking out of its Lombardy-Venetia heartland and winning the mayoralties of the seaports of Genoa, Venice and Trieste? What would happen in the three big southern cities: Would the DC's networks of client voters enable it to retain its position as the leading party south of Rome? In Rome and Naples in particular, the MSI believed it had a chance to capitalize on public disgust at *tangentopoli*. Naples had been in tumult all Fall over the inadequacies of the city administration, which was deemed unfit to run the city by the central government in October. The MSI's candidate for the mayoralty in Naples was the glamorous Alessandra Mussolini, the grand-daughter of the Duce and niece of Sofia Loren. In Rome, the MSI's intelligent, youthful and comparatively presentable leader, Gianfranco Fini, was the party's candidate. In both cities, left coalitions based on the PDS were expected to challenge the DC and the MSI hard. Leftist coalitions were also the League's main opponents in the North. The third big question hanging over the poll was: Would the PDS's strategy of forming progressive coalitions achieve the same success as in June? This question was by no means susceptible to an easy answer. The national hierarchy of the PDS had been touched by the *Mani pulite* scandal in October 1993, when one of the junior prosecutors associated with the Milan pool sent an *avviso di garanzia* to the PDS's treasurer, Marcello Stefanini. After a bitter public row between themselves the Milan prosecutors later concluded that there was insufficient evidence to support the hypothesis that the PDS had been taking illegal contributions. Disgruntled voices were heard, however, insinuating that the pool's senior members were protecting the PDS.

In the event, the *Lega*, the MSI and the PDS all did well in the first ballot on November 21, 1993, though all three, especially the League, were left less than fully satisfied. The League became the largest single party in Genoa, Venice and Trieste, taking more than 25 percent of the vote in all three cities, but, lacking coalition partners, found itself out-gunned in the mayoral races. The League's candidates entered the run-offs in Genoa and Venice (in both cases well behind the united left's candidate), but managed to come only third in Trieste, being overtaken on the right by a candidate supported by the MSI and a civic list. The success in Trieste for the MSI, however, was eclipsed by its triumphs in the South. In Naples, the neo-fascists reached 31 percent (up from 9 percent in the 1992 national elections), and Alessandra Mussolini entered the mayoral run-off against the PDS's candidate, Antonio Bassolino. The MSI was largest party in the city. In Rome, Fini emulated Mussolini's feat, surging to 35 percent of the vote and finishing a close second to Francesco Rutelli, the Green minister for a day in April 1993, who was supported by the PDS, among other progressive forces. Again, the MSI, with 30.3 percent, was the largest party. Elsewhere in the *Mezzogiorno* and the Center-South the party also did well, entering mayoral run-offs in Latina and Benevento, for instance. The lees in the MSI's cup of victory came from its failure, Trieste apart, to make an impression in the North. The MSI's share of the vote in Genoa, Venice (where it was a derisory 2.9 percent) and other northern cities such as Alessandria, La Spezia, Trento and Lodi hardly budged from the levels obtained in April 1992.

The PDS, unlike both the League and the MSI, emerged from the ballot with a legitimate claim to be called a national party. The candidates it backed finished first in the poll in Rome, Naples, Genoa, Venice, and Trieste, not to mention any number of smaller cities. Yet a close look at the results, city by city, shows that the PDS would have been unable to win any of these municipalities on its own. Only in Genoa did the party obtain a fraction more than 25 percent of the vote.

The big loser of the November 21 poll was the DC. Despite the fact that most of the cities under contention were in South, the party's loss of dominance within the political system was underlined even more cruelly than in June 1993. In Naples, for instance, the DC took just 10 percent of the vote, down from 31 percent in April 1992. In Rome, the DC's candidate got a mere 12 percent of the vote, down from 27.5 percent. Elsewhere, the collapse was even more dramatic. In Caserta, a largeish town near Naples, the DC's vote fell from 48 percent in 1992 to less than 20 percent. In the Sicilian provincial capital of Caltanisetta, the fall was from 54 percent to 22 percent. The biggest blow of all, however, came in Palermo, where the DC lost the mayoralty for the first time since the war. There, the DC's vote plunged from 35 percent to just 13 percent as Leoluca Orlando's *Rete* party swept the poll. Orlando scored 75 percent in the mayoral race, the only candidate in a major city to be elected in the first ballot. For the DC, the lesson of the November 21 poll was that its vaunted strength in southern Italy was much less imposing than it seemed. Deprived by *Mani pulite* and the Ciampi government's austerity policies of their habitual injections of cash and jobs, the client networks built up by DC in the previous 40 years saw no reason to maintain their loyalty to a party manifestly in need of the last rites.

The second round of balloting exalted and enthused the left. Progressive candidates were victorious in the run-offs in all the major cities being contested. In Rome, Rutelli held off Fini; in Naples, Bassolino kept Mussolini from adding the tricolor sash worn by an Italian *sindaco* from her already imposing wardrobe of designer clothes. The *leghisti* were kept at bay in the three northern ports. All in all, the PDS added 47 more mayors to the large numbers it had won in June 1993. This result was widely interpreted as a vote for stability. The lire and the stockmarket both rose sharply upon news of Italy's likely turn leftward: An unprecedented event in modern Italian history. In the aftermath of the poll, the conviction was strong that the PDS, together with *Alleanza democratica*, *La Rete*, the Greens and (more dubiously) *Rifondazione comunista*, would get its chance to govern once national elections were held. The collapse of the DC (and the political peregrinations of Segni, who had broken with *Alleanza democratica* in October, pronounced himself the man who could stop the *Lega* in November, but who then opened negotiations with the League after the December results) meant that there was no coherent centrist force to draw voters away from the left. The MSI's surge was widely regarded as a protest vote that could be reversed by clean government; the League seemed destined, all of a sudden, to play a role resembling that of the Bavarian CSU in Germany. Instead of the Leviathan fondly predicted by Bossi in June, the League now seemed condemned to remain a right-wing regionalist party commanding massive levels of support within certain geographical boundaries, but incapable of projecting its values on a national scale.

Forza Italia!

This prospect of a coherent and relatively purposeful left confronting a fragmented and divided right alarmed the media mogul Silvio Berlusconi. On November 23, Berlusconi announced his preference for Fini over Rutelli in the run-off for the mayoralty of Rome.This was not (or not just) a knee-jerk aversion to liberal ideas. The following day, he gave voice to a rumor that had been circulating for several months and announced that he was thinking of establishing a new political party to represent the center-right viewpoint. For the next few weeks, Berlusconi's television networks, his newspapers and magazines, and other media under his control, disseminated propaganda on behalf of *Forza Italia* (Come on, Italy!), as the new party was unoriginally dubbed. The fact that the party name recalled the DC's uninspiring 1987 election slogan, however, did little to brake the enthusiasm of Berlusconi's supporters. By January 1994, 1300 *Forza Italia* clubs had sprung up around the country and Berlusconi and his executives were at work choosing possible parliamentary candidates.

Silvio Berlusconi is a Milanese entrepreneur who made his first fortune in the construction industry, building -- with the help of mysterious funds from a secretive Swiss holding company -- the upscale housing complex known as Milano II in the early 1970s. From construction, he branched into television, advertising, marketing, insurance and super-markets. Fininvest, Berlusconi's holding company, is one of the world's largest private firms. In the 1980s,

Berlusconi became one of the emblematic figures of Italian life. Favored with Craxi's friendship (Craxi was best man when Berlusconi re-married in 1990, and Berlusconi was one of the few people, as Craxi liked to put it, with "access to the fridge," in the Socialist leader's home), Berlusconi took advantage of television deregulation to establish a rival television monopoly to the state television service. His three channels, Canale 5, Rete 4 and Italia 1, by serving up a relentless diet of action movies, sport and naked women, rapidly won a large segment of the television audience from a viewing public tired of the politicized boredom of the RAI channels, though attempts to export his formula to France and Spain were less rewarding. In the mid-1980s, Berlusconi raised his public profile by buying the historic AC Milan soccer club and turning it into the most successful team in the world in the late 1980s and early 1990s. AC Milan's huge network of supporters' clubs would become a useful conduit for *Forza Italia* publicity after Berlusconi's decision to diversify his activities into politics. In 1990, to complete his media colossus, he added the Mondadori publishing company to his empire, though he was compelled to disgorge *La Repubblica* and *L'Espresso* after Andreotti voiced his preoccupation that the concentration of media businesses in Berlusconi's hands was too great.[18] After the passage of a somewhat toothless law regulating the media later in 1990, Berlusconi was also obliged to cede nominal control of the Milanese daily *Il Giornale* to his brother Paolo, though nobody had any illusions that he had renounced his control over the paper.

Politically, Berlusconi never fully exposed his hand. Except for the businessman's standard rhetoric in praise of private enterprise, his deepest political views were not widely known. He was a member of the P2 masonic lodge, but his chief motive for joining seems to have been a desire to network with Italy's rich and powerful, not a marked sympathy for the neo-fascist extremism that permeated that organization. When his three national TV channels began broadcasting news bulletins, moreover, they were somewhat less sycophantic to the parties than the party-controlled state TV service. Certainly, Berlusconi's flagship evening news program on Canale 5 gave generous and supportive space to the *Mani pulite* investigation -- *Il Biscione*'s concern for Craxi's individual plight did not extend to diminishing the audience ratings. In fairness, it should be said that the Milanese entrepreneur was one of the few businessmen and media figures whose friendship with the Socialist leader did not waver after Craxi's disgrace in the Spring of 1993.

Berlusconi, in short, should be seen as less an ideologue than an opportunist. He cosied up to the political elite because he knew, Italy being Italy, that he would never be able to fulfil his business goals without political backing. To the same end, Berlusconi was also careful to give cheap advertising during electoral campaigns to all the principal parties. This practice, incidentally, may well explain why, of the major Italian corporate bosses, he alone has hitherto managed to stay out of *tangentopoli*. His brother -- who is widely regarded as a front man for his more famous sibling -- has not been so lucky. He was arrested in February 1994, and charged with passing a $700,000 bribe to the parties. Indeed, Berlusconi's motive for entering politics in November 1993 was arguably motivated as much by business as ideological reasons. Like most self-made men, Berlusconi had built his empire with the help of debt -- more than $2 billion, if reports are to be believed.[19] The election of a PDS-dominated government would therefore have spelled disaster for Fininvest. The PDS made no bones of the fact that they intended to strip Berlusconi of at least one of his TV networks and make him slim down the rest of his media operations. Shorn of his most valuable assets, *Sua Emittenza* might have struggled to keep his organization solvent.

Events both prior and subsequent to the second round of balloting in the municipal elections only encouraged him to press ahead with the new political formation. The scandal of the League's involvement in *tangentopoli* erupted on December 7, when the party treasurer was arrested, leaving opposition to the PDS suddenly looking weaker than ever. In the meantime, the Cusani trial had begun in earnest, with the testimony of the main party leaders. The trial must have squashed any lingering doubts in Berlusconi's mind that the political old guard who had been his protectors might be capable of mounting a comeback. One by one they came before Di Pietro and Cusani's advocate Giuliano Spazzali, in theory to give evidence, in practice to be judged by the watching millions on TV. Carlo Vizzini of the PSDI admitted taking 200 million lire; so did Giorgio La Malfa of the PRI, whose dignified performance won him many friends. Claudio Martelli appeared in court and admitted to having taken 500 million lire. Severino Citaristi, the DC's unfortunate treasurer, clearly anxious to unburden himself and retire to private life, revealed that the DC's main party organization (not to mention individual politicians and *correnti*) had required 85 billion lire per year in illegal contributions. He had been instructed by both De Mita and Forlani to raise this money through illegal donations. In particular, he had taken several billion lire from the Ferruzzi group in January 1991 and before the 1992 elections. Paolo Cirino Pomicino admitted to taking 5 billion lire from Montedison, but also cast the inquiry's net wider, alleging that Giuliano Amato had been involved in the scheme to block Gardini's takeover of Enimont.

On December 17, Forlani and Craxi gave evidence. Interrogated first, Forlani was humiliated by Di Pietro's incisive questioning. A line of froth was visible at his mouth as he denied the undeniable and insisted that he recalled nothing about the Enimont affair, nor knew anything of the staggering sums of money that were flowing through a party administration nominally under his supervision. Forlani's embarrassing performance was followed by an arrogant and assertive Bettino Craxi. Showing unusual forbearance, Di Pietro allowed Craxi to speechify rather than testify. The former Socialist leader argued that the illegal system of financing had been common to all the parties, including and especially the PCI, which had taken money from Moscow for decades, and was "on a par" with the parties in *tangentopoli*. Without offering a shadow of proof, Craxi named Giorgio Napolitano and Giovanni Spadolini of the PRI as prominent politicians who should have received *avvisi di garanzia*. On January 5, the parade of top politicians came to an end with the testimony of Umberto Bossi. The leader of the *Lega* affirmed that its treasurer had taken Sama's 200 million lire, which had in any case been stolen from the League's headquarters shortly after the money was paid, but that he himself had been unaware of the payment until afterward.[20] This unlikely story weakened Bossi's main argument: That Sandro Patelli, the treasurer, had been right to accept an illegal offer of cash because in that "historic moment" before the 1992 elections, they had needed it to mount some sort of competition to the big spending electoral machines of the thoroughly corrupt *partitocrazia*. Giorgio La Malfa's defense had always been a less defiant version of the same theme. Not the least of the ills of money politics, Italian style was the fact that the corruption of the DC and the PSI had meant that nobody else could stay clean.

In mid-January, Scalfaro dissolved parliament. The day of the election was set for March 27, which coincided with the Jewish feast of Passover and aroused objections from Italy's small Jewish community. Ciampi solved the problem by allowing voting on March 28 as well. Scalfaro's long-awaited move initiated a month of febrile political activity. On January 22, Martinazzoli announced that the DC would fight the elections as the *Partito Popolare Italiano* (PPI): After 50 years, the DC was no more. As it died, long-suppressed ideological controversies came bubbling to the surface. A splinter group of anti-communist rightists, convinced that Martinazzoli and the party's reformist wing were leaning towards a post-election pact with the PDS, left noisily to form the Christian Democratic Centre (CCD). Meanwhile, Gianfranco Fini of the MSI announced that the neo-fascists would be fighting the elections as the *Alleanza Nazionale* (AN). Fini had long planned this gesture. More a conservative than a fascist, he had long edged the party toward shedding its blackshirt image and its nostalgia for Mussolini, and casting itself as a modern force of government. Segni and Roberto Maroni, Bossi's deputy and the acknowledged leader of the League's left, were meanwhile holding talks over a possible electoral pact between the *Lega* and Segni's reformers. On January 25, it seemed that the two sides were close to an agreement. Bossi, however, brusquely switched horses in mid-stream and announced that the League was interested in collaborating with Berlusconi, who officially entered the lists in the last week of January. By the end of the first week of February, Berlusconi had cobbled together an electoral agreement with the League in northern Italy, and a similar deal with the National Alliance, the CCD and a group of ex-Liberals known as the Union of the Center (UC) in the South and Center of the country. The hard bargaining over who would run candidates in which constituencies was still to come, but the right had at least assured that it would not split its vote. Segni, hung out to dry, was forced to return to Martinazzoli and the PPI to create the "Pact for Italy." For the referendum movement's leader, this was a personal and political defeat. It is hard, however, to dispute the conclusion that Segni had got his just political deserts. Segni left *Alleanza democratica* in the lurch, but then relied entirely on his reputation to keep him at the center of the political scene. By the time he was driven to treat with Bossi, he looked like "a colonel without troops."[21] Unlike Berlusconi, with his three TV channels, Segni brought no reinforcements to the League. Moreover, if Bossi had not agreed to cooperate with Berlusconi, he risked a three-way fight in the League's heartland with the PDS and *Forza Italia*. Sensibly, Bossi decided to cut his losses, though allying the League to a man who had been so close to Craxi and the old PSI went against the grain for many *Lega* activists. Bossi also flatly refused to harness the *Carroccio* to Fini's *Alleanza Nazionale*. At any rate in February 1994, the League was insistent that its federalist ideology was not compatible with the MSI's strident nationalism.

While Berlusconi had been busy achieving at least a semblance of unity on the right, the left had been equally active. At the beginning of February, Occhetto presented the Progressive Alliance, together with its symbol, a stylised ocean wave about to break upon the shore. The progressive pact was composed of six parties and two splinter groups: the PDS, *Rifondazione comunista*, *Alleanza democratica*, *La Rete*, the PSI, and the Greens were recognized forces; the Social Christians and Socialist Renewal added some slight weight to the progressive slate. These parties were no less uncomfortable bed-fellows than the three main groupings in the right-wing pacts. The chief source of trouble was the presence of *Rifondazione comunista*. Many of *Alleanza democratica*'s activists were unhappy about sharing the ballot with unreconstructed supporters of Brezhnev and Andropov, but electoral arithmetic allowed no other solution. *Rifondazione* could count on about 6 percent of the national electorate and was very strong in a number of industrial cities the left had to win if it was going to take power.

At the beginning of the campaign, the progressives were confident that the elections would be the crowning conclusion of the Italian revolution. The left would win, even if it had to rely on the goodwill of Pact for Italy for a safe parliamentary majority. Martinazzoli had similar expectations. The reason that the PPI abstained from coming to terms with either the right or the left is that its leaders assumed, especially after Segni rejoined their ranks, that the ex-DC would hold the balance of power within the new parliament. As soon as the campaign began, however, it became clear that the tide was ebbing to the right. The presence of *Rifondazione comunista* was to some degree responsible for this, especially after *Rifondazione*'s newly elected leader, Fausto Bertinotti, proposed taxing income from government bonds and leaving NATO. The campaign, however, was won by the right for other reasons. Berlusconi unsurprisingly marketed himself shrewdly, sticking to sound bites and prepared speeches, and avoiding direct debates. He handled the arrest of his brother with skill. The comprehensive party networks of the League, the MSI and the CCD, plus *Forza Italia*'s hundreds of clubs, gave the right an organizational edge over the left and center. More painfully for the progressives, the right won the ideological battle. Berlusconi made a number of seductive, but unsound policy statements (suggesting, for instance, that unemployment could be reduced by one million by the simple expedient of each small business hiring one worker), but he also articulated a competent-sounding program of measures to slim down the state and to introduce private competition in the health service, the schools and the pensions system. The "progressives" found themselves defending the status quo, and thus stamped themselves as opponents of change among millions of Italians fed up with the wastefulness, patronage politics and inefficiency of the Italian state.[22] Berlusconi also probably won sympathy from what, rightly or wrongly, appeared to be a coordinated attempt to discredit him. Rumors that Berlusconi was under investigation for having made payoffs to the Mafia in Sicily were attributed to Luciano Violante of the PDS; while on March 23, the *procura* of Palmi made a dramatic search of *Forza Italia*'s headquarters. The ostensible purpose of this search was that of obtaining a full list of *Forza Italia*'s activists and candidates as part of the Palmi attorneys' investigation into illegal freemasonry, but there was no reason why this document could not have been sent through the post. If the Palmi authorities were seeking to discredit the Milanese entrepreneur, the attempt backfired: Berlusconi treated the prosecutors' move as a golden opportunity to denounce the intimidatory tactics being used against him.

The Counter-Revolution

As part of the new electoral law, the last two weeks of the campaign were conducted without opinion polls. This absence of official polling data to a certain extent disguised the gains being made by the right-wing pacts, though by mid-March, it was becoming obvious that early expectations of a Progressive victory would need to be drastically revised. In the event, the *Polo della libertà* ("Liberty Pole"), as Berlusconi's set of alliances was named, won a stunning victory. Even the darkest forecasts of the Italian left had not anticipated the right-wing grouping obtaining a huge majority in the Chamber of Deputies, and being within a handful of seats of winning an overall majority in the Senate as well.

The right's triumph was especially sweet for Berlusconi. On the day the results came in, *La Voce*, a new center-right newspaper edited by Indro Montanelli, whom Berlusconi had forced from *Il Giornale* in January, featured a clever photo-montage of *Il Cavaliere* holding Achille Occhetto's severed head.[23] Measured by the percentage of preferences cast for the PR redistribution, *Forza Italia* emerged as the biggest party in Italy with a stunning 21 percent: An amazing result for a party formed just three months before the poll. It had pulled off the difficult feat of outscoring the League in most of Lombardy and Venetia, run a good second to the PDS in the central regions (and proved able to take votes away from traditional leftist voters), and upset *La Rete* in Sicily, taking more than 30 percent of the vote throughout the island. All told, Berlusconi could count on just over 100 *Forza Italia* deputies and about 40 senators. Berlusconi's support had also helped the election of more than 30 CCD members, along with a handful of Marco Pannella's followers, and members of the UC. Only the generosity of his deals with the AN and the Northern League in the pre-electoral negotiations prevented him from amassing more representatives at Rome than any other party.

In terms of parliamentarians, the League was the largest component of the "Liberty Pole." The League's representation at Montecitorio advanced from 55 in 1992 to 106. The League also obtained more than 50 senators. This huge surge in numbers, however, was a product of the FPTP system. In percentage terms, the election was a setback for the League. The *Lega*'s share of the national vote was only 8.4 percent, down slightly from April 1992, and down dramatically from the huge victories of June and December 1993. In Milan, the League's vote collapsed from the 40 percent obtained by Formentini, to just 16 percent. In only one electoral college (Lombardy 2, which contains Varese, Sondrio and Como, the League's birthplace and heartland) was the *Carroccio* the most popular party, though Bossi's movement ran a close second to *Forza Italia* in the rest of Lombardy and in Venetia and Friuli Venezia Giulia. Robbed by Berlusconi of its monopoly on neo-conservative economic rhetoric, the League's bubble of support was deflated, and Bossi's movement was unambiguously reduced to the status of a purely regional power.

The AN, by contrast, did moderately well all over the country, and spectacularly well in parts of the Center and South. With 13.5 percent of the PR preferences, the ex-MSI became the third largest party in the country. In the North, the party scored steadily in the 5-10 percent range, doing slightly better than in December 1993. In the Center, it did surprisingly well in "red" bastions like Umbria and the Marche. Elsewhere in the Center-South, Fini could gloat over five major victories. In the electoral colleges of Abruzzo, Molise, Lazio 1, Campania 2 and Puglia, the former neo-fascists emerged as the largest party. The high point was reached in Puglia, where the AN took 26.5 percent of the PR preferences, though this figure was inflated by the fact that *Forza Italia* did not manage to get on the ballot. In Lazio 1 (which contains Rome), 26 percent of the electorate preferred the ex-MSI. These results, which were easily the best of the post-war period for the Italian far right, enabled the AN to march a parliamentary contingent of 150 on Rome. Table 8.1. shows the margin of the right's overall victory.

Table 9.1: The Italian Elections of March 1994

List	Percentage Share of PR preferences	No. of seats	
		Chamber	Senate
Liberty Pole	42.9	366	156
Pact for Italy	15.7	46	31
Progressive Alliance	32.2	213	122
Others	9.2	5	6

Source: The *Italian Journal*, (8) 1994. No 1&2, p 3.

The biggest loser of the election was Pact for Italy. Mario Segni was personally and politically humiliated by the results. Segni's own list scored just 4.6 percent of PR preferences, and thus made the 4 percent threshold only by a whisker. All the party's deputies, including Segni himself, were elected by proportional representation. The PPI plunged to a mere 11.1 percent, much less than half of the figure obtained by the DC in April 1992. It won a mere four constituencies directly. Pact for Italy's vote in regions such as Venetia, Molise, and Basilicata, which historically had given 45-50 percent pluralities to the DC, slumped to well under 20 percent. The PPI did not win a plurality of PR preferences in any region, and came second in only one (Basilicata). The DC's hegemony of the South was splintered four ways, with the AN emerging as the largest party, slightly ahead of the PDS, and quite a way ahead of *Forza Italia*. The PPI scored a dismal 12.3 percent to finish a humiliating fourth.

The elections were clearly a tremendous delusion for the Progressive Alliance. As in 1948 and 1976, the Italian middle-class, faced with a genuine opportunity of giving the left a chance to govern, had scuttled away to the safety of the center-right. As Achille Occhetto scornfully commented in the aftermath of the poll, the Italians, having lost "Mother DC," had gone running after "a new daddy."[24] The PDS itself did not badly: Overall, it obtained 20.4 percent, up 4 percent from 1992. The Progressive Alliance, however, was a one-man team. Unlike Berlusconi, who had the luxury of two powerful allies with strong regional bases of support, Occhetto was hampered by the dismal performance of his partners. *Rifondazione comunista*, with 6 percent of the PR preferences just succeeded in reaching the 4 percent cut; *La Rete*, the PSI (just 2.2 percent, down over 12 percent from 1992), the Greens, and *Alleanza democratica* did not. As a consequence, nearly three million "progressive" votes failed to contribute to the election of a single deputy.[25]

The votes counted, the next task was to form a government. There were two chief difficulties. First, could Berlusconi become prime minister? How could anyone who already owned most of the private sector media be placed in charge of running the state? Many worried (and still worry) that the *partitocrazia* would be replaced by a *telecrazia* if Berlusconi's power to influence his business concerns was not curbed. Second, how could the *Lega Nord* and the ex-MSI be welded into a governing coalition? On the morrow of the election results, Bossi immediately raised the stakes by proclaiming that the League would not join a government that included the "hangman right."[26] For a few days, the possibility of forming a new administration dangled tantalisingly out of Berlusconi's reach. The familiar ritual of the *giro di consultazioni* began; Bossi, Fini and Berlusconi squabbled and negotiated in the best tradition of Craxi, Andreotti, Forlani, and De Mita. And as usual, the crisis was resolved. With ill grace, the *Lega* came to terms. Bossi's position was numerically strong in terms of parliamentarians, but electorally weak. Many of the *leghisti* were very well aware that they owed their place in parliament to Berlusconi as much as Bossi; the leader of the *Lega Nord* could not be sure that there would not be a split in his ranks if he failed to honor the spirit of his agreement with *Forza Italia*. Moreover, *Forza Italia* had already showed that it could take votes from the League in its heartland. Bossi doubtless realized that from his point of view it was better to lie low for a while and not run the risk of provoking fresh elections. After all, Berlusconi's past is not pristine and his electorate is volatile. The fact that this meant swallowing the AN's participation in the government was, however, genuinely unsettling to many of the League's senior members, Bossi included. Bossi's post-electoral posturing was doubtless partially tactical: He wanted as many top ministries as he could get and threatening to break the electoral alliance was one way of achieving his objectives. At the same time, the League has always been adamant that its decentralizing, anti-statist philosophy is the ideological polar opposite of the corporatism and nationalism of Italian fascism. The AN also, as a mainly southern party, was unlikely to go along with the League's long-standing plans to halt the drain of resources to the *Mezzogiorno*; nor was the CCD, which largely consists of veteran DC hack politicians with substantial client networks. After a few days of reciprocal insults, however, the League seemed to win a promise from both Berlusconi and Gianfranco Fini that federalism in some form would be on the new administration's agenda, and the League bit the bullet of the AN's taking a government role.

The new right-wing *maggioranza* was thus able to elect Irene Pivetti, a 31-year-old woman who is one of the few devout Catholics in the *Lega Nord*'s hierarchy, as the new Speaker of the Chamber of Deputies. The new President of the Senate is Giuseppe Scognamiglio (*Forza Italia*), a former chancellor of the Rome university and Liberal senator. Once it had been decided that a committee of wise men would make recommendations to ensure that Berlusconi's business interests would be separated from his new political power, Scalfaro entrusted the "burden" of forming the new government to Berlusconi on April 30 (more than a month after the election). After nearly a fortnight's consultations Berlusconi was able to present his cabinet, which shared the senior posts out between the parties with scrupulous fairness. The League had good reasons to be satisfied. Roberto Maroni became minister of the interior and deputy prime minister. The League also gained the ministries dealing with European unity and regional affairs, the universities and science, industry and budget. Francesco Speroni became minister for institutional reform. The AN obtained fewer of the top jobs. Admittedly one deputy prime ministership was reserved for the AN, but otherwise the party had to content itself with second rank posts (agriculture, environment, transport, cultural affairs). Fini ensured that all AN ministers were conservatives untainted by a fascist past, but this did not stop outsiders such as Jacques Delors and François Mitterrand voicing their preoccupation at the spectacle of fascism once again being in the saddle in Italy.

Forza Italia -- justly -- reserved the lion's share of the top jobs for itself. The new foreign minister, Antonio Martino, hailed from Forza Italia. Martino immediately began taking a more assertive line than his predecessors in the post. Forza Italia also took control of defence, justice, public works and a number of other cabinet seats. Several top ministers were formerly connected to Fininvest. Gianni Letta, Berlusconi's right-hand man at the TV company, became the Prime Minister's parliamentary secretary; Cesare Previti, Fininvest's lawyer, was appointed minister for defense. Most egregiously of all, the new minister for relations with parliament was television personality Giuliano Ferrara, of colpo di spugna fame.

Despite the familiar horsetrading between the parties of the maggioranza, the plethora of small parties in the new parliament, and the dismaying prominence of men as closely associated with the worst features of the old regime as Ferrara, the novelty of Berlusconi's administration was unquestionable. Italy had chosen the most right-wing government in its post-war history; more rightist even than the 1960 Tambroni administration. Neither the AN nor Forza Italia have convincing democratic credentials. The AN is full of people who sincerely believe that Mussolini was the greatest political figure of the twentieth century, and while Fini insists that his party is a "post-fascist" movement, his supporters' often fanatical attachment to the symbols and mythology of Italian fascism throw his assertions into doubt. When the membership of the AN gather together, black shirts, Roman salutes and apologetics for the death squads of the Salò Republic abound. Forza Italia appears undemocratic in a different way. Any movement that is so blatantly the vehicle for the ambitions of a single man cannot but arouse disquiet. Berlusconi's recent triumph is also the most striking instance hitherto recorded of the power of the media and skilful marketing to affect the political debate.

True, *Forza Italia* could not have won without a program capable of attracting support among a broad segment of the electorate, but long before Berlusconi had even announced his legislative priorities, clever advertising had carved out a niche for his embyronic party. *Forza Italia* did not so much win the 1994 elections in Italy, as obtain significant market share.

Notes

1. I owe this analysis of the Rauti interlude's influence on the development of the MSI to Piero Ignazi's chapter on the Italian neo-fascist movement in his recent *L'Estrema destra in Europa*, Bologna (Il Mulino), 1994, especially pp 183-184.
2. Opinion poll in *La Repubblica*, April 23, 1993.
3. A full list of Bossi's intemperances before the poll in Milan is recounted in Giampaolo Pansa, *L'Anno dei barbari*, Milan (Sperling & Kupfer) 1993, pp 305-311.
4. Mino Martinazzoli, quoted by the *Indipendente*, May 27, 1993.
5. A "historic shove" is my translation of "una storica spallata," which was the headline for Eugenio Scalfari's comment on the first round of balloting in the municipal elections in *La Repubblica*, June 8, 1993.
6. Umberto Bossi, quoted *La Repubblica*, ibid.
7. Umberto Bossi, interview in *Panorama*, July 4, 1993.
8. By way of explaining the new system for the Senate, imagine a region with six seats in parliament, four of which are to be awarded by FPTP, and two by PR. The following results are obtained (winners are in bold):

		Party		
Constituency	A	B	C	D
One	**12,000**	10,000	9,000	6,000
Two	10,000	9,000	**13,000**	7,000
Three	10,000	11,000	4,000	**12,000**
Four	9,000	6,000	**14,000**	5,000
Total Votes	41,000	36,000	40,000	30,000
Subtracted	12,000	0	27,000	12,000
Eligible for PR	29,000	36,000	13,000	18,000

The D'Hondt formula is then applied:

	Divider	
Party	1	2
A	29,000 (2)	14,500
B	36,000 (1)	18,000
C	13,000	6,500
D	18,000	9,000

Party A thus takes two seats, as does party C. Parties B and D each get one seat.

For elections to the *Camera dei deputati*, the following technique would have been used. Let us imagine a party that obtained 200,000 PR preferences in one of the 27 electoral colleges, but won only one constituency directly, by a margin of 40,000 votes to the 24,999 votes obtained by its nearest rival. This party would lose 25,000 preferences from its total (24,999+1) and would thus transfer 175,000 votes to the single national constituency, if the party had met the 4 percent threshold requirement on the national level. The system "corrects," in other words, at the expense of parties that have won directly. Notice, however, that this is partially compensated for by obtaining a big majority. Obviously, the larger the winner's majority is, the fewer votes will be subtracted. To adjust for this possibility, the new electoral law subtracts a minimum of 25 percent of the total ballots cast from the winner's total. Thus in a constituency where 80,000 votes are counted, 20,000 will be subtracted from the winning total, regardless of the score of the second-placed party. A further complication arises from the fact that the seats available by direct election were contested by coalitions of parties (ie. The *Polo della libertà*) while the PR votes were cast for individual parties. This difficulty was avoided by sharing out the loss of preferences among the constituent parties of such a coalition in proportion to their share of its joint PR preference total in the college. The method of subtracting part or all of the winners' totals is known in Italian as *lo scorporo* (the subtractor).

9. My source for this discussion of the electoral system was *L'Italia vota: una guida alle elezioni politiche del 27-28 marzo*, Rome (Office of the Prime Minister) 1994. A full-length English language guide to the new system is Richard S. Katz, "The 1993 Parliamentary Electoral Reform," in Carol Mershon and Gianfranco Pasquino (eds), *Italian Politics A Review*, (vol 9), Boulder (Westview), Bologna (Il Mulino) 1994.

10. For an account of the charges directed at De Lorenzo, see Leo Sisti, "Ladri di pillolette," *L'Espresso*, July 4, 1993.

11. *L'Espresso* published the confession of the official, Duilio Poggiolini, in its November 28, 1993, edition.

12. Cagliari's suicide note was reported by Claudio Rinaldi, "Anche gli eroi si stancano," *L'Espresso*, August 1, 1993.

13. Quoted Marcella Andreoli, *Processo all'Italia*, Milan (Sperling & Kupfer) 1994, p 155.

14. For details of the Enimont scam -- the word is used deliberately -- see Antonio Carlucci and Leo Sisti, "La madre di tutti i tangenti," *L'Espresso*, August 8, 1993; Giuseppe Turani, "La favola di Ravenna finita in carta straccia," *La Repubblica*, August 2, 1993; Marcella Andreoli, *Processo all'Italia*, is a useful source of "color" on the Enimont scandal's protagonists, but it frustratingly lacks a solid chapter explaining the financial intricacies behind the *maxi-tangente*. Another excellent recent book on the Cusani trial that remedies this deficiency is Andrea Pamparana, *Il Processo Cusani: politici e faccendieri della prima repubblica*, Milan (Mondadori) 1994.

15. Roberta Visco, "La Lega vince ma non convince," *La Repubblica*, October 3/4, 1993.

16. Text of the televised appeal to the nation made by President Scalfaro on the evening of November 3, 1993. "Stand for" is my translation of "io non ci sto."

17. Sebastiano Messina, "I deputati mondiali," *La Repubblica*, October 13, 1993.

18. For an account of Andreotti's role, see Giampaolo Pansa, *L'Intrigo*, Milan (Sperling & Kupfer), especially Chapter 13.

19. An in depth inquiry into the state of Fininvest's finances is to be found in Giovanni Ruggieri and Mario Guarino, *Berlusconi Inchiesta sul signor TV*, Milan (Kaos edizioni) 1994. See especially Chapter 11, "L'ultima spiaggia nel mare dei debiti," especially pp 255-260. Berlusconi, in the past, unsuccessfully sued the two authors for alleging that he was a member of the P2. The theme of the book is that Berlusconi was far closer to the upper reaches of the P2 than he has admitted and that his strategy of building an alternative media pole to the state-dominated RAI was in keeping with the P2's plans. The two authors also give an outstanding description of how Berlusconi's political contacts enabled him to first flout Italy's laws giving monopoly television rights to the state and then shape the legislative constraints on private media groups.

20. These paragraphs on the Cusani trial draw on Andreoli, *Processo all'Italia*, pp 149-170.

21. Gianfranco Pasquino, "The Unexpected Alternation," paper presented to the Pennsylvania Political Science Association, April 8-9, 1994, at Duquesne University, Pittsburgh PA, p 11.

22. Ibid., p 24-25.

23. "Vince la Destra," *La Voce*, March 29, 1994. Montanelli's editorial was titled "Chaos as predicted." Montanelli called Berlusconi's coalition "a right-wing facsimile."

24. Achille Occhetto, interview in *La Repubblica*, March 30, 1994.

25. My analysis of the election results owes much to Pasquino, "The Unexpected Alternation," and to the post-election surveys of *La Repubblica, La Voce* and *Corriere della Sera* on March 29-30. Discussions of the Italian election and their significance in English are: Robert H. Evans, "Italy, Quo vadis?" *Italian Journal*, 1994, No 1 & 2, pp 4-12; Edmondo Berselli, "Solution on the Right: The Evolving Political Scenario," Ibid., pp 13-21; Mark Gilbert, "Italy Turns Rightwards," *Contemporary Review* (128) July 1994, pp 4-10.

26. Bossi's actual words were "la destra forcaiolo."

10

Premier Berlusconi

Even the best advertising and slickest media presentation cannot indefinitely disguise a bad product from the consumer. From the moment it took office, Berlusconi's administration was plagued by two uncomfortable truths that even Fininvest's image-polishers were unable to hide. First, Berlusconi is too profoundly implicated with the old regime to pass himself off as a breath of fresh air in Italian political life. Second, the Milanese entrepreneur is both afraid and unable to separate his business persona from his new political duties.

Berlusconi's government began with a dramatic victory in the elections to the European parliament held at the beginning of June 1994. *Forza Italia*'s share of the vote leaped to over 30 percent, mostly at the expense of his two main coalition partners. Berlusconi also had the satisfaction of seeing his main political rival, the PDS, briefly split in two by the Euro-poll results. The PDS lost ground relative to March 1994, a defeat that left Achille Occhetto, Italy's most battered politician, with no option but to resign. Two candidates presented themselves as Occhetto's replacement: Walter Veltroni, the editor of *L'Unità*, and Massimo D'Alema. Occhetto supported Veltroni, who is associated in the public mind with the notion of continuing the Italian left's troubled passage to the political center still further by creating a Democratic Party embracing all of Italy's progressive parties, but not *Rifondazione comunista*. The party machine, however, was in favor of D'Alema. Occhetto's long-time deputy is arguably too much a creature of the party apparatus, but he is undeniably clever and is fully seized of the necessity for further modernization of the PDS's ideology and political program.

Nevertheless, the PDS's latest defeat left Berlusconi emperor of all he surveyed. Flushed with victory, Berlusconi undertook a series of ill-judged and arrogant measures that by the beginning of August had severely tarnished his image and had thrown into doubt the long-term survival of his government. Firstly, in June, Berlusconi compelled the resignation of the committee of business and economics professors that had been appointed by the Ciampi administration to oversee the state television network's restructuring program. By bringing standard business techniques to bear, the "professors" had already rooted out much waste, over-manning and inefficiency in the RAI hierarchy. The result of this company re-engineering was that by the Spring of 1994, RAI was competing ruthlessly with Fininvest for advertising revenues. By halting the professors in their tracks, the suspicion grew that Berlusconi was using his government role to favor his private interests. None of the parties in his government, however, can claim to be entirely innocent of trying to influence the RAI. The League and the AN both insisted on their fair share of patronage in the television service and in the state sector more generally.

Berlusconi's next false step was to introduce his own version of the *colpo di spugna* decree. In mid-July, Berlusconi and his justice minister, the ex-PLI grandee Alfredo Biondi, introduced a decree that would have outlawed the use of preventive detention for a number of offences, including corruption and extortion. A by now familiar sequence of events followed. The *Mani pulite* team in Milan held a press conference at which they effectively announced their resignation by publicly asking to be transferred to other duties. The press, led by *La Repubblica*, subjected the proposed decree to destructive criticism. Thousands of faxed messages of outrage began pouring into government offices, newspapers and the presidential palace. A rejuvenated Umberto Bossi blasted the decree, especially after the League's chief representative in the cabinet, Roberto Maroni, insisted that Biondi had circulated a different and less controversial version of the proposal to his ministerial colleagues. The AN, while more supportive of Berlusconi than the *Lega Nord* had been, made their lack of enthusiasm for Biondi's move abundantly clear. Faced with the collapse of his government, Berlusconi floundered badly and with ill grace consented to transform the decree into a parliamentary bill, effectively killing all hope of its ever being made law.

Why had Berlusconi made such a blatant political gaffe? In effect, he had voluntarily exposed himself to widespread condemnation and had also allowed himself to be humiliated in public by his coalition's junior partners. Bossi and Fini, who had seemed like dwarves after the European elections, suddenly loomed large as equal members of the government. To use a business analogy, Berlusconi had been brutally reminded that in the government he was not a majority shareholder and could not, therefore, do as he pleased. Within a week, however, Berlusconi's haste to introduce the Biondi decree was explained. The *Mani pulite* team's investigations, which were now centered on corruption within the *Guardia di finanza* (the division of the Italian police that concerns itself with tax and financial fraud and auditing), led to a spate of arrests among the top ranks of Fininvest. A number of executives were accused of paying off the tax authorities in return for carrying out a merely superficial review of the media conglomerate's affairs. Bad though this development was for Berlusconi, he immediately worsened his own position by convening, on the evening of July 24, a secret meeting in his villa with his principal advisors (including government ministers) as well as *the lawyers of the arrested executives*. When, subsequently, the arrested men claimed that they had been authorized to pay bribes by Berlusconi's brother Paolo, public opinion was inclined to be skeptical. To many, it looked as if the informal Fininvest board meeting had decided to make Berlusconi junior into a scapegoat. Even more worrying, however, was the ethical laxity Berlusconi had shown by holding the meeting, and the inability of the prime minister to cut himself loose from his holdings. Berlusconi does not want an American-style blind trust to control his media empire, nor does he want to sell off his assets, for the very good reason that he does not want analysts and auditors poking their noses into the amazingly complex network of companies that he owns. This attitude was not good enough for the League at least, which promised to introduce an anti-trust law for the media, and by August was extending to the government only its critical support.

Berlusconi's relations with Bossi worsened still further in the Fall of 1994. The League distanced itself from the government's proposal to take an axe to Italy's over-generous pensions system when a million-strong demonstration in Rome on November 12, 1994, demonstrated how strongly ordinary tax-paying Italians rejected the notion that they should pay for the accumulated deficit of the Craxi-Andreotti years. This blatant opportunism infuriated Berlusconi (and did nothing for the government's economic credibility with the financial markets), but he was forced to bite on the bullet, by agreeing to a modified package of pensions reforms with the unions on December 1. Bossi's objections to *Forza Italia*'s administration, however, were not confined to populist sniping at Berlusconi's economic strategy. In common with much of the Italian left and center, the leader of the League rightly or wrongly seems to have convinced himself that the Berlusconi-AN pact represents a genuine threat to liberal democracy in Italy.[1] This conviction was formed by the reluctance of *Forza Italia*'s leadership to allow the judicial investigations into Fininvest to continue unhindered. Berlusconi became ever more deeply immersed in the *Mani pulite* inquiry in November 1994, and on November 22 was formally warned that he was being investigated for his role in Fininvest's corruption of the tax authorities. Within days, the Court of Cassation -- notoriously open to political pressure -- had provisionally transferred the inquiry away from Milan to the nearby town of Brescia, and Antonio Di Pietro and his colleagues had been subjected to an unprecedented wave of abuse in the media from Berlusconi's closest political allies. Sickened and frustrated by these developments, Di Pietro (who had already been subjected to a pointless two-month investigation by Ministry of Justice inspectors earlier in the Fall) announced his irrevocable resignation from the judiciary on December 6, 1994. In an affectionate yet nonetheless bitter letter to Francesco Saverio Borrelli, the magistrate expressed his dismay at the way in which his impartially conducted investigations had been misrepresented as political acts.

Round one had gone to Berlusconi, but the arrogance with which *Forza Italia* was challenging the judiciary seemingly brought to the boil Bossi's doubts. Combining forces with the PDS and the PPI (which is now led by a Catholic philosopher, Rocco Buttiglione), the League tabled a vote of confidence in the government on December 13 which specifically called into question the political pressures that had been brought to bear against magistrates in Milan and elsewhere. As is his wont, Berlusconi responded with hyperbole to the League's move. The Italian premier described opponents of his government as "enemies of democratic stability" and proclaimed that he was the victim of a vast plot that could reasonably be compared to "a downright coup d'état." Berlusconi's spokesman, Giuliano Ferrara, was even more graphic in his denunciation of the parliamentary maneuvering of Bossi and the opposition. He warned that any new government that "overturned" the right's victory in March 1994 would be regarded as the beneficiary of an "institutional coup." In ominous tones, he additionally warned that there would "shortly" be "a storm of unprecedented violence" that would "clear the air" of "accumulated poisons." Other AN and *Forza Italia* personalities threatened that any center-left administration that emerged from the crisis would be a "governo Facta" (the last Liberal government prior to Mussolini's seizure of power).[2] Such lurid threats were to no avail. The confidence debate, on December 21, 1994, ended in defeat for Berlusconi and his neo-fascist allies.

It is possible that the violent imagery of *Forza Italia*'s spokesmen prior to the confidence debate was mere posturing. *Forza Italia* is full of self-publicists for whom media attention seemingly is an unusually addictive drug. That parliamentarians should even be flirting with undemocratic language and sentiments, however, is a deeply worrying sign. Deputies from the AN and *Forza Italia* show no sign of recognizing that Bossi, in a representative democracy, had the right to withdraw the support of his party's parliamentary contingent from Berlusconi's government. In the consultations that President Scalfaro set in motion after Christmas, the two chief parties of government, egged on by a vociferous faction of self-proclaimed anti-communists within the League, argued that parliament had been "delegitimized" by Bossi's actions and pressed Scalfaro to reappoint Berlusconi as premier, if necessary as head of a minority administration, for a transitional period before fresh elections. The League, the PPI, the PDS and *Alleanza democratica* sustained, by contrast, that the President should appoint a government of experts, presided over by a neutral figure of international standing, which would enact an anti-trust law for the media, restore the confidence of the financial markets in the Italian state's fiscal and monetary policies, and repeal the 1993 electoral law by introducing a fully FPTP system on the French dual ballot model. In his New Year's Eve address to the nation, Scalfaro appeared to lean toward this latter proposal, by insisting that it was "dangerous" for democracy to go to the polls in the absence of "parity of conditions," and by explicitly denying that parliament had been delegitimized by the events of December.

On January 13, 1995, Scalfaro put forward a compromise solution to the crisis. The "burden" of forming a new government was given to the treasury minister in the outgoing Berlusconi administration, Lamberto Dini, a former senior official from the Bank of Italy. Dini is associated with *Forza Italia*, which made his appointment relatively acceptable to the right, but was explicitly given the task of constructing a Ciampi-style government of non-party experts that would institute an anti-trust law and an alteration to the electoral system. Whether this compromise will prove acceptable to the main political forces remains to be seen. Berlusconi at once made it clear that he expected the Dini government to be a short-lived interlude before fresh elections; Umberto Bossi warned, by contrast, that the country would face "devastating tensions" if the Dini administration did not endure.[3] A realist would add that Italy is likely to face great tensions even if the government does endure. It is hard to see the AN and Berlusconi passively accepting changes to the electoral rules that severely reduce their chances of winning an outright majority, or allowing elections to be postponed until Berlusconi's media monopoly has been weakened.[4]

The Italian Revolution

In the Spring of 1994, it seemed as if the biggest gainer from the traditional parties' debâcle would prove to be the AN, which for all the efforts of its leaders to bring it out of its intellectual ghetto, was addicted to shouting anti-immigrant slogans and hailing Mussolini, and Berlusconi, the smooth opportunist whose interest in political reform had always been zero. Italy's progressives could not call this development anything other than a usurpation of the process of institutional and political reform. The widespread habit of referring to the political upheaval of the previous months as the Italian "revolution" consequently dropped out of use. This semantic shift was arguably premature. It presupposed that the right's victory in the 1994 elections was likely to be both long-lasting (a view that rested upon the conviction that the League's neo-conservative economic ideas would bind it to the right) and that Berlusconi's media clout and transcendent personal popularity would render him immune from judicial inquiry. Both of these presuppositions have proved to be in error. The League is ideologically restless, as ill at ease on the right as on the left. It seems unlikely, moreover, that the Italian premier will emerge spotless from continued investigations by the *Mani pulite* pool. Berlusconi's satellites have attempted to diffuse the perception that the Milanese attorneys are political liberals whose judicial activism is aimed at advancing the PDS's cause. This is self-serving nonsense, but there is some truth in the charge that the prosecutors have a political agenda. Operation Clean Hands is, to a certain extent, judicial retribution for the suppressed scandals of the late 1970s and early 1980s; for the aborted or curtailed investigations into the collapse of the Banco Ambrosiano, the death of Roberto Calvi, the occult power of the P2 masonic lodge. It is also a conscious crusade against the business-politico-criminal network, epitomized by Bettino Craxi, that transformed the Italian legislature into, to quote Antonio Di Pietro, "a democracy for sale."[5] If it is proved that Berlusconi was part of this network; if the judiciary advance convincing proof that Berlusconi (for instance) flouted the laws governing monopolies in the media, paid bribes in exchange for political favors, or abused his powers on behalf of Fininvest after becoming prime minister, his popularity will fade away, in Orwell's phrase, like "breath off a razor blade." Many Italians find Berlusconi's media-savvy political style engaging, but they do not want a return to the *affarismo* of the past.

At least one aspect of Italy's political revolution, however, will be unaffected by Berlusconi's political survival or demise. The crucial point to grasp about the huge changes that Italy has undergone since the election of April 1992 is that the ideological dimension has been restored to politics. For most of the post-war epoch, anti-communism gave the principal political parties a sense of purpose. The goal of the leading figures in the DC, in particular, was keeping Italy within the democratic camp and excluding the PCI from power. In the 1980s, as ideological concerns loomed less large, the short-sighted greed of the political class turned politics into a souk: Transforming political influence into hard cash became the *raison d'être* of the whole system. Naturally, such practices could not last. Clientelism and patronage are part and parcel of politics, but no country, in the long run, will tolerate leaders that are content merely to feed off the labors of more productive citizens. Following the collapse of the "regime," Italy's political parties are once more bitterly divided over substantive issues of the country's identity. As much as in the 1940s, or the 1970s, who wins the political struggle really matters. An Italy guided by Gianfranco Fini would be radically different in kind from an Italy governed by a centrist-left coalition based on the PDS, the PPI, and *Alleanza democratica*. To use an over-worked metaphor, Italy is at a crossroads, and its people are likely to become embroiled in a bitter -- perhaps even violent -- argument over the route it should take.

188

Notes

1. See Guido Panalacqua, "Bossi avvisa: mi sento con le mani libere," *La Repubblica*, December 5, 1994, for a short but convincing report of Bossi's fears.
2. All the quotations in this paragraph are from Giampaolo Pansa, "E un giorno Er Pecora violenterà il Casini," *L'Espresso*, December 23, 1994.
3. Quoted, Celestine Bohlen, "Italy Names Banker With No Party Ties New PM," *New York Times*, January 14, 1995.
4. In December 1994, Italy's Constitutional Court ruled that Berlusconi's possession of three television networks was illegal and gave him until December 1995 to rectify the situation. It is obviously in Berlusconi's interests to force an election while his monopoly over the airwaves is still complete.
5. In his last duty as a prosecutor, Antonio Di Pietro appealed in court for severe sentences for politicans involved in the Enimont *maxi-tangente*. In his peroration, the Milanese attorney said that the evidence he had advanced during the trial demonstrated that Italy had been "una democrazia venduta" (literally, a "sold democracy") in the late 1980s. Di Pietro asked that Craxi be sentenced to 3 years and 4 months imprisonment; that Forlani should receive 2 years and 6 months; that Bossi should get 10 months; and that numerous other politicians, including Martelli, LaMalfa, Vizzini, Cirino Pomicino and Citaristi should also be condemned. Whether sentencing the politicians to time in gaol is anything more than a gesture is unclear. Craxi has already been condemned to a long prison sentence for his role in the Banco Ambrosiano affair, but continues to reside, pending appeal, in his luxury villa in Tunisia. It is claimed that the former premier is seriously ill.

Appendix

Presidents of Italy 1978-1994

1978-1985:	Sandro Pertini (PSI)
1985-1992:	Francesco Cossiga (DC)
1992-1994:	Oscar Luigi Scalfaro (DC)

Italian Governments 1976-1994

Andreotti III:	DC	July 1976 - March 1978
Andreotti IV:	DC	March 1978 - January 1979
Andreotti V:	DC- PRI - PSDI	January - August 1979
Cossiga I:	DC - PLI - PSDI	August 1979 - March 1980
Cossiga II:	DC - PSI - PRI	April 1980 - September 1980
Forlani I:	DC - PSI - PRI - PSDI	October 1980 - June 1981
Spadolini I :	DC - PSI - PRI - PLI - PSDI	June 1981 - August 1982
Spadolini II :	DC - PSI - PRI - PLI - PSDI	September 1982 - November 1982
Fanfani V:	DC - PSI - PRI - PLI - PSDI	November 1982 - April 1983
Craxi I:	DC - PSI - PRI - PLI - PSDI	August 1983 - August 1986
Craxi II:	DC - PSI - PRI - PLI - PSDI	August 1986 - April 1987
Fanfani VI:	DC	April 1987 - July 1987
Goria I:	DC - PSI - PRI - PLI - PSDI	July 1987 - April 1988
De Mita I:	DC - PSI - PRI - PLI - PSDI	April 1988 - July 1989
Andreotti VI:	DC- PSI - PRI - PLI - PSDI	July 1989 - March 1991
Andreotti VII:	DC - PSI - PLI - PSDI	April 1991 - June 1992
Amato I:	DC - PSI - PLI - PSDI	June 1992 - April 1993
Ciampi I:	DC - PSI - PLI - PSDI	May 1993 - May 1994
Berlusconi I:	FI - LN - AN - CCD - UC	May - December 1994

The Twilight of the First Republic
Governments and Ministers July 1989 - May 1994

Andreotti VI: July 1989 - March 1991
DC - PSI - PRI - PLI - PSDI

Prime Minister: Giulio Andreotti (DC)
Deputy Prime Minister: Claudio Martelli (PSI)
Foreign Affairs: Gianni De Michelis (PSI)
Interior: Antonio Gava (DC)*
Budget: Paolo Cirino Pomicino (DC)
Justice: Giuliano Vassalli (PSI)
Mezzogiorno: Riccardo Misasi (DC)

* From October 1990, Gava was replaced by Enzo Scotti (DC)

Andreotti VII: April 1991 - June 1992
DC - PSI - PLI - PSDI

Prime Minister: Giulio Andreotti (DC)
Deputy Prime Minister & Justice: Claudio Martelli (PSI)
Foreign Affairs: Gianni De Michelis (PSI)
Interior: Enzo Scotti (DC)
Budget: Paolo Cirino Pomicino (DC)
Treasury: Guido Carli (DC)
Mezzogiorno: Calogero Mannino (DC)

Amato I: June 1992 - April 1993
DC - PSI - PLI - PSDI

Prime Minister: Giuliano Amato (PSI)
Foreign Affairs: Emilio Colombo (DC)
Interior: Nicola Mancino (DC)
Budget & Mezzogiorno: Franco Reviglio (PSI)*
Justice: Claudio Martelli (PSI)**
Treasury: Piero Barucci (DC)

* replaced by Beniamino Andreatta (DC) March 1993
** replaced by Giovanni Conso (No Party Affiliation: NPA) February 1993

Ciampi I*: May 1993 - May 1994
DC - PSI - PLI - PSDI

Prime Minister: Carlo Azeglio Ciampi (NPA)
Foreign Affairs: Beniamino Andreatta (DC)
Interior: Nicola Mancino (DC)
Budget: Luigi Spaventa (NPA)
Justice: Giovanni Conso (NPA)
Treasury: Piero Barucci (DC)

* The original Ciampi government, containing the three PDS ministers, is not officially counted since it collapsed before the ministers could take the oath of office.

Berlusconi I : May 1994
FI - LN - AN - CCD - UC

Prime Minister: Silvio Berlusconi (FI)
Deputy Prime Minister & Interior: Roberto Maroni (LN)
Deputy Prime Minister
 & Post & Telecommunications: Giuseppe Tatarella (AN)
Foreign Affairs: Antonio Martino (FI)
Budget: Giancarlo Pagliarini (LN)
Justice: Alfredo Biondi (FI)
Institutional Reform: Francesco Enrico Speroni (LN)
Treasury: Lamberto Dini (NPA)

Select Bibliography

This bibliography is not intended to be exhaustive. It gives a list of books in English and Italian that I found to be particularly useful and thought-provoking. I have included several collections of articles, notably the series *Italian Politics: A Review*, but have not listed publications in scholarly journals.

Andreoli, Marcella. 1994. *Processo all'Italia*. Milan: Sperling & Kupfer.

Arlacchi, Pino. 1983. *La Mafia Imprenditrice: L'etica mafiosa e lo spirito del capitalismo*. Bologna: Il Mulino.

Bellu, Giovanni Maria and Sandra Bonsanti. 1993. *Il Crollo: Andreotti, Craxi e il loro regime*. Bari: Laterza.

Bocca, Giorgio. 1990. *La Disunità d'Italia*. Milan: Garzanti.

Bossi, Umberto (with Daniele Vimercati). 1992. *Vento Dal Nord*. Milan: Sperling & Kupfer.

_____, 1993. *La Rivoluzione: La Lega Storie e idee*. Milan: Sperling & Kupfer.

Chimenti, Anna. 1993. *Storia dei referendum*. Bari: Laterza.

Cossiga, Francesco. 1993. *Externator: discorsi per una repubblica che non c'è*. Rome: Panorama.

Dalla Chiesa, Nando. 1990. *Storie di boss ministri tribunali giornali intellettuali cittadini*. Turin: Einaudi.

Di Nicola, Primo. 1992. *Mario Segni*. Milan: Sperling & Kupfer.

Einaudi, L'Ente Luigi. 1991. *Il disavanzo pubblico in Italia* (2 vols). Bologna: Il Mulino.

Farneti, Paolo. 1993. *Il sistema dei partiti in Italia 1946-79*. Bologna: Il Mulino.

Galli, Giorgio. 1991. *I partiti politici italiani 1943-1991*. Rome: Rizzoli.

Ginsborg, Paul. 1990. *A History of Contemporary Italy: Society and Politics 1943-1988*. London: Penguin.

Hellman, Stephen. 1988. *Italian Communism in Transition: The Rise and Fall of the Historic Compromise in Turin 1975-80*. New York. Oxford University Press.

_____, 1992. "Italy" in Mark Kesselman & Joel Krieger (eds) *European Politics in Transition*. Lexington: Heath.

Hine, David. 1993. *Governing Italy: The Politics of Bargained Pluralism*. Oxford: OUP.

Ignazi, Piero. 1992. *Dal PCI al PDS*. Bologna: Il Mulino.

_____, 1994. *L'Estrema destra in Europa*. Bologna. Il Mulino.

Istituto Cattaneo. 1986. *Italian Politics: A Review*, (vol 1: 1985), eds. Robert Leonardi and Raffaella Nanetti. London: Pinter. Bologna: Il Mulino.

_____, 1988. *Italian Politics: A Review*, (vol 2: 1986), eds. Raffaela Nanetti, Robert Leonardi and Piergiorgio Corbetta. Same publishers.

_____, 1989. *Italian Politics: A Review*, (vol 3: 1987), eds. Robert Leonardi and Piergiorgio Corbetta. Same publishers.

_____, 1990. *Italian Politics: A Review*, (vol 4: 1988), eds. Raffaela Nanetti and Raimondo Catanzaro. Same publishers.

_____, 1991. *Italian Politics: A Review*, (vol 5: 1989), eds. Filippo Sabetti and Raimondo Catanzaro. Same publishers.

_____, 1992. *Italian Politics: A Review*, (vol 6: 1990), eds. Robert Leonardi and Fausto Anderlini. Same publishers.

_____, 1992. *Italian Politics: A Review*, (vol 7: 1991), eds. Stephen Hellman and Gianfranco Pasquino. Same publishers.

_____, 1993. *Italian Politics A Review*, (vol 8: 1992), eds. Stephen Hellman and Gianfranco Pasquino. Same publishers.

_____, 1994. *Italian Politics A Review*, (vol 9: 1993), eds. Carol Mershon and Gianfranco Pasquino. Boulder: Westview Press.

Kogan, Norman. 1983. *A Political History of Italy*. New York: Praeger.

Locatelli, Goffredo. 1990. *Irpiniagate: Ciriaco De Mita da Nusco a palazzo Chigi*. Rome: Newton Compton.

LaPalombara, Joseph. 1987. *Democracy, Italian Style*. New Haven: Yale University Press.

Mannheimer, Renato. 1991. *La Lega Lombarda*. Milan: Feltrinelli.

McCarthy, Patrick and Gianfranco Pasquino. 1993. *The End of Post-War Politics in Italy: The Landmark Elections of 1992*. Boulder: Westview Press.

Messina, Sebastiano. 1992. *La Grande Riforma*. Bari: Laterza.

_____, 1992. *La Nomenklatura: Come sopravvive in Italia la specie politica più antica nel mondo*. Milan: Mondadori.

Miglio, Gianfranco. 1992. *Come cambiare*. Milan: Mondadori.

Pamparana, Andrea. 1994. *Il Processo Cusani*. Milan: Mondadori.

Pansa, Giampaolo. 1992. *I Bugiardi*. Milan: Sperling & Kupfer.

Pasquino, Gianfranco. 1985. *Restituire lo scettro al principe. Proposte di riforma istituzionale*. Bari: Laterza.

_____, 1991. *La Repubblica dei cittadini ombra*. Milan: Garzanti.

Ruggeri, Giovanni and Mario Guarino. 1994. *Berlusconi: Inchiesta sul signor TV*. Milan: Kaos.

Sabbatucci, Giovanni. 1991. *Il riformismo impossibile*. Bari: Laterza.

Sassoon, Donald. 1986. *Contemporary Italy: Politics, Economy & Society since 1945*. London: Longman.

Sales, Isaia. 1988. *La Camorra, le camorre*. Rome: Riuniti.

Savelli, Giulio. 1992. *Che cosa vuole La Lega*. Milan: Longanesi & Co.

Scoppola, Pietro. 1990. *La Repubblica dei partiti*. Bologna: Il Mulino.

Teodori, Massimo. 1993. *Come voterai*. Rome: Panorama.

Tranfaglia, Nicola (ed). 1992. *Mafia, politica e affari 1943-91*. Bari: Laterza.

_____, 1994. *Cirillo, Ligato e Lima: Tre storie di mafia e politica*. Bari: Laterza.

Turani, Giuseppe and Cinzia Sasso. 1992. *I Saccheggiatori*. Milan: Sperling & Kupfer.

Veltri, Elio. 1993. *Da Craxi a Craxi*. Bari: Laterza.

Vimercati, Daniele. 1990. *I Lombardi alla nuova crociata*. Milan: Mursia.

About the Book and Author

Since 1992, Italy has been rocked by the disintegration of its traditional ruling elite as dozens of leading politicians have been accused of corruption, extortion, and Mafia ties. The two linchpins of the former governing coalition, the Christian Democrats and the Socialists, have been shattered by scandal and humiliated at the polls, leaving a vacuum that new political forces, such as the Northern League, have rushed to fill. Taking place against a backdrop of mounting economic worries and an internecine war between the state and the Mafia, these political convulsions could well be designated a revolution. This clear and balanced book provides both a historical account of the circumstances that led to *la rivoluzione italiana* and an explanation of why it took place after decades of complacency.

Mark Gilbert is assistant professor of political science at Dickinson College, Pennsylvania.

Index